Disciplined by Race

Disciplined by Race

Theological Ethics and the Problem
of Asian American Identity

KI JOO CHOI

CASCADE *Books* • Eugene, Oregon

DISCIPLINED BY RACE
Theological Ethics and the Problem of Asian American Identity

Cascade Books
An Imprint of Wipf and Stock Publishers
199 W. 8th Ave., Suite 3
Eugene, OR 97401

www.wipfandstock.com

PAPERBACK ISBN: 978-1-5326-3472-7
HARDCOVER ISBN: 978-1-5326-3474-1
EBOOK ISBN: 978-1-5326-3473-4

Names: Choi, Ki Joon, author.
Title: Disciplined by race : theological ethics and the problem of Asian American identity / Ki Joo Choi.
Description: Eugene, OR : Cascade Books, 2019 | Includes bibliographical references and index(es).
Identifiers: ISBN 978-1-5326-3472-7 (paperback) | ISBN 978-1-5326-3474-1 (hardcover) | ISBN 978-1-5326-3473-4 (ebook)
Subjects: Asian Americans—Social conditions. | Asian Americans—Ethnic identity. | Identity (Psychology)—Religious aspects—Christianity. | Christian ethics. | Racism—United States.

Classification: E184.A75 C45 2019 (print) | E184.A75 C45 (ebook)

Manufactured in the U.S.A.   JANUARY 27, 2020

For
Nate and Sammy

Contents

Acknowledgments | ix

Introduction | xi

1 Identity | 1

2 Culture | 36

3 Racism | 67

4 Agency | 109

5 Relationality | 147

Bibliography | 179

Index of Subjects and Names | 189

Acknowledgments

PARTS OF THIS BOOK received initial consideration in a variety of forums. A section of chapter 4 was presented in a spring 2016 colloquium on race sponsored by the Center for Literature and the Public Sphere (now called the Center for the Humanities and the Public Sphere), which is supported by the Department of English at Seton Hall University. My colleagues from the English and History Departments who participated in this colloquium provided invaluable perspective. Another portion of chapter 4 was presented at the Asian American Theology and Ethics Colloquium sponsored by Princeton Theological Seminary in spring 2017. Responses from participants in this colloquium sharpened my thinking about the racial character of Asian American identity.

Two other chapters of the book develop several themes explored in previous essays. Chapter 2 is a wholly revised version of my essay "After Authenticity: Clarifying the Relevance of Culture as a Source of Moral Reflection in Asian American Christian Ethics," published in the *Journal of Race, Ethnicity, and Religion* 7.2 (August 2016) 1–30. Chapter 2 also includes a revision of one section from my essay "Should Race Matter? A Constructive Ethical Assessment of the Post-Racial Ideal," published in the *Journal of the Society of Christian Ethics* 31.1 (Spring/Summer 2011) 79–102. I thank both journals for allowing me to include revised portions of these two articles. Chapter 3 is a thorough reexamination of a question that I first broached in my essay "Racial Identity and Solidarity" that appeared in *Asian American Christian Ethics: Voices, Issues, Methods*, edited by Grace Y. Kao and Ilsup Ahn (Waco, TX: Baylor University Press, 2015) 131–15. No section of this essay, however, is reprinted in chapter 3 of this book.

The initial groundwork for this book was made possible by release time granted to me by former provost Larry Robinson of Seton Hall University. Dean Peter Shoemaker of Seton Hall University's College of Arts and Sciences provided additional support, which allowed me to prepare the manuscript for publication. I am especially grateful to David Gushee for reading the entire manuscript and sharing his assessment of it with me. Matthew Wimer, Karl Coppock, and George Callihan of Wipf & Stock deserve special recognition for responding to all my questions and concerns patiently and graciously. I am also indebted to my friends and colleagues in the Asian American Working Group of the Society of Christian Ethics, especially Jonathan Tran, Grace Y. Kao, Ilsup Ahn, and Hak Joon Lee for their support and fellowship. I would not have found my voice as an Asian American theological ethicist were it not for the many conversations we have shared over the years.

A final thanks goes to my indefatigable wife and partner, Mandy, and our two children, Nate and Sammy, who kept me on task by asking me (almost) every day whether I am finished with the book. Ultimately, this book is for them; it is about my children's future, the kind of questions and choices they will have to navigate. Will they be able to decide what it means to be Asian American on their own terms? I hope we can struggle with that question together.

Introduction

As I SET OUT to write an Asian American theological ethics, I quickly came to the realization that such a task is more daunting than I initially thought it would be. I began with the primary aim of mapping out what thinking theologically and ethically can look like from an Asian American perspective. That goal was motivated by the belief that Asian American life, as a collective experience, is theologically and ethically substantive and as such necessarily challenges, deepens, and expands the way the general discipline of theological ethics or, for a lack of a better descriptor, mainstream theological ethics approaches fundamental questions that would not be available otherwise.

I am convinced more than ever that mainstream theological ethics cannot do without the perspective of Asian American theological ethics. It is through theological particularities, which must include the theological particularities underlying Asian American experience, that we are able to better view the larger whole of Christian truthfulness. That is especially true when it comes to one of the more difficult moments that contemporary theological ethics finds itself in, the task of assessing, integrating, and learning from contemporary debates on racism in the United States and the implications of those debates for the work and vocation of theological ethicists. Building on the momentum initiated by the volume of essays on Asian American Christian ethics coedited by my colleagues Grace Y. Kao and Ilsup Ahn, *Asian American Christian Ethics: Voices, Methods, Issues*, it is my hope that this book provides yet another convincing case as to why an Asian American perspective matters in the ongoing articulation and implementation of that task.

However, the challenge in writing this book from the very start has been articulating what that Asian American perspective is. What about being Asian American is critical to theological ethics? How is the wild diversity of Asian American identities to be accounted for? Is that very diversity itself an argument against the prospects for an Asian American perspective? Can the diverse experiences of Asian Americans be described and interpreted in such a way that a coherent Asian American identity can be defined? Or is being Asian American so hopelessly nebulous that defining what it means to be Asian American and thus articulating what an Asian American perspective might be for theological ethics is an interesting intellectual proposition and no more than that? Responses to such questions are hardly self-evident given the caution of many scholars of Asian American life in avoiding essentializing Asian American experience.[1] That there is no one way of being Asian American is a given. Yet, simply resting on that given presents an obvious problem since the prospects of Asian American theological ethics is premised on the notion that there is something distinctively tangible to being Asian American in the first place, which constitutes the source of its moral salience.[2] The question, then, of what it means to be Asian American (or what defines Asian American experience) is the primary methodological challenge that confronts those who are interested in advancing Asian American theological ethics as a discipline and integral mode of moral reflection.

That methodological challenge proved to be a significant undertaking, which has unexpectedly but necessarily recast the initial aims of this book. So, while this book still aims to be a book on Asian American theological ethics, its primary focus has turned out to be one of making a case for what it means to be Asian American; not just any sort of case but one that warrants and, more strongly, demands theological-ethical scrutiny. While I will draw out the key theological-ethical implications of my description and interpretation of Asian American identity toward the end of this book, I take those concluding sections as primarily proposals for what I hope will be more systematic theological reflections and positions for the future. In

1. For instance, Ho, *Racial Ambiguity in Asian American Culture*, and Lowe, "Heterogeneity, Hybridity, Multiplicity."

2. This is not to say that this is the only premise to Asian American theological ethics, but it is one that requires greater sustained attention, especially given the emphasis on the diversity of Asian American experiences in the volume *Asian American Christian Ethics*, edited by Kao and Ahn. While Asian American experience is hardly singular, there is also a need for examining what binds Asian Americans together (or what constitutes Asian Americanness), otherwise the very idea of identifying as Asian American would seem to border on triviality. My aim is to hold together two seemingly opposite aims, to explore the prospects for a common Asian American identity while at the same time underscoring the inherent diversity of Asian American life.

that way, I see this book more as a prolegomena rather than a sustained theological argument from an Asian American perspective. The latter can only come about until the substantial lacuna in articulating or narrativizing what it means to be Asian American in a manner that is distinctively relevant to theological-ethical inquiry can be filled.

To start filling that lacuna, this book is an attempt at working out two interrelated convictions. The first is that we need to move away from a cultural understanding of Asian American identity and second that we need to think about Asian American identity in distinctly racialized terms. These two convictions should not be taken as suggesting that culture is irrelevant to Asian American identity; culture of course matters. But a singular focus on culture inevitably runs up against the problem of cultural multiplicity; there is no one Asian American culture but Asian American cultures, which tends to make talking about Asian American identity in a coherently collective sense too unwieldy. That, then, tends to establish unnecessary obstacles to recognizing the ways in which Asian American identity is socially delimited. More specifically, a too narrow focus on Asian American as a cultural identity inhibits the assessment of how Asian Americans are racially delimited or, simply, racialized. Asian Americans as racialized beings is one fundamental thread that is woven through the diverse fabric of Asian American life and identifying this thread and naming it for what it is merits a long overdue theological-ethical reckoning. While the diversity of Asian American cultural forms may rightly support an ambivalence about who we are as Asian Americans in at least cultural ways, we cannot be ambivalent about who we are as Asian Americans in racialized ways. To reflect on how Asian American identity is racialized—specifically, how Asian Americans inhabit bodies or forms of life that are molded by racial hierarchies of value and relationship—is to locate Asian Americans squarely at the center of contemporary discourses on race, and it insists that unless an Asian American voice is heard, how theological ethics discusses, in particular, questions of racism will be incomplete.

The book's focus on mapping the racialization of Asian Americans takes several forms, but they all pivot on the proposition that the self-determinative possibilities of Asian Americans cannot be understood or accounted for apart from Asian Americans' uneasy relationship with whiteness. By whiteness, I mean primarily the following accepted sociological description. First, the "compilation of institutional privileges and ideological characteristics bestowed upon members of the dominant group in societies organized by the idea and practice of pan-European supremacy." Second, the corresponding "white racial frame" or the "use of stereotypes, metaphors, images, emotions, and narratives" that "both emanate from and support [the] systemic racism [of whiteness]."[3] The author and journalist Ta-Nehisi Coates concretizes or particularizes this account of whiteness by referring to the socially formative power of "the Dream," the values, practices, privileges and racial hierarchies underlying the aspirational vision of post–World War II middle-class Americana.[4] It is Asian Americans' problematic relationship with such an account of white ascendency and its underlying vision of what constitutes the good life that interests me in particular. A primary thread in this book is to examine how whiteness positions Asian Americans relative to white Americans and non-Asian persons of color and what such positioning reveals about the ideological justifications of (or the strategies employed to buttress) whiteness or, more specifically, white racism in the modern United States.

The unease that characterizes the relationship between Asian Americans and whiteness moves beyond the observation that scholars within and outside theological ethics have made about the ways in which Asian Americans, corresponding to their purported economic ascendency,[5] are increasingly identifying as white or, if not identifying as white, increasingly *identifiable* as white. The latter description reflects what some have described as Asian Americans' "adjacency" to white Americans given the increasing numbers of Asian Americans living in affluent urban and suburban communities.[6] Such migration into white communities intimate a sense of shared values between Asian Americans and white Americans, in actuality or aspirationally. Such ways of thinking about the relationship between Asian Americans and whiteness, however, is too narrow and unrevealing. In subjecting the Asian American relationship with whiteness

3. Bush, *Everyday Forms of Whiteness*, 3.

4. Coates, *Between the World and Me*, 11.

5. Pew, "Rise of Asian Americans." I say the "purported" ascendency of Asian Americans not to discount the gains that Asian Americans have indeed made economically and educationally, but to signal that this ascendency is more complicated than commonly understood. Disaggregating Asian Americans, that is, making distinctions between various Asian American communities (e.g., South Asians from East Asians, etc.), provides a picture of Asian American ascendency that is far from evenly distributed. The unevenness of Asian American social gains will be highlighted throughout the book.

6. The notion of adjacency is from Kang, "How Should Asian Americans Feel about the Peter Liang Protests," *New York Times*, February 23, 2016.

to closer scrutiny, I argue that the self-determinative possibilities of Asian Americans are not only limited, if that merely connotes a smaller range of possibilities, but more properly, are deeply disciplined by whiteness. In other words, whiteness does not only limit the range of what is possible for Asian Americans especially in terms of their identity, but whiteness molds if not manipulates the choices of those identities themselves; as disciplined by whiteness, Asian Americans bear the social pressures of being habituated into certain identities that fit the social and cultural visions and assumptions of whiteness.

Such a proposition is not meant to displace what may be more familiar narratives of Asian American identity, such as Asian Americans as other or perpetual immigrants or foreigners who are subject to the enduring strands of American nativism.[7] And then there is of course the narrative of Asian Americans as the hard(est)-working persons of color: the model minorities. These narratives, as I will show throughout this book, are critically relevant to understanding the racialized character of Asian American life. However, those narratives by themselves, or at least in their more familiar versions, do not tell the whole story of Asian Americans as racialized persons. Recognizing the way in which Asian American identity is positioned or disciplined by whiteness reconfigures those narratives within a distinctly racialized framework or "color axis."[8] That reconfiguration pertains in part to how the perception of immigrant otherness and the model minority designation are not mutually exclusive. Furthermore, that reconfiguration diverts efforts away from simply drawing parallels of how racial discrimination is felt between Asian Americans and other nonwhite communities of color, especially Asian Americans and African Americans. I will, when necessary, try to draw such parallels at least for the sake of complicating popular perceptions, especially within theological ethics, of Asian Americans as somehow either immune from the marginalizing dynamics of whiteness or only sporadically afflicted by them given, again, our so-called ascendency into the white American mainstream. However, the more pertinent and unsettling point is that those popular perceptions of racial immunity and transcendence are in fact integral features of how Asian Americans are racialized by whiteness. Thus calls since at least Ferguson that Asian Americans must stand as allies to non-Asian persons of color,

7. See, for instance, Ancheta, *Race, Rights, and the Asian American Experience*; Park and Park, "Race Discourse and Proposition 187," 175–204.

8. Kim, "Are Asians Black?," 331–53.

in their racial afflictions, while indeed crucial and morally and politically urgent, do not adequately identify the basic racial forces at play in Asian American life and how they operate on Asian American self-understanding in relation to other non-Asian persons of color.[9] Moreover, I do not want to contravene instances of racial solidarity and cooperation between Asian Americans and other racial groups; those instances should be made known, affirmed, celebrated, and multiplied.[10] However, my concern is mapping the racializing pressures that make such cooperation challenging; those pressures should not be underestimated.

To work out these convictions on Asian American identity and race, I will rely on insights primarily from the discipline of Asian American studies and to a lesser degree the emerging field of Asian American food studies. I also engage a number of prominent Asian American journalists who have been playing significant roles in crafting a public dialogue on what it means to be Asian American as we negotiate the political, economic, and cultural shifts or trends defining US society in the early twenty-first century. Since dimensions of my attempt at mapping the racialization of Asian American identity have also been navigated by works from these three sources, my aim is not to provide sustained expository reviews of these works but to employ and interpret them in a way that narrates a cohesive account of what the racialization of Asian American identity means for the nature or status of Asian American agency. The question of Asian American agency, I aim to show, indicates at least one vital way that Asian American theological ethics is relevant to contemporary debates on the relationship between race and the task of theological ethics. It also reveals the import of Asian American theological ethics to mainstream theological ethics well beyond issues of race.

Lastly, I will also rely heavily on contemporary Asian American fiction. While the use of literature is not uncommon in related fields of theological-ethical inquiry, especially in black and womanist theology and ethics,[11] the use of literature in Asian American theological ethics is scant. This book aims to shift perception of Asian American literature, specifically

9. See, for instance, Punongbayan, "What Asian Americans Owe African Americans," *Huffington Post*, October 2, 2015.

10. For instance, see Lee, *Civility in the City*.

11. For one of the more prominent and influential engagements with black women's literary traditions, see Cannon, *Black Womanist Ethics*. See also Bantum, *Redeeming Mulatto*, especially chapter 2. My turn to contemporary Asian American fiction is especially influenced by Bantum's use of African American literature, including Charles Chestnutt's

contemporary Asian American fiction, toward its viability and relevance as a critical source for Asian American theological ethics. For reasons I will discuss later in this book, I am somewhat reluctant to refer to novels that I will focus on simply as works in Asian American fiction. While the question of what it means to be Asian American is not the sole focus of any of these novels, it is significant that they do not ignore that question. I am primarily interested in how these novels articulate that question and respond to it. It is noteworthy that these novels, even in their overarching thematic diversity, speak to the question of Asian Americanness as fundamentally restrictive. As such, contemporary Asian American fiction provides alternative pathways to imagining what it means to embody an Asian American identity that is not simply "of culture" but, more significantly, "of race."

The chapters of this book proceed as follows. Chapter 1 begins to chart the path toward a racialized interpretation of Asian American identity by asking what it means to be Asian American in the post-Proposition 209 and post-Ferguson era. That question to an important extent has been answered in theological ethics in the turn to whiteness as specifically antiblackness. Certain accounts of this turn situate Asian Americans as tangentially relevant to the task of racial and social justice, if not, at least, a part of or contributing to, wittingly or not, the problem of racial and social injustice. In response to such troubling characterizations of Asian Americans, I argue that our contemporary discourses on race are deficient when Asian Americans are effectively sidelined form those discourses given what is often intimated as the inscrutability of Asian Americans as persons of color. The success of this argument requires a more sophisticated account of how Asian Americans are related to whiteness and the continuing relevance of the black-white paradigm to understanding who Asian Americans are. While the black-white paradigm is often criticized for marginalizing Asian Americans from racial debates in the United States, chapter 1 concludes that this paradigm is necessary as a means of focusing attention on the ways in which Asian Americas are disciplined by whiteness and, correspondingly, for providing a fuller account of what white racism as antiblackness means.

The House Behind the Cedars, James Weldon Johnson's *Autobiography of an Ex-Coloured Man*, and Nella Larsen's *Passing*.

Chapter 2 turns to the question of Asian American identity as a cultural identity versus a racial identity. The fullness of Asian American identity as couched within the dynamics of white racism requires displacing the notion that being Asian American is primarily about inhabiting a particular cultural form. A point of departure for that displacement is a critique of cultural authenticity. Behind this critique is the premise that culture, rather than as self-contained, is necessarily an expression of the social perspective of a person or particular persons. Another way of putting it is that culture is a crucial form of *negotiating* the social dynamics or realities that persons are situated within. Such a conception of culture accounts for Asian American as encompassing a pluralism of cultural identities while providing a conceptual framework that accounts for Asian American as also a collective identity defined by the racial logics of whiteness.

Chapter 3 examines the extent to which Asian American identity is subject to such racial logics by taking as a point of departure the concept of Asian American hybridity. My interest here is specifically examining certain Asian American accounts of hybridity, from both theological and non-theological voices, as a mode of resisting and transcending the discriminatory dynamics of whiteness, and whether they underestimate the force of those racial dynamics. It is ironic that hybridity is often regarded as a path toward dissembling conventional and essentialized race-talk when its prospects face considerable racial headwinds. But I am not suggesting that hybridity as intercultural innovation is an impossible prospect. I also do not think that hybridity so defined is a false or misguided aspiration; it does, at least formally, intersect with my concern for the integrity of Asian American self-determination or agency, a matter to be explored in chapters 4 and 5. In this chapter, however, assessing the kind of liberating optimism that is typically placed on hybridity is critically instructive in revealing a social dimension to Asian American life that requires careful, nuanced, and reasoned confrontation beyond what is typically given, if given at all: how Asian American life relates and, more consequentially, yields to the social visions and values of whiteness. Articulating the nature of the tug and pull of whiteness on Asian American self-understanding clarifies a mutually reinforcing complicity: the Asian American complicity in their own social invisibility and marginalization and the Asian American complicity in maintaining (or reinscribing) the hierarchical status of whiteness. This twofold complicity pivots on how the model minority myth reflects a white racial strategy of deploying Asian Americans in the service of its own social interests. Thus, the notion that Asian Americans are model minorities is not only a myth (and not only a benign myth at that, not unlike the very "normal" human tendency to generalize about people, such as all Texans like barbecue) but, more problematically, it is a racialized attribution with a particular marginalizing *telos*. To be rendered as model minorities is to be put in our proper place in American society; while not entirely white (whether Asian Americans realize that or not), Asian Americans are bestowed social privileges that engender the perception that we are not like other minorities (and they not like us). Such a rendering of Asian Americans is a critical feature of white racism's tenacity in the contemporary United States and indicative of how Asian Americans are very much a part of an ongoing American tragedy.

While the language of complicity paints a picture of willful participation, my aim in using that language is to suggest the opposite. The model minority myth is one important instantiation of how being Asian American is not necessarily a self-directed project but one that is persistently configured within white racial logics; the notion that Asian Americans are complicit in such a dynamic is intended to underscore the depth of whiteness's disciplining influence on Asian Americans; its influence is of the sort that recognition of whiteness's hold on Asian Americans and our conformation to it is oftentimes disguised, which underscores the social success of whiteness. Against this account of Asian Americans as model minorities, chapter 4 raises the question of what kind of agency Asian Americans possess or are afforded in society and turns to contemporary Asian American fiction to sort through this question.

To what extent can Asian Americans be counted as self-determining persons? In turning to a select number of novels mostly published in the last decade by Asian American authors, my interest is in detailing how their Asian American characters are identified as Asian American. The argument that I will advance is that these novels taken together depict a world in which Asian Americans can either be white or Asian. While the former choice may sound unsurprising, especially given the discussion in chapter 3, the latter choice is unsettling. The choice of being Asian is not so much a choice if by choice we mean the ability to determine for oneself what one desires to be. But rather, the choice of being Asian amounts to choosing an Asian or Asian American identity that is already defined within a racially stereotypical and, thus, ultimately racially marginalizing matrix. Just as the white identities these characters adopt are really not their identities (but presented and foisted onto them as normative modes of life), so too their Asian American identities.

In chapter 5, I conceptualize the constrained nature of Asian American agency within the principle of relationality. If Asian Americans are hampered in their ability to choose, if not precluded from choosing, their identities, then what does that lack of agential freedom imply about the notion that all persons are fundamentally relational beings? I argue that paying close attention to the nature of Asian American agency, that is, the kind of attraction and hold that the logic of whiteness has for modern Asian American life, pushes us to reexamine the meaning of relationality as a nonnegotiable feature of human personhood and renews attention to the importance of autonomy, not to displace relationality but as an integral principle in the refinement of what it means to be relational beings.

But in making a theological-ethical case for the importance of autonomy for relationality, my aim is to also raise the question of what resistance to whiteness should look like for Asian Americans. I will focus on one argument that advocates for the principle of radical self-love. To resist the expectations and demands of whiteness, Asian Americans must fiercely insist on and protect the expression of their own imagination and desires, so the argument goes. While I will draw positive linkages between my advocacy for autonomy and this kind of defense of self-love, I will also register a deep unease with any singular advocacy for self-love, for it does not sufficiently account for how the line between self-love and conformity to whiteness can be easily blurred. As an alternative, I will propose the priority of an expansive, other-regarding self-love, which is intended to place importance on cultivating the self-determinative capacities of Asian Americans in the face of whiteness while doing so in the service of the larger good of society.

Yet, in proposing the salience of an outward-moving self-love from an Asian American perspective, I do not want to underestimate or undermine the force of the argument that I level against hybridity in chapter 3 and the nature of the agential constraint that chapter 4 maps out. It would be too easy to simply conclude that a path of resistance is clear and traversing that path is realistically possible so long as Asian Americans are committed to staying on that path. That of course requires the awareness that resistance is necessary in the first place and the willingness to acknowledge that its converse is, to say the least, morally problematic. But such optimism is itself theologically problematic. This book concludes by reflecting on how that theological problematic is "the problem" that Asian American identity poses to theological ethics as a whole.

While the pessimistic tone of this conclusion might be interpreted as less than liberating, that would be far from my intention. The persistence and pervasiveness of whiteness in determining the kind of persons we desire and ought to be demands an Asian American theological ethics that is emancipatory in its fundamental orientation and goal. But a too optimistic assessment of such emancipatory possibilities is just as naïve and problematic as one that is overly pessimistic. Simply desiring visibility as Asian American and demanding due recognition as Asian American in public life is complicated by the fact that being or defining oneself as Asian American on one's own terms is a tenuous prospect at best. Such precariousness in self-determination is the tragedy of Asian American life that warrants close theological-ethical inspection and interpretation. In short, being clearheaded about what it means to be Asian American in modern US society is tantamount. Reckoning with how being Asian American is a deeply racialized reality—that is, how Asian American life fits into as well as complicates our contemporary discourse on race—and grappling with the theological-ethical implications and meanings of that reality is one important step in averting cheap optimism and, we can hope, unreasonable pessimism.

1

Identity

The majority of Americans regarded us with ambivalence if not outright dis-
taste . . . We threatened the sanctity and symmetry of a white and black America
whose yin and yang racial politics left no room for any other color, particularly
that of pathetic little yellow-skinned people pickpocketing the American purse.

—*THE SYMPATHIZER*[1]

WHILE I IDENTIFY AS an Asian American, I do so with some ambivalence.
That ambivalence is a reflection of my personal history as an immigrant
to the United States who has struggled since early childhood to find my
place in American society. While many Asian Americans with similar
backgrounds have found life outside the immigrant home strange and even
alienating, my experience was more than simply about not "fitting in." It
was also colored by a profound sense of puzzling disconnection between
life at school (public and then parochial) and life at home. By puzzling I
mean the experience of wondering why my parents so firmly held onto
being Korean even though they decided to uproot themselves from South
Korea and bring me and my brother (at the ages of 4 and 1, respectively) to
live permanently in the United States, first in California and then in New
York City. I often wondered, shouldn't they try to be American or, perhaps
more generously (so I thought), just a little *more* American by speaking

1. Nguyen, *Sympathizer*, 117.

1

English in addition to Korean at home and socializing beyond Korean circles, especially beyond the Korean churches we attended? Of course, it is entirely possible that my parents thought of themselves as quintessentially American; after all, they were, like so many Americans, immigrants trying to make a better life for themselves and their children. But I remember fixating on the perceived differences: since they were not like other typical (non-Korean, non-Asian) parents in our predominantly white middle-class neighborhood of Newbury Park, CA, or working-class Irish-Italian-German neighborhood of Ridgewood, Queens, and Bushwick, Brooklyn, they were in my mind strictly Korean, no more no less. From grade school to high school, partly due to youthful contrariness but also out of a genuine desire to be "American," I was resolutely focused on trying to be like most other kids in the neighborhoods I lived in (that is, not too Korean).

However, my sense of myself as Asian and Korean American began to change later in life, to some degree, forced by the birth of my children who are multiracial: of not only Korean ancestry but also English, German, and Norwegian. Their multiraciality has occasioned a number of questions about who they are. I have found amusing the extent to which my parents see my children as Korean, or perhaps insist on treating them as Korean, primarily, for instance, calling them by their Korean middle names. Then there are my in-laws, who rarely fixate on my children's race or multiraciality, perhaps out of politeness or out of a genuine feeling that their race is irrelevant, though that has not tempered the desire to purchase American Girl dolls that are Asian-esque. While it is amusing to see how various family members navigate the multiraciality of my children, less amusing have been instances in which strangers have asked my spouse about her "adopted" children or when others (non-Asian Americans and Asian Americans alike) occasionally stare at me and my children with curiosity, engaging in a subtle and sometimes not so subtle compare-and-contrast.

In taking note of the kind of responses my children have elicited from various persons, I am often reminded of my own uncomfortable experiences with racial slurs (often linked to my so-called "slanted" eyes), stereotypical assumptions (as an Asian, I must be skilled in kung fu), and questions about my genuine origins (saying California and then New York has been less than satisfying to many who have asked, leading to the follow-up question, "Where are you *really* from?"). Such reminders have encouraged me to think more sharply about my own assumptions about race and racial identity and what I have taken to mean by Asian American. Are my multiracial children Asian American, and if so, in what sense? I often wonder if I am doing my children a disservice by not introducing them in a more regular and intentional manner to traditional Korean customs, or by not speaking to them in Korean at home (which is a tad ironic given my desire for my parents to speak more English at home). I readily admit that I have tried to assuage such doubts by coaxing my children to eat more Asian food as a subtle, perhaps accessible means of encouraging them to be conscious of themselves as Asian American and of Korean descent. But is that all there is to being Korean, to being Asian American? Is it simply a matter of performing a few conventional (or what is taken as typically traditional) cultural practices from time to time?[2] How many practices does one need to perform in order for one to be meaningfully identifiable as Asian American?

I have struggled with those kinds of questions for quite some time, and they have escaped easy resolution. If I feel uncomfortable speaking Korean to another Korean at a Korean restaurant (given my poor Korean language abilities), does that mean I am somehow less Korean, less Asian— maybe more troubling, not Asian at all? Why am I any less Asian if I do not do this or that? But why should any of this matter anyway, given that I am more than my Korean and Asian identities? Korean and Asian, yes, but a New Yorker and now also a New Jerseyan, husband, father, and academic, among other identities. It would seem that obsessing over what it means to be Asian American, like any racial identity, only ensnares Asian Americans into being over-, if not solely, determined by parochial definitions of that identity. So what, then, does it mean to be Asian American?

ASIAN AMERICAN IDENTITY
AND THE COSTS OF AMBIVALENCE

To be sure, my own ambivalence with my identity as an Asian American is not unique, and for some, such ambivalence has moved in the direction of overt dismissal of Asian American as a coherent racial identity, or at the very least cautiousness over its prospects.[3] Such an attitude is partially fueled by a conceptual objection to the idea that Asian American corresponds

2. Given that my children, by way of their mother, are also of white American identity, what it might mean to be Asian American is made more perplexing and challenging.

3. See again, for instance, Ho, *Racial Ambiguity*, and Lowe, "Heterogeneity, Hybridity, Multiplicity."

to a discernible biological or even an ontological reality. While not addressing the nature of Asian American identity per se, when US Supreme Court
Justice Clarence Thomas referred to race-based affirmative action policies
as an exercise in classroom aesthetics, the implications for racial identity,
including Asian American identity, were clear.[4] Racial identity is no more
than appearing a certain way, or being perceived a certain way based on
how one looks; I am Asian American only because my skin tone and facial
features suggest Asian in some typically accepted, aesthetic manner, which
only undermines the idea that there is something inherent to being of a
particular race.

But it is also the case that one can want to appear a certain way for particular reasons (or want to have one's appearance recognized in a particular
way), even if that appearance may lack concordance with a "real" racial
identity. Telling, for instance, is the fact that Asian American is a category
of identity that came into existence in the late 1960s, created by the historian and activist Yuji Ichioka, to mobilize Asians from diverse backgrounds
as a visible political, social force.[5] Since then, Asian American has come to
be an umbrella category of identity that mobilizes a wide array of nationalities and cultures under a single ethno-racial consciousness.

Yet, consider that many of these nationalities or cultures cannot be
regarded as interchangeable or complementary, and the deeply contested
nature of which nationalities and cultures are appropriately Asian American. Typical is the association of Asian American and those of East Asian
origins or heritages such as Korea, Japan, China, and Taiwan. More recently, those of Southeast Asian origins such as Thailand, Singapore, Myanmar,
Malaysia, and Vietnam are readily acknowledged as Asian American, and
increasingly too, South Asians such as Indians. But the inclusion of other
South Asians such as Pakistanis and Bangladeshis is still not uncontroversial, and recent scholarship on Asian Americans and Islam has raised
questions about the intersections of religion, politics, and Asian American

4. "A distinction between these two ideas (unique educational benefits based on
racial aesthetics and race for its own sake) is purely sophistic—so much so that the majority [deciding in favor of Michigan Law School's use of affirmative action] uses them
interchangeably . . . [Michigan] Law School's argument, as facile as it is, can only be understood in one way: Classroom aesthetics yields educational benefits, racially discriminatory admissions policies are required to achieve the right racial mix, and therefore the
policies are required to achieve the educational benefits." See *Grutter v. Bollinger*, 539
U.S. 306, 355 (2003) (Thomas, C. dissenting opinion).

5. Zhou, "Are Asian Americans Becoming White?," 354.

identity.[6] And consider that only 19 percent of Asian Americans describe themselves as Asian American, with 62 percent of Asian Americans preferring to identify primarily with their country of origin, according to the 2010 US census.[7]

There are good reasons to be cautious about identifying as Asian American, that is, to resist defining what it means to be Asian American. As I will discuss at greater length in chapter 2, monolithic accounts, especially monolithic cultural accounts, of Asian American identity only capture a single dimension of experience while falsely universalizing it, which perpetuate the dubious notion of cultural authenticity. Nevertheless, ambivalence over what it means to be Asian American, or whether there is in fact a meaningful Asian American identity to speak of, is not without social liabilities.

One significant cost is how "outside" perceptions of Asian Americans necessarily end up filling the definitional-identity void that such ambivalence leaves. The journalist Wesley Yang articulates well one widespread perception of Asian Americans in society and popular culture:

> Here is what I sometimes suspect my face signifies to other Americans: an invisible person, barely distinguishable from a mass of faces that resemble it. A conspicuous person standing apart from the crowd and yet devoid of any individuality. An icon of so much that the culture pretends to honor but that it in fact patronizes and exploits. Not just people "who are good at math" and play the violin, but a mass of stifled, repressed, abused, conformist quasi-robots who simply do not matter, socially or culturally.[8]

To be sure, such a perception of Asian Americans has been fueled by Asian Americans themselves. Amy Chua's infamous *Battle Hymn of the Tiger Mother* is one striking instance of such self-inflicted perpetuations of Asian Americans as a sea of disciplined, STEM-bound, and dutiful machines. But whether such an image of Asian Americans is self-perpetuated or imposed on us from "outside" is not the primary point (at least not for now; later the idea of such images of Asian Americans as imposed will be treated at

6. This is particularly so within the British context, regarding the meaning of British Asian. See Sardar, "Who Are the British Asians?" Consider also essays from Junaid Rana, Asha Nadkarni, Rajini Srikanth, and Candace Fujikane in Schlund-Vials, *Flashpoints for Asian American Studies*, 101–74.

7. These numbers are according to a Pew Research Center study of the 2010 US Census, "Rise of Asian Americans."

8. Yang, "Paper Tigers."

greater length). The more immediate point is signaled in Yang's suspicion that Asian Americans are perceived as simply not mattering. Such a perception—which is rooted in caricatures of segments of the Asian American population—only serves to sequester Asian Americans as a group from public life. The repercussions of that segregation are numerous.

(1) Ferguson and Baltimore. Consider, first, the place of Asian Americans (and how Asian Americans are perceived) in public discourse on racism and the peculiar spot Asian Americans occupy especially around the issue of discriminatory policing. More specifically, street protests in Ferguson, MO, and Baltimore, MD, spurred by the deaths of Michael Brown (August 9, 2014) and Freddie Grey (April 19, 2015), respectively, have resurrected questions about the state of relations between Asian Americans and African Americans with the looting of some Asian American businesses during those protests.[9] For some Asian Americans, those events recalled bitter memories of violence in Los Angeles's Koreatown in the wake of the Rodney King verdict in late April 1992. What is noteworthy is the way mainstream media approached the looting of Asian American businesses. It was either given little to no coverage or approached as "collateral damage," suggesting that they were one of many kinds of businesses caught in the looting crossfire and, therefore, not specifically targets by some African American protestors.[10] Adjudicating the question of whether Asian American (especially Korean American) businesses were directly or unintentionally targeted during the Ferguson and Baltimore protests is not the aim here. But noting the fact that Asian American businesses were harmed by Ferguson and Baltimore protesters recalls the legacy of tense relations between Asian Americans and African Americans and raises once again in a striking way the question of where Asian-black relations and perceptions of each other stand today. In other words, what is the status of Asian Americans as persons of color relative to non-Asian persons of color, and what role do Asian Americans play in current racial controversies and debates?

(2) Charleston and the Alt-Right. Mainstream media avoidance of the question of what role Asian Americans have in current racial debates leaves Asian Americans subject to one-dimensional interpretations of who we are. A case in point: when it was discovered that Dylann Roof, who murdered

---

9. Cf. Aizenman, "Baltimore Unrest"; and Mak, "Ferguson's Other Race Problem."

10. See, for instance, Yang, "Black-Asian Tensions"; Yang cites Lee, *Civility in the City*, to bolster his claim.

nine African Americans at the Emanuel African Methodist Episcopal Church in Charleston, SC, on June 17, 2015, believed that Asian Americans would be good allies of the white supremacist cause.[11] Then there was the widely circulated article on the so-called "yellow fever" of the white supremacist movement. The article describes one alt-right forum as advocating that "'exclusively' dating Asian women is practically a 'white-nationalist rite of passage.'" It also highlights the viral hit of a photo of Tila Tequila, a "Vietnamese-American star of the short-lived MTV reality show 'A Shot at Love With Tila Tequila,'" giving the Nazi salute "at a dinner the night before the [November 2016] conference of Richard Spencer's white-supremacist think tank, the National Policy Institute."[12] Both instances, the discovery of Roof's manifesto and Tequila's salute, were treated as either a curiosity or reinforced quiet suspicions of the inscrutability of Asian Americans as persons of color. (Perhaps Asian Americans are not really persons of color after all?)

(3) Brooklyn. The question of who Asian Americans "really" are, especially vis-à-vis other persons of color, was brought to the fore more intensely with the conviction of New York City police officer Peter Liang on February 11, 2016. Liang was found guilty for the accidental shooting death of Akai Gurley. On November 20, 2014, Liang and his partner, Shaun Landau, began their nightly vertical patrol of a predominantly African American housing project in East New York, Brooklyn, the Louis H. Pink Houses. At about 11:15 p.m., as the Asian American studies scholar Cathy J. Schlund-Vials recounts, "As per established vertical patrol protocol, Liang had his 9mm Glock drawn in his left hand; he steadied a small, police-issue flashlight in his right. Startled by a noise approximately one flight below, Liang—without specific target, with no visibility, and sans probable cause—discharged his weapon." The bullet ricocheted off a wall and struck and killed Akai Kareem Gurley who "had entered the complex just minutes after Liang and Landau; it was afterward reported that Gurley was at the Pink Houses to have his hair braided in anticipation of the upcoming Thanksgiving holiday."[13] Magnifying the tragedy of this incident,

> Gurley was unaware of the seriousness of his injuries; attempting to run from his then-unknown assailants, Gurley sought refuge in the Pink Houses, though he only made it to the project's fifth

11. O'Connor, "Here Is What Appears to Be Dylann Roof's Racist Manifesto."
12. Lim, "Alt-Right's Asian Fetish."
13. Schlund-Vials, "Crisis, Conundrum, and Critique," 6.

7

floor hallway. According to after-the-fact eyewitness accounts and trial transcripts, Liang and his partner, oblivious to the fatal detail that Gurley had been hit and unmindful that their unintended target was in dire need of emergency care, argued for almost four minutes about whether or not they should call their supervisor to report the incident. At no point did either officer provide Gurley with medical assistance, who—without basic CPR and the benefit of rudimentary first aid—quickly succumbed to the gunshot wound to his chest.[14]

The New York City police commissioner at the time, William Joseph Bratton, judged the event an unfortunate accident, yet the Brooklyn district attorney eventually indicted Liang and was found guilty of manslaughter and official misconduct.[15]

The conviction led to sizeable protests among Asian Americans in New York City and beyond.[16] For many Chinese Americans in New York City, Liang was regarded as a scapegoat. It was not lost on many that "Liang would . . . be the first NYPD officer to be convicted for a shooting that occurred in the line of duty in over a decade."[17] The Brooklyn district attorney, an African American, was accused of trying to rectify a New York grand jury's decision (on December 3, 2014) to not indict a white NYPD officer, Daniel Pantaleo, for the chokehold death of Eric Garner on July 17, 2014.[18] Schlund-Vial also notes that in addition to the failed indictment of Pantaleo, the Liang shooting was preceded only two days prior by the shooting of Tamir Rice in Cleveland, OH. The two officers involved escaped indictment. Then on November 24, 2014, it was announced by the St. Louis County prosecutor that Ferguson police officer Darren Wilson would not be indicted for shooting and killing Michael Brown.

Protests against the Brooklyn district attorney for pursuing Liang's conviction raised questions of whether Asian Americans were in solidarity with African Americans or, at the very least, understood the fullness of the distressed state of black lives in the United States. Were Asian Americans insensitive to the loss of life at the hands of Liang, simply because the shooter was Asian? Were Asian Americans unduly siding with Liang

14. Schlund-Vials, "Crisis, Conundrum, and Critique," 7.

15. Schlund-Vials, "Crisis, Conundrum, and Critique," 8.

16. Consider Philadelphia, where Asian Americans protested in support of Liang. See Swanson, "Thousands in Philadelphia Protest."

17. Schlund-Vials, "Crisis, Conundrum, and Critique," 8.

18. See Rojas, "In New York, Thousands Protest."

because Gurley was black? New York state assemblyman Ron Kim, after the Liang conviction, asserted: "Our system failed Gurley and it failed Liang. It pitted the unjust death of an innocent young black man against the unjust scapegoating of a young Asian police officer who was frightened, poorly trained, and who committed a terrible accident."[19] Such appeals to Liang's situation as demanding the attention of the civil rights movement were perceived as strained and fell flat, if not altogether ignored by many outside the Asian American community, especially among African American community leaders.

(4) Milwaukee. The questions emerging from the Liang-Gurley tragedy—the location of Asian Americans in contemporary racial discourse and whether Asian Americans are relevant voices in the struggle for racial and social justice—have persisted well after the Liang case. Revealing is the first-person account of an Asian American journalist with the *Milwaukee Journal Sentinel* who was sent to cover the shooting of Sylville Smith on August 13, 2016. The account underscores vividly the uneasy, fraught relationship between Asian Americans and the Black Lives Matters movement. The journalist, Aaron Mak, recalls his anxiety over the potential for violence in the wake of that shooting in Milwaukee. An African American community activist spotted him and called him over, "I can see from your face that you don't think you're safe." Mak identified himself as Chinese American and the community activist retorted, "You're a minority, too." After a strange turn of events, however, Mak soon found himself chased by a group of African Americans. They eventually caught up to him and landed blows on his back, head, and torso. He then heard someone yelling, "Stop! He's not white! He's Asian!" Reflecting on that moment and the events that followed, Mak writes the following: "The voice that stuck in my head over the next few days, as I talked to relatives and friends about it, belonged to a woman who'd come up to me in the afternoon scrum: 'You're Asian, right?' she said to me. 'Why are you even here?'"[20]

(5) College Campuses. And then there is the question of Asian Americans' place, if any, in protests over issues of racial discrimination, inequality, and appropriation that has roiled many US college campuses. In reflecting on her Asian American students' experience with this question, Nitasha Sharma of Northwestern University writes, "Black student activists told one Asian American student that he was not a minority, he was not Black, and

---

19. As cited in Schlund-Vials, "Crisis, Conundrum, and Critique," 9.

20. Mak, "You're Asian, Right?"

therefore was, like White students, there to listen rather than to speak."[21] Such an attitude underscores the kind of challenges that Asian Americans face in making sense of "when and where to enter conversations on race," if they figure into that conversation at all.[22] In an aptly titled *Atlantic Monthly* essay, "What Role Do Asian Americans Have in the Campus Protests?" posted not too long after student protests at Princeton University demanding the removal of the name Woodrow Wilson from campus buildings, Asian American students are quoted as suggesting that they are perceived, at best, as ancillary and, at worst, irrelevant to that conversation.[23] The essay notes Asian American students who felt ignored by the Black Justice League, the Princeton student group that led the protests, as they finalized an agreement with Princeton's president on how to promote a culture of racial justice on campus. The article quotes Hunter Dong, a Princeton University junior and member of its undergraduate government. When asked about his view on the protests, the essay registers, "he highlighted his frustration with the oftentimes-overlooked Asian American perspective during discussions of minority rights. 'It seemed like there wasn't any room in there for any other minority or culture groups to attend these meetings and talk with the administration,' Dong said."[24]

(6) Affirmative Action. That Asian Americans are perceived (or, at the very least, susceptible to being perceived) as *negatively* relevant to the adjudication of contemporary racial issues is visible in how Asian Americans are situated within contemporary debates on affirmative action. The controversial position that Asian Americans find themselves over questions of affirmative action are not new; Asian Americans are familiar players since at least the passage of Proposition 209 in the state of California in 1996. Proposition 209 added a new section to the California state constitution, part of which reads: "The state shall not discriminate against, or grant preferential treatment to, any individual or group on the basis of race, sex, color, ethnicity, or national origin in the operation of public employment, public education, or public contracting" (Section 31, Article 1). Subsequent to the approval of this amendment, Asian students have gone from 29.8 percent (11,085) of the freshman admits to 37.47 percent (22,877) at California

21. Sharma, "Racial Studies Project," 56.
22. Sharma, "Racial Studies Project," 56.
23. Cheng, "What Role Do Asian Americans Have."
24. Cheng, "What Role Do Asian Americans Have."

public universities,[25] fueling perceptions that Asian Americans are one of the primary beneficiaries of Proposition 209 perhaps at the expense of other minority populations.[26]

Consider also a 2015 lawsuit against Harvard University regarding its undergraduate admissions and its effects on Asian American applicants.[27] The complaint reignites the question of the status of Asian Americans as persons of color. The complaint against Harvard, brought by a coalition of sixty-four Asian American organizations to the US Departments of Education and Justice, alleges "unlawful racial discrimination that led to the rejection of admission of highly qualified Asian American applicants."[28] As

25. *Ballotpedia*, https://ballotpedia.org/California_Affirmative_Action,_Proposition _209_(1996).

26. On this issue, it is interesting to note that "the only major category that declined in percentage terms was whites, who went from 44% (16,465) of the freshmen admits to 34% (20,807)," *Ballotpedia*, https://ballotpedia.org/California_Affirmative_Action,_Proposition_209_(1996). It is important to note that such perceptions of Asian American self-interest was stoked by many groups who sought the end of affirmative action policies. As the political scientists Claire Jean Kim and Taeku Lee note: "During the controversy over Asian American admissions quotas at selective universities in the 1980s, conservatives depicted Asian Americans as victims of pro-Black affirmative action programs, when they were actually being harmed by quotas intended to preserve the whiteness of student bodies (Takagi 1992). Similarly, proponents of Proposition 209 in California insisted that 'preferential treatment' for Blacks and Latinos rendered Asian Americans victims of 're-verse discrimination' (Park and Park 1999)" (Kim and Lee, "Interracial Politics," 547). In the latest affirmative action case in the US Supreme Court, it is noteworthy that Associate Justice Samuel Alito, in his dissent in the 2016 *Fisher v. The University of Texas at Austin* case, referred to possible discrimination against Asian American students. In his dissent, he "emphasized that the University of Texas—which automatically admits students from the top 10 percent of each public high school . . . enrolls fewer Asian Americans than it does Hispanics. Unless the university is illegally massaging the racial composition of its student body so that it reflects the state's population, in which Hispanics outnumber Asians, he argued, 'it seemingly views the classroom contributions of Asian-American students as less valuable than those of Hispanic students'" (Wong, "Asian Americans and the Future of Affirmative Action"). Alito's comments suggest that the University of Texas at Austin is engaging in a kind of race-conscious admissions policy that is unfairly keeping Asian American students away from the university, adding to the evidence that affirmative action policies are generally suspect.

27. Brought by the Asian American Coalition for Education, http://asianamerican-foreducation.org/en/hime/. See also the *Chronicle of Higher Education* for text of the complaint, http://www.chronicle.com/blogs/ticker/asian-american-groups-seek-federal-investigation-of-alleged-bias-at-harvard/99053. These citations originally accessed from Chuh, "Asians Are the New . . . What?," 233.

28. Citations from the 2015 complaint are from Chuh, "Asians are the New . . . What?," 220.

the Asian American Studies scholar Kandice Chuh exposits, "By way of introduction, the complaint explains that 'over the last two decades, Asian American applicants to Harvard University and other Ivy League colleges have increasingly experienced discrimination in the admissions process.' It continues: 'It has become especially difficult for high-performing male Asian American students to gain admission to Harvard University and other Ivy League colleges.'"[29] This complaint supports itself with the claim that preeminently qualified Asian Americans being denied admissions to Harvard creates racial barriers between racial groups. Again, referring to Chuh's citation of the complaint, "In its subsection titled 'Creating racial barriers between Asian-Americans and other racial groups,' the complaint further explains that 'most Asian-Americans want to merge into the American melting pot and to develop pleasant relationship [sic] with other racial groups. However, the discrimination by Harvard University and other Ivy League Colleges is creating a racial divide between Asian-Americans and other racial groups.'"[30] While the 2015 lawsuit was dismissed later that year, findings that were made public in June 2018, stemming from an earlier 2014 lawsuit against Harvard University by a group called Students for Fair Admissions (or SFA),[31] show, according to claimants, that Asian American applicants to Harvard were consistently rated as having lower personality traits such as likability and being widely respected.[32] Those findings, according to SFA, prove the merits of their lawsuit that Harvard discriminates against Asian American applicants, echoing the claims registered in the 2015 lawsuit.

The arguments advanced against Harvard by both lawsuits revolve around the suspicion that Asian American applicants are being disadvantaged relative to white applicants. The 2015 lawsuit, as Chuh points out, cites Thomas J. Espenshade and Alexandra Radford's study *No Longer Separate, Not Yet Equal*.[33] But to the extent that Espenshade and Radford also note that African American and Latino/a applicants are afforded a relative advantage in admissions compared to white applicants, the per-

29. Chuh, "Asians are the New . . . What?," 220.

30. Chuh, "Asians are the New . . . What?," 229.

31. For more information on Students for Fair Admissions, see their website, https://studentsforfairadmissions.org.

32. Hartocollis, "Harvard Rates Asian-American Applicants Lower." See also Hartocollis, "Asian Americans Suing Harvard."

33. Chuh, "Asians Are the New . . . What?," 234n6; Espenshade and Radford, *No Longer Separate, Not Yet Equal*.

ception that Asian American students think of themselves as besieged by both whites *and* other persons of color is not unreasonable, or so those behind the 2015 lawsuit suggest.[34] According to Chuh, the 2015 complaint "submits that 'Asians have the lowest acceptance rate for each [SAT] score bracket, lower than Whites, Blacks, and Hispanic [*sic*].'"[35] As such, "the complaint describes Asian Americans as targets of racial discrimination akin to antiblack and antibrown racism and as suffering from being not-white, not-black, and not-brown[, while] deftly erasing the access that affirmative action politics have afforded Asian Americans."[36] That erasure, however, circles back to the question of Asian American alignment with (or distance from) other minority communities.[37] Moreover, inasmuch as Students for Fair Admissions, the group that initiated the 2014 lawsuit against Harvard, is led by Edward Blum, a scholar at the conservative think tank the American Enterprise Institute and noted anti-affirmative action advocate, the 2014 lawsuit, at least, has raised suspicions of the integrity and seriousness of Asian American claims for wanting the elimination of racial barriers, further underscoring the inscrutability of Asian Americans as persons of color.

(7) Standardized Testing. Those suspicions have also surfaced, perhaps more as resentful innuendos, in New York City over debates on the

34. See, for instance, the opinion piece by Joshi, "Stop Anti-Asian Bias."

35. Chuh, "Asians Are the New . . . What?," 221.

36. Chuh, "Asians Are the New . . . What?," 229.

37. While the perception that Asian Americans are disinclined to affirm affirmative action policies to address discrimination against African Americans and Latinos/as have been aided by such lawsuits, as well as Asian Americans who have expressed disapproval of the University of Texas at Austin's affirmative action policies in the 2016 *Fisher* case, organizations such as Asian Americans Advancing Justice, Asian American Legal Defense and Education Fund, and scholars such as Karthick Ramakrishnan at the University of California at Riverside have argued that Asian Americans as a whole affirm affirmative action; those who oppose represent a small minority. As Alia Wong reports, "In 2012, the National Asian American Survey found that three in four Asian Americans support affirmative action. The 2016 Asian American Voter Survey similarly found substantial support when it asked respondents, 'Do you favor or oppose affirmative action programs designed to help blacks, women, and other minorities get better access to higher education?' A majority of respondents—64 percept—said they think it's a good thing. . . Such broad support for race conscious admissions policies sends a clear message that AAPIs [Asian Americans and Pacific Islanders] overwhelmingly support these policies and will not be used as a racial wedge to disenfranchise other communities of color,' Laboi Hoq, the litigation director at Asian Americans Advancing Justice-Los Angeles, said" (Wong, "Asian Americans and the Future of Affirmative Action").

fairness of the admissions test (the Specialized High Schools Admissions Test or SHSAT) for entry into the City's elite specialized high schools, such as Stuyvesant, Bronx Science, and Brooklyn Technical. Demographics of student enrollment in these specialized public high schools show 51.7 percent of the 5,067 offers of admissions for incoming 9th graders in 2018 went to Asian Americans, while only 6.3 and 4.1 percent went to African Americans and Latino/a students, respectively.[38] Aiming to bolster nonwhite and non-Asian student admissions to these public schools, the mayor of New York City has proposed the elimination of the standardized entrance exam, which currently serves as the sole criteria for admissions. In response, Peter Koo, a New York City councilman whose district includes sizeable Asian American communities in the City's borough of Queens, stated, "The test is the most unbiased way to get into a school . . . It doesn't require an interview. It doesn't require a resume. It doesn't even require connections . . . [The mayor of New York City, Bill DeBlasio,] wants to stop this and build a barrier to Asian Americans."[39] The remark by Richard A. Carranza, the New York City school's chancellor, was found particularly offensive and enflaming: "I just don't buy into the narrative that any one ethnic group owns admissions to these school." The former city comptroller John C. Liu called those remarks "the most offensive and irritating comments that Asian-Americans have heard in quite some time."[40]

While such comments captured the concerns of many within Asian American communities across New York City, at the same time, they raised questions, similar to those raised with the Harvard affirmative action lawsuits, about whether Asian Americans are uninterested in the question of fair access to New York City's specialized public high schools. Implied in such questions is whether Asian Americans are more interested in advancing their interests and, in the process, aligning themselves with white New Yorkers at the expense of African Americans and Latino/a communities in New York City. The *New York Times* Editorial Board's endorsement of the elimination of the SHSAT is revealing of how those questions are received. In noting how the admissions test has "unfairly denied so many black and Latino New Yorkers," the Editorial Board's opinion essay displays a picture of graduating Stuyvesant seniors in June 2018, zeroing in on two smiling

38. *New York Times* Editorial Board, "It's Time to Integrate." See also Brody, "Who Got Into Stuyvesant."

39. Harris and Hu, "Asian Groups See Bias."

40. Chen, "Huge Blind Spot."

Asian American students posing for a picture with two (presumably) white students; in the background, somewhat blurred (but certainly not the primary focal point of the image), is a group of three graduates, one who appears black or Latina and another wearing a hijab. The message of the image is rather unambiguous; Asian American and white New Yorkers, together, have benefited from the admissions policy for New York City's specialized high schools, whereas "the admissions policy is flawed and unfair to other children." It further notes that "the current testing regime is not 'race-blind,' since it can't be separated from the reality of unequal schools and the disadvantages of generations of poverty and racism,"[41] intimating that white New Yorkers, but more notably Asian American New Yorkers, are not necessarily the ones who have been trapped in such inequality and disadvantages. How else to interpret the editorial essay as advancing a perception of Asian Americans as disconnected to the realities facing other communities of color in New York City? More to the point, perhaps Asian Americans are a different social breed altogether?

ASIAN AMERICANS, THE QUESTIONABLE MINORITY: ANTIBLACKNESS IN THEOLOGICAL ETHICS

If the controversy surrounding admissions standards to New York City's specialized high schools, just like the affirmative action complaints against Harvard University, sharply bring to the fore the question of the status of Asian Americans as people of color vis-à-vis other minority communities in the United States, then the move, especially within certain sectors of theological ethics, to articulate the nature of white racism as distinctively antiblackness encapsulates that status for Asian Americans as essentially different and, thus, immaterial to the struggle for racial justice in the United States, and quite possibly part of the problem. To presume difference between Asian Americans and other communities of color is not to deny our minority status; in terms of absolute numbers Asian Americans are minorities. Yet, whether Asian Americans occupy the same social situation or face similar social pressures as other persons of color at the level of political, economic, and cultural status, privilege, and opportunity is a different question, and it is one that is especially pronounced in Katie Walker Grimes's articulation of antiblackness.

41. *New York Times* Editorial Board, "It's Time to Integrate."

Vincent W. Lloyd and Andrew Prevot describe antiblackness as "the key term employed in struggles for racial justice today. The key term for an earlier generation was racism." The switch from simply racism to anti-blackness calls attention, they claim, to at least two limitations to the term racism. First, "conversations about racism can tend . . . to remain at an unhelpful level of abstraction," distracting from the actual harm of white racism by sometimes leading to appeals to reverse racism.[42] Second, the term racism does not necessarily focus attention on the structural causes of racism and instead can lead to a myopic focus on individual prejudices, however important that may be. Grimes follows this definition of anti-blackness, which is certainly not without merit. But Grimes takes it a step further by proposing that antiblackness obscures the actual harms of white racism if it is not specified as "antiblackness supremacy." A critical part of that specification is a critique of the term white privilege, which she argues is conceptually deficient in its ability to establish "*white* privilege [as] more oppressive than other forms of privilege, especially if every one experiences different amounts and bundles of privilege."[43] Her emphasis on white is key, for it underscores Grimes's primary concern for switching antiblackness to antiblackness supremacy. "[Unlike other] forms of asymmetrical power relations, anti-blackness alone bears the imprint of black slavery." It is the enslavement of black bodies—its history and sustained legacy—that is at the center of the unique violence of racism on black bodies. Grimes continues, "Because it recognizes the singularity of the black experience, the expression 'anti-blackness supremacy' in fact surpasses 'white supremacy' in both rhetorical power and descriptive precision."[44]

Consequently, following the philosopher George Yancey, Grimes advocates for a black-nonblack framework for discussing race rather than a white-nonwhite dichotomy as a way of calling attention to the singularity of black experience formed by slavery. In addition, the black-nonblack framework sheds light on how not all persons of color occupy the same racial position. In fact, Grimes suggests, not only are the racial realities different, many nonblack persons of color must be recognized as having social status at the expense of black lives: "Thus, even if nonblack people of color do not occupy the ontological position of 'master,' they enjoy immunity from the

42. Lloyd and Prevot, introduction to *Anti-Blackness and Christian Ethics*, xxi.

43. Grimes, "Black Exceptionalism," 44, emphasis original. Themes in this essay are treated further in Grimes, *Christ Divided*.

44. Grimes, "Black Exceptionalism," 45.

ontological position of 'slave.' We might be tempted here to describe this reality of 'nonblack privilege.' But more than simply enjoying nonblack privilege, nonblack people accrue power over and at the expense of blackness."[45]

The temptation, to highlight a word she uses in the foregoing citation, to claim nonblack privilege to nonblack persons of color is the temptation to explicitly call out Latinos/as and Asian Americans as those who are increasingly adjacent to white privilege at the expense of black empowerment. (She does not necessarily say whether experiencing nonblack privilege is a mark of nonblack minority populations essentially having entered whiteness as an identity category, such as many European immigrants to the United States.) But to some extent, Grimes is not simply tempted, for she makes it abundantly clear that at least with reference to Asian Americans, they are not only different in their racial positioning from African Americans (that is, differential experiences of racial violence), but are in possession of a kind of social power and freedom that marks them as participating in antiblackness. As she asserts, "Because the expression 'anti-blackness supremacy' names power as the essence of racial evil, it maintains the link between the oppression of black people and enslavement in a way the appellation 'anti-blackness' cannot. It points out not just what black people endure, but also what nonblack people gain."[46] Such gain is what frames the racial realities of Asian Americans, as a community immune from racial discrimination. Minimizing, but perhaps more accurately trivializing, the plight of Asian Americans of Southeast Asian descent such as Laotians and Cambodians (interestingly she does not mention Hmong, Malaysians, and Bangladeshis, among other Asian groups), she notes, "Asian Americans end up in prison at lower rates than everyone else."[47] To acknowledge the gains of nonblack persons of color such as Asian Americans sheds light on how "the relative affluence and educational success of Asian Americans" contributes to or "partake[s] in the discourse that purports to unmask the inherent weaknesses of African Americans."[48] Lastly, the gains of nonblack persons of color such as Asian Americans are indicative of the pervasive tug of antiblack racism, even on nonblack persons of color: "Besides, one does not have to be white to be anti-black. Asian Americans and nonblack Latino/as desire residential distance from native-born blacks at rates that

45. Grimes, "Black Exceptionalism," 45.
46. Grimes, "Black Exceptionalism," 47.
47. Grimes, "Black Exceptionalism," 54.
48. Grimes, "Black Exceptionalism," 54.

approach and sometimes even surpass those of Anglo whites. Judging by their residential behavior, nonblack people place the definitive color line not between white and nonwhite, but black and nonblack."[49]

The assimilationist pressures on Asian Americans are not insignificant and, as chapter 3 will outline in more detail, the racial consequences of such pressures, especially via the model minority myth, uncomfortably situates Asian Americans in the marginalizing dynamics of white racism. But black-Asian relations do not simply move in the direction of Asian Americans purportedly surpassing African Americans economically and, thus, participating in the suppression of black freedom; the dynamic also moves in the other direction. Grimes in only giving perfunctory gloss to Asian American social gains too easily ignores and, perhaps, absolves black insensitivity to and, thus, perpetuation of the stereotyping of Asian Americans (or what we might call the Chris Rock syndrome).[50] Such oversight of, or maybe even refusal to acknowledge, the more nuanced and discomfiting character of interracial relations is part and parcel of the larger trivialization of the complicated political, economic, and social realities that Asian Americans confront. For instance, as the political scientists Claire Jean Kim and Taeku Lee note, "Not all scholars agree that Asian Americans are advantaged relative to Blacks. For instance, a few argue that Asian Americans (specifically Korean Americans) stand in a horizontal relationship with Blacks insofar as Korean Americans have economic power but lack political power and Blacks have political power but lack economic power."[51] We can also add Pew Research Center findings that income inequality increased most among Asian Americans between 1970 to 2016, surpassing African

---

49. Grimes, "Black Exceptionalism," 59-60.

50. See Liu, "Why Chris Rock's Asian Joke Was Such a Disappointment." The public stereotyping of Asian Americans is not unique to Chris Rock, however. Among other instances, one that also stands out given the mainstream media coverage it received is Steve Harvey's segment on his eponymous television show that perpetuated the emasculation of Asian American males. As the celebrity chef Eddie Huang recounts in an opinion piece expressing his deep disapproval of Harvey's segment, "On Jan. 6 [2017], Steve Harvey did a roundup of dating books on his talk show, displaying an image of the cover of 'How to Date a White Woman,' and said the book could be only one page long: "'Excuse me, do you like Asian men?' 'No.' 'Thank you.'" He then asked an imaginary black woman if she liked Asian men, and acted out her response: 'I don't even like Chinese food, boy. It don't stay with you no time. I don't eat what I can't pronounce'" (Huang, "Hey, Steve Harvey").

51. Kim and Lee, "Interracial Politics," 55on4.

Americans.[52] Even with respect to racial profiling, while focus is rightly placed on how African Americans are unjustly targeted, Asian Americans are hardly immune to the same.[53] Lastly, in the midst of current conflicts over the question of due process and deportations, that question is rarely regarded as an Asian American one, but it is.[54] But adjudicating who is more harmed or at a social disadvantage is not the primary point, nor should it be; it is ultimately fruitless, further pitting one community of color against another, jeopardizing racial solidarity. The more salient and consequential point is that Grimes fails to account for the complexity of Asian American social realities due to the insistence on the Manichaean dichotomy of black versus nonblack.

To acknowledge the complicated social realities of Asian Americans is more than to simply call attention to the fact that Asian Americans are in a more economically, politically, and culturally precarious situation than is commonly recognized. More importantly, such insistence pertains to the notion that the very *opacity* of the complicated social realities of Asian Americans is *itself* a function of white racism working on both Asian Americans and African Americans alike. While this point will be elaborated more deeply in chapters 3 and 4, suffice it to say here that in focusing primarily on the social gains of Asian Americans at the purported expense of African American freedom—ostensibly by channeling the power of the slave master *through* Asian Americans against the slaves, who are still African Americans—the racial situation of Asian Americans is not given (nor can it be given) a fuller accounting and, thus, serves to marginalize Asian Americans as irrelevant to discussions on racism (or, at least, relevant only to extent that we are now part of the problem). That marginalization of Asian Americans in racial discourse, paradoxically, grants more power to whiteness since it obscures the fullness of the logic of white racism, that is, how white racism

52. Kochhar and Cilluffo, "Income Inequality in the U.S."

53. See, for instance, the ACLU's website, https://www.aclu.org/racial-profiling-definition; cf. Linshi, "Why Ferguson Should Matter to Asian Americans."

54. Indonesians, for instance, have been the target of recent Immigration, Customs, and Enforcement activities. See Sherman, "In 'Life and Death' Stakes." Also, a sizeable number of Vietnamese Americans are at greater risk of deportation proceedings due to immigration policies adopted by the Trump administration. See Denyer, "Thousands of Vietnamese." Also consider that "roughly twenty percent of Korean immigrants are unauthorized. Immigrants from South Korea make up the fifth-largest share of DACA recipients, and the number of undocumented immigrants coming from the country has increased by more than 700 percent in the last 30 years." See Medina, "Awe, Gratitude, Fear."

operates to further its colonizing reach.[55] Such obscurity is inevitable when racial discourse is singularly focused on how white racism pivots on, to borrow a description from Ta-Nehesi Coates, the plundering of black bodies. This is not to deny that black bodies have been subjugated and that they continue to be systemically threatened and harmed; that white racism is antiblack racism is unassailable. But the very fact that such a qualification or disclaimer must be made, by an Asian American, to indicate the veracity of white racial evil suggests how nonblack persons of color, especially Asian Americans, are only given the choice to arrive to the conversation on racism in an inherently different position, one that is secondary or minor at best, that is, as having ancillary experiences to the true force of white racism. In that respect, it is interesting to note Sharma's experience in advocating for comparative race studies, which methodologically prioritizes studying racism intersectionally, which moves slightly differently than the premise that "anti-Blackness is global and foundational to the formation of society . . . [,]the basis from which other racisms, such as Islamophobia, Native genocide, and immigrant nativism, emerge."[56] Sharma notes that for some of her students, "Blackness, or rather, anti-Blackness, trumps any and all other kinds of racisms (if, indeed, critics acknowledge the reality of any other kind of racism)." She then recounts how they "interpreted [her] presentation of comparative race studies as 'anti-Black' . . . as a move away

---

55. Asian American scholars also fall into this trap. Consider Minh-Ha T. Pham's reflection on the need to eliminate the standardized test for entry into New York City's specialized public high schools. She writes, "For school admissions to be truly unbiased, all students would need to have equal access to elementary schools and middle schools that receive equal shares of property taxes and state and federal aid and have the same cultural, educational and social resources. That kind of equality doesn't exist, in large part because of the anti-Black racism that has been a defining feature of this country since its inception. This deep-seated and well-documented force, which fuels employment discrimination and keeps neighborhoods and schools segregated, has not kept Asian-Americans from getting access to public resources to the same extent that it has African-Americans" (Pham, "De Blasio's Plan for NYC Schools"). While I agree with Pham that standardized tests are not unbiased and merit elimination or at least ought to be only one factor among many for admissions purposes, the larger point to be drawn here is that she too simplistically insulates Asian Americans from the force of white racism. White racism is certainly antiblack, but to suggest that white racism, therefore, has been less anti-Asian obscures the complexity of how Asian Americans are subject to the grip of white racism.

56. Sharma, "Racial Studies Project," 56.

from the specificity and exceptionalism of the Black condition as one of abjection."[57]

To the extent that antiblackness, in its emphasis on the singular experience of black persons and how nonblack persons reinscribe white freedom at the expense of black bodies, displaces Asian Americans from the center to the periphery of discussions on racism, the black-nonblack dichotomy ends up no more than perpetuating the black-white dichotomy that has traditionally framed how race is discussed in the United States. The primary difference with Grimes's iteration of the black-white dichotomy is that she makes more explicit the idea that nonblack persons of color such as Asian Americans are more appropriate to the white pole of the dichotomy.

ASIAN AMERICANS IN THE MIDDLE OF BLACK AND WHITE?

The pervasiveness of thinking about racism between the poles of black and white only serves to buttress Asian American ambivalence, that is, the uncertainly of what it means to be Asian American within the larger conversation on race in the contemporary United States. Asian Americans have never easily figured into the black-white paradigm, as US legal history makes clear. According to Kandice Chuh and Karen Shimikawa's account of that history, the 1854 California Supreme Court case *People v. George C. Hall* ostensibly begins the legal wrestling over what Asian Americans are or, more specifically, "the content of the category 'Asian' (figured variously as 'Chinese,' 'Asiatic,' 'Mongolian,' 'Yellow')."[58] The *People* case involved a defendant's appeal of a conviction that "rested on the testimony of three Chinese witnesses."[59] The appeal was based on "an 1850 statute that barred testimony for or against a white person by a 'Black or Mulatto person, or an Indian.' The Court was asked to determine what 'specific typ[e] of the human species' Chineseness was in relation to this statute."[60] While the court ultimately decided that Chinese persons are suitably "Indian" given their prehistorical ties to Native Americans who migrated across the Bering Strait, the larger significance of the case is that it "inaugurates a string of cases in which the courts must determine what Asianness is in relation to

57. Sharma, "Racial Studies Project," 56.
58. Chuh and Shimikawa, "Adjudicating Asian America," 31.
59. Chuh and Shimikawa, "Adjudicating Asian America," 31.
60. Chuh and Shimikawa, "Adjudicating Asian America," 31.

the categories of blackness and whiteness."[61] As the decision of the *People v. George C. Hall* case demonstrates, US courts struggled with such determination. Determining what made Asian persons Asian was made more difficult by the way in which the rights that came with being naturalized citizens of the United States was "restricted to 'free white person[s]' and (following the ratification of the Fourteenth and Fifteenth Amendments to the US Constitution) to 'aliens of African nativity, and to persons of African descent.'"[62] Chinese applicants were often rejected for naturalization on the basis that they were neither white nor black, being deemed of the "Mongolian race" in the federal circuit court case *In re Ah Yup* in 1878.[63]

It was not until 1922 and 1923 in *Takao Ozawa v. United States* and *United States v. Bhagat Singh Thind*, respectively, that "the U.S. Supreme Court 'settled' the question," as a matter of constitutional law, of what Asian Americans are, "establishing categorically that whiteness excludes Asians, thereby constituting Asianness as a distinct racial category."[64] Since these

61. Chuh and Shimikawa, "Adjudicating Asian America," 32.

62. Chuh and Shimikawa, "Adjudicating Asian America," 32. According to the historian Charles J. McClain, the restriction of naturalized citizenship to white persons dates back to 1790 when the first federal naturalization statute was enacted, restricting the "right of naturalization to 'any alien, being a free white person.'" McClain then explains that "Congress revisited the question of racial eligibility for naturalization in 1870 . . . In Congress, versions of a new naturalization statute were discussed that would have eliminated the word 'white' from the provision defining classes of persons eligible for naturalization. However, Westerners and other representatives objected on the grounds that this would extend the naturalization privilege to Chinese immigrants, and the change in wording was voted down. The new naturalization statute that was ultimately enacted did contain a section extending the privilege of naturalization to 'aliens of African nativity, and to persons of African descent'" (McClain, "Tortuous Path, Elusive Goal," 35).

63. Chuh and Shimikawa, "Adjudicating Asian America," 32. The attorney for the four Chinese immigrants who filed naturalization petitions in the federal circuit court in San Francisco "contended that the term 'white persons' was vague and indeterminate and could not be taken literally, since within the class of persons called 'white' could be found individuals of many different shades—'from the lightest blonde to the most swarthy brunette.'" The court's response defined white person in such a way as to make clear that Asians were of another race altogether: "The words 'white person,' said the court, had a well-settled meaning in both common speech and scientific literature and were seldom if ever used in a sense so comprehensive as to include individuals of the Mongolian race" (McClain, "Tortuous Path, Elusive Goal," 36).

64. Chuh and Shimikawa, "Adjudicating Asian America," 33. These Supreme Court decisions, therefore, can be considered as finally catching up to or affirming the longstanding federal statutory designation of Asians as Asians or distinct from whites that was definitively spelled out in the first Chinese Exclusion Act of 1882. See McClain, "Tortuous Path, Elusive Goal," 37–50. McClain notes that the designation of Chinese

two cases involved the racial status of Japanese and (South Asian) Indian persons, the court's decision made clear that whiteness excludes not only Chinese but also other Asian persons. Being deemed as such, the legal basis for universal Asian American exclusion, that is, irrespective of national origin with respect to immigration and especially citizenship, was established, which "further sedimented the status of Asians as suspect or altogether ineligible for U.S. American identity."[65] When the Immigration and Nationality Act was passed in 1965, only then did the *exclusion* of Asians shift to the *regulation* of Asian entry into the United States.[66]

If the dominance of the black-white paradigm has for most of American legal history placed Asian Americans in a kind of racial limbo, neither black nor white, but something entirely different—that is, Asian—then that legal history indicates how Asian Americans have been susceptible to being "middle minorities." Drawing from Andrew Sung Park, the theologian Jonathan Y. Tan describes what it means to be a middle minority or "middle-agent minority." "Specifically, the middle minority group acts as a buffer in turbulent sociopolitical or economic moments between the dominant elite who holds the levers of power on the one side, and the exploited and oppressed groups on the other side."[67] This is not to be a buffer in the more familiar mode of the middle child, who, as such, is capable of empathizing with both older and younger siblings and serving as a bridge for sibling cooperation and peace.[68] Instead, Asian Americans as middle minorities, or buffer between black and white persons, are present "as an attractive target for the anger and frustrations of the oppressed, but is itself also discriminated against, and unprotected by the dominant elite."[69]

---

immigrants as of the Mongolian race in the 1878 federal circuit course case *In re Ah Yup*, as noted above, was never taken up by the Supreme Court and was thus not binding on other federal or state courts when it came to questions of Asian eligibility for citizenship. The *In re Ah Yup* decision was affirmed, however, through various federal statutes, most prominently in the 1882 Chinese Exclusion Act that specifically forbade US courts from granting Chinese citizenship since they were not white. With the *Ozawa* and *Bhagat* Supreme Court decisions, a federal constitutional ban, and not only a federal statutory ban, on citizenship for Asian Americans was established.

65. Chuh and Shimikawa, "Adjudicating Asian America," 34. On the legal status of Filippinos, see McClain, "Tortuous Path, Elusive Goal," 50–53.

66. Chuh and Shimikawa, "Adjudicating Asian America," 34.

67. Tan, *Introducing Asian American Theologies*, 39–40. Cf. Park, *Racial Conflict and Healing*, 35–37.

68. Sternbergh, "Extinction of the Middle Child."

69. Tan, *Introducing Asian American Theologies*, 40.

Asian Americans, therefore, are literally caught in the middle like a Ping-Pong ball bandied about between two competing players in American racial politics. Not only has there been legal resistance to accepting Asian Americans into mainstream American society (i.e., citizenship, since they are not white), Asian Americans also serve as convenient scapegoats for the injustices suffered by African Americans at the hands of white society, as some Asian Americans have argued in the case of Peter Liang, as we saw earlier. The casting of Asian Americans as scapegoats is also related to the casting of Asian Americans as perpetuators of racism rather than its victims.[70] For instance, the contention that Asian Americans in Hawaii benefit from "settler colonialism" is one provocative instantiation of Asian Americans serving as buffer. "While Asian Americans in Hawai'i frequently complain about anti-Asian discrimination on the part of haoles [or white Hawaiians]," the idea of settler colonialism highlights how "they are much less willing to acknowledge their own role in dispossessing Native people of their resources and benefiting from the latter's political, economic, and social subjugation."[71] The merits of such dispossession notwithstanding, the critique of settler colonialism also distracts from the negative impact of white Hawaiians as the original colonizers and how the legacy of colonialism and imperialism undergirds the multivalent forms of dispossession in Hawaii, as well as in other Pacific islands, Native American communities, and, to be sure, among African Americans.

While Asian Americans may be caught in the middle between black and white, is that characterization of the state of Asian American life adequate? Part of the problem with being descried as middle minorities is that it maintains the notion that Asian Americans are essentially different from other communities of color. That is true in at least a literal sense, just as Latinos/as are not the same as African Americans, African Americans are not the same as Latinos/as, Asian Americans are not the same as African Americans, and so on. At the same time racial essentialism is conceptually as well as descriptively suspect as any other form of essentialism. The concern in raising the question of difference is more precisely a concern over whether Asian Americans are in some meaningful or nontrivial way a part of the narrative of racism in American society. If Asian Americans are only

70. Kim and Lee, "Interracial Politics," 546; they refer to Kim, "Korean Americans in U.S. Race Relations," 69–78, and Matsuda, "We Will Not Be Used," 79–84.

71. Kim and Lee, "Interracial Politics," 546. See also Chuh and Shimikawa, "Adjudicating Asian America," 36.

middle minorities, then it would seem that Asian Americans are part of that narrative only when one side or another—black or white—forces our participation in the narrative for a specific, momentary reason, one that serves the interests of either blacks or whites. As an Asian American Princeton University student is quoted as saying about Asian Americans' relationship to racial protests on college campuses, "Asians are minorities whenever it's useful for people to frame them as such."[72] If only instrumental players in the ongoing narrative of race in American society, Asian Americans, then, are merely interlopers of this narrative whose primary place is, recalling Sharma's anecdote about her Asian American students' work with the Black Lives Matter movement, to simply listen to what is said about race—what is offered as firsthand testimony of the realities or effects of racism—rather than active storytellers of our own realities of race in American life. To be given the opportunity to be active storytellers would assume that Asian American experiences of race are pertinent to begin with. But the common view of our insignificance only reinforces the perception of Asian Americans as non-Americans. It quite possibly also reinforces the correlative notion that African Americans are more American than Asian Americans and "the[ir] demand for equal rights, opportunities, and privileges appears more legitimate than when immigrants demand those same things."[73]

NEITHER IN THE MIDDLE OF NOR BEYOND BLACK AND WHITE, BUT RATHER BLACK AND WHITE IN AN ASIAN AMERICAN KEY?

To be rendered as interlopers or as spectators not only trivializes Asian American experiences of race but, significantly, also trivializes the pervasiveness of racism in American life. If so, then the question of how Asian

72. Cheng, "What Role Do Asian Americans Have."

73. Kim, "Are Asians Black?," 344. My reference to Kim in this sentence turns on its head the arguments she cites (disapprovingly) that claim the black-white paradigm of racial discourse is inapplicable to Asian Americans. While I will say more about the applicability of the paradigm later, I dispute those arguments that claim "the discrimination experienced by Asian Americans follow not a color axis but a 'foreigner axis'" (Kim, "Are Asians Black?," 344). My point, with Kim, is that the refusal to acknowledge Asian American experiences of discrimination as racial experiences of discrimination only perpetuates Asian Americans as outsiders, essentially foreigners, and thus not as rightful, full members of the United States who are tangled in its social realities. Moreover, the perpetuation of Asian Americans as foreigners masks how the perception of our otherness as foreigners is itself a fundamentally racialized dynamic.

Americans too experience white racism takes on renewed urgency. Consider Lloyd and Prevot's more capacious sense of antiblackness, claiming that antiblackness cannot be considered in isolation from other social problems. They specify,

> On the contrary, it examines concrete connections between antiblackness and colonialism, capitalism, patriarchy, and homophobia, to mention but a few, and it relates anti-blackness to similar harms done to other nonwhite groups, such as immigrant communities from Latin America and Asia and indigenous peoples of the Americas. Clarity about the role of anti-blackness in this interconnected web of social crises and oppressions is possible only if we can appreciate anti-blackness as a distinct category of critical analysis that is not reducible to the others.[74]

The interconnectedness of antiblackness to the racial harms of other non-white groups speaks to the ubiquitous and entrenched hold of whiteness on modern society and all its inhabitants. While that does not mean that experiences of racial violence and harm are identical across communities of color, it does open up the need to appreciate how other persons of color articulate their experience of race. Antiblackness may not be the only relevant articulation of racism today,[75] but additional articulations of racism cannot be nor should it be taken as diminishing both the entrenchment of white racism as well as the effects of white racism on black bodies and selfhood. Rather these additional articulations of racism underscore the importance of an "intersecting, expansive, and multiscalar approach to various racialized groups in the United States." As Sharma states, "To center any one group is necessarily an incomplete project."[76]

To make the project of understanding white racism's hold on life in the United States more complete, paying attention to how Asian Americans necessarily fit into the racial narrative of the United States is required. But in so doing—in paying attention to an Asian American articulation of white racism—it is not simply about filling in the historical gaps of racism's genesis and legacy. Consider as an example the theological ethicist Bryan Massingale's historical review of how "social policies, institutions, and procedures . . . deliberately created a system to advance the welfare of

---

74. Lloyd and Prevot, introduction to *Anti-Blackness*, xxiv.

75. This is a paraphrase of Sharma, "Racial Studies Project," 61.

76. Sharma, "Racial Studies Project," 57.

white Americans and impeded the opportunities of persons of color."[77] That review includes, among other events, *Plessy v. Ferguson* and the redlining practices of the Federal Housing Administration in the 1940s and 1950s.[78] Only one event pertaining to Asian Americans appears in his review, the 1923 Supreme Court case *United States v. Bhagat Singh Thind*, which we noted earlier ruled that South Asians were not white and thus ineligible for citizenship.[79] To be sure, many more events that were consequential to Asian American well-being could and should be added to Massingale's historical review (some of which were noted in the previous section), and he intimates as much when he admits broadly, "Many more historical examples can be cited."[80] But what is gained in insisting that those events should be included, lest Asian Americans are, as usual, ignored or remain invisible? Note Massingale's point on offering his historical review, even in its limitations; it is simply to "demonstrate how pervasive beliefs about the inadequacies of people of color . . . become expressed by or entrenched in our [society] . . . for the purpose of maintaining white group privileges and advantages."[81] Massingale's point is well taken. At what point does a historical review sufficiently or insufficiently demonstrate the pervasiveness of the "privilege state of whiteness"?[82] Ten historical events, fifteen, twenty? To insist that Asian American experiences of race in the United States requires greater attention cannot simply be an insistence for historical accuracy, however important that may be, especially in making clear that Asian Americans are also rightly "people of color" who have been on the receiving end of white racism. More importantly, the insistence must be based on calling attention to the salience of the following question: what is lost if Asian Americans are not intentionally and more fully accounted for in how whiteness has and continues to shape institutional and cultural life in the United States? This question does not call into question the realities of white racism for persons of color, including Asian Americans, but it calls into question whether the nature of white racism, its logics or strategies for privileging whiteness over nonwhiteness, can be accounted for in its

---

77. Massingale, *Racial Justice and the Catholic Church*, 37.

78. Also see Rothstein, *Color of Money*; Coates, "Case for Reparations."

79. Massingale, *Racial Justice and the Catholic Church*, 58.

80. Massingale, *Racial Justice and the Catholic Church*, 39.

81. Massingale, *Racial Justice and the Catholic Church*, 39–40.

82. Massingale, *Racial Justice and the Catholic Church*, 37.

fullness unless Asian American experiences of race are attended to specifically and intentionally.

But does that mean the narrative, as traditionally defined within a black-and-white paradigm, requires revision at least in terms of its fundamental premises and assumptions? In other words, is the black-white dichotomy more trouble than it is worth? To jettison the black-white dichotomy, however, would be premature, for it would undermine the essential point that is right about antiblackness: white racism is about the violence against black bodies; it always has been and always will be. But such a point in itself does not necessarily preclude the realities of white racial violence against other persons of color; at the very least, that would be a logical, conceptual overreach. Consider, for instance, the theologian James Cone's provocative assertion that if God of the Hebrew and Christian Bible is to be faithfully of that Bible, then God must be black. But does this mean that God is only of and for black persons? Cone anticipates such suspicions by elaborating that the blackness of God does not elevate blackness above and beyond others but serves as an ontological symbol of the systemic evil of whiteness:

> The focus on blackness does not mean that only blacks suffer as victims in a racist society, but that blackness is an ontological symbol and a visible reality which best describes what oppression means in America.
>
> The extermination of Amerindians, the persecution of Jews, the oppression of Mexican-Americans, and every other conceivable inhumanity done in the name of God and country—these brutalities can be analyzed in terms of the white American inability to recognize humanity in persons of color. If the oppressed of this land want to challenge the oppressive character of white society, they must begin by affirming their identity in terms of the reality that is antiwhite. Blackness, then, stands for all victims of oppression who realize that the survival of their humanity is bound up with the liberation of whiteness.[83]

Cone's reference to blackness as an ontological symbol suggests the continued relevance or applicability of the black-white paradigm for nonblack persons of color in a manner that is non-exclusionary. Thus, Cone avoids the liabilities of talking about racism in a manner that connotes racism as simply a white person's problem and a black person's problem; it is a

83. Cone, *Black Theology of Liberation*, 7.

28

problem with wide-ranging reach, disciplining the self-understanding of and interrelations between persons and communities.

Given the resiliency and entrenchment of white ideologies of power and privilege throughout American life, to talk about how black persons are subject to such ideologies also necessitates how Asian Americans are subject to such ideologies so long as Asian Americans are recognized as part and parcel of American life.[84] One way of gaining a handle on the realities of racism in American life, therefore, is to view it through the lens of Asian American experiences of race, just as one can and must through the lens of blackness. (So just as "blackness is an ontological symbol and a visible reality which best describes what oppression means in America," as Cone proposes, we ought to be interested in asking what that oppression might mean in the United States if Asian Americanness is also regarded as a kind of ontological symbol and visible reality that critically describes that oppression.) In short, if racism is an inescapable feature of life in the United States, then racism is as much an Asian American problem as it is an African American problem, problem in the sense that the evil of *white* racism is the reality that demands attention and displacement. As both their problems, to ignore Asian American experiences of race would be to miss if not forego an expansive, fuller narrative of how white racism operates. Thus, it is insufficient to simply focus on the antiblackness of racism if the logics, aims, and depths of racism in the United States are to be understood; a focus on the anti-Asianness of white racism must be included.

84. That said, it is interesting to recall the essay "Do Not Forget Us!" written by Bayard Rustin, a senior black minister who was an organizer of Martin Luther King Jr.'s March on Washington in 1963, and published in the Carnegie Council's *Worldview Magazine* in 1978. Written in response to the Southeast Asian refugee crisis in the mid and late 1970s, Rustin underscores the Asian American community's many historical ties to the African American community and the imperative of recognizing and attending to each other's social struggles: "A new 'invisible man' has been born within our midst—the Southeast Asian refugee. Shunted from country to country, over 150,000 of these 'invisible people' cling to a precarious existence in scores of refugee camps that dot non-Communist Asia. They have a simple and solitary message for the international community: 'Do not forget us!' Some well-meaning people have said to me: 'The black community suffers from record high unemployment. Why should blacks be concerned about Southeast Asian refugees? They'll only take jobs and housing that black people desperately need.' Such an attitude is understandable, but allow me to describe the enormity and urgency of the refugee problem" (Ruskin, "Do Not Forget Us!").

AFTER AMBIVALENCE

If the "traditional" black-white paradigm does not necessarily have to be seen as excluding the racial realities of Asian American life, then what is gained by insisting on the paradigm's continuance? That is a question that is obliquely raised by Chuh and Shimikawa when they turn to Asian American literary voices that "explore the possibilities of knowing the self by securing a stable meaning for Asianness without regard to blackness and whiteness."[85] They highlight perspectives that emphasize how racial categories established by legal and political determinations only "offer limited self-knowledge . . . [Such] racial designations serve as obstacles to rather than windows into the self."[86] Yet, the very fact that Asianness emerges as a category of identity constructed and sanctioned by a state that is rooted, from its inception, in the paradigm of black and white should give us pause. Therefore, being Asian American cannot neatly be divorced from the legacy of black-white racial discourse, since that discourse is the very framework within which the history of Asians as Asians in America is forged.[87]

That said, to take Asian Americans more seriously as indeed an integral part of (rather than a bystander to) the narrative of racism in the United States is to not only demand a more complete American narrative on race, but it is also to demand that Asian Americans take themselves more seriously with respect to that narrative. In other words, being ambivalent about our identity is no longer a viable option. (This of course does not preclude the possibility of denial, but denial does not negate the veracity of the kind of racial realities Asian Americans confront; denial is simply to refuse either by ignorance or decision to acknowledge that veracity.) The task, however, is to articulate what it means to say that racism is an Asian American problem. In other words, what exactly are the contours of the racial cartography Asian Americans navigate? Above, I mentioned in passing the proposition that white racism is also anti-Asianness. That is easier to say than to define, to be sure. At the very least, to consider how Asian Americans are very much a part of the American discourse on race reorients a

85. Chuh and Shimikawa, "Adjudicating Asian America," 32.

86. Chuh and Shimikawa, "Adjudicating Asian America," 32.

87. As Janine Young Kim observes, "[The black-white] paradigm's persistence in race relations and discourse attests to its continuing relevance and growing complexity . . . Indeed, an alternative theory cannot emerge unless people of color dismantle the current organization and vocabulary of race, which have been articulated through the paradigm" (Kim, "Are Asians Black?," 349).

sense of who we are as more than (or as something other than) innocent or irrelevant bystanders to the black-white tug-of-war in the United States. Again, not that we are caught in the middle of that tug-of-war, but to consider how we are one of the participants in that tug-of-war. That distinction between being caught in the middle versus being participants matters to the extent that it signals the prospects that Asian Americans, far from living an alternative racial reality or one that is insulated from the dominant racial narrative of American society or, further still, being a casualty of that racial struggle, are a vital part of that struggle. In other words, it signals the prospects that the prevailing black-white discourse on race is already entrenched in Asian American life, experience, or self-understanding, but not in an either-or Manichaean way. Perhaps one could argue that the deficiency of the use of a black-white paradigm, even within Cone's context, is that it necessarily requires nonblack persons of color to articulate their experiences of race within a distinctively black discourse on race (that is, racial oppression must be measured against the realities of black lives). But it would be insufficient to wrestle an account of Asian American experiences with race as simply identifiable to the experiences of black persons, because they are not, at least not so obviously; to think otherwise would trivialize the distinctiveness of Asian American experiences, as well as the distinctiveness of black experiences. Nor would it be accurate to say, as Kim and Lee note, that Asian American experiences with race is "virtually 'white' in terms of their status in American society." While Gary Okihiro's answer to his own "now-famous question—'Is yellow black or white?'—is 'neither,'"[88] Kim and Lee observe that "Asian American experience has been at once distinct from [sic] the white and Black experiences and *importantly conditioned by them*."[89] Both whiteness and blackness are central to Asian Americanness, but the difficulty is understanding how that is the case, how Asian Americans are, to reiterate, "importantly conditioned by them," both whiteness and blackness.

If not as middle minority, then one alternative is to examine how the disciplining force of white racism on black bodies is also *the same* force that operates on Asian bodies. This alternative echoes the spirit of theologian Grace Ji-Sun Kim's critique of Hollywood's representation of Asian Americans: "If Hollywood is supposed to be a representation of our larger

88. Kim and Lee, "Interracial Politics," 546; they cite Okihiro, *Margins and Mainstreams*, 62.

89. Kim and Lee, "Interracial Politics," 546, emphasis added.

society, invisibility of all people of color should cause an uproar. In the battle against racism, to ignore other affected groups can serve to further white supremacy and white privilege."[90] This criticism is not unlike one that is leveled by the anthropologist Jorge Klor de Alva. In mapping out how nonwhite groups of color can forge a durable alliance to address social injustice in the United States, Klor de Alva insists, "At the core of that effort lies the capacity to address common suffering, regardless of color or culture. And that cannot be done unless common suffering, as the reason for linkages across all lines, is highlighted in place of the very tenuous alliances between groups that identify themselves by race or culture."[91] Like Kim, Klor de Alva finds it necessary to move beyond the black-white binary; the racialization of social injustice, more generally, serves as an impediment to recognizing that nonwhite persons, as well as women, whether white or not, are marginalized. The insistence that the story of marginalization in the United States is primarily one that takes place around the poles of black and white is to obscure the breadth of social injustice; discrimination is an equal opportunity force in the United States.[92] Kim differs from Klor de Alva in at least one important respect; she does not shy from identifying and emphasizing white racism as one of the driving forces of social injustice in the United States, whereas Klor de Alva's primary concern is calling attention to the issues of class that underlie social fragmentation, marginalization, and inequality. In that respect, Kim's critique of the black-white binary is more about the inadequacies of the privileged place that black occupies in the binary and, thus, the need to broaden the paradigm to include all nonblack persons of color, including Asian Americans.

Yet, the insistence that moving past the black-white binary altogether or revising it to include all nonblack persons of color is critical to making visible the work of white racism on all people of color is not unproblematic. Such an insistence makes it too easy to insulate Asian Americans (or any other nonblack person of color) from reflecting on how the disciplining force of white racism may work on nonwhite bodies in a tandem, concerted, or *integrated* way.[93] Simply stating that white racism marginalizes Asian

90. Kim, "Chris Rock Should Know."

91. West and Klor de Alva, "On Black-Brown Relations," 516.

92. For a prominent version of this argument from a legal perspctive, see Chang, "Toward an Asian American Legal Scholarship."

93. See Kim, "Are Asians Black?" She echoes a similar argument by noting, for instance, the ways in which the manipulation of Asian Americans to serve the interests of mainstream white America is at its core a white-black dynamic. To abandon the

Americans *and* marginalizes African Americans obscures the possibility that the disciplining of black bodies and the disciplining of Asian bodies do not simply move along parallel lines but, more worrisomely, go *hand-in-hand*. In other words, the marginalizing of African Americans is lessened unless Asian Americans are also marginalized, and the marginalization of Asian Americans is stunted without the marginalization of African Americans. Maintaining the relevance of the black-white binary for Asian Americans aids in the excavation of how white racism advances itself through the *interdependent* marginalization of both African Americans and Asian Americans. But that excavation will not happen by itself; it requires Asian Americans to actively engage in that work of excavation, to make the case that both Asian Americans and African Americans are in the thick of white racism together because that is the modus operandi of white racism.

Recognizing how white racism is a discourse that includes the mutually reinforcing marginalization of nonwhite persons does and should not discount the ways in which Asian Americans, as advocates of antiblackness such as Grimes points out, have benefited from the hegemony of whiteness in the United States. As I noted earlier, Asian Americans do have a peculiar and unsettling relationship with the concept of whiteness. That relationship is not without historical provenance. We need only to recall the precedent of employing whiteness, both in terms of culture and physical appearance, to describe and assess South Asians and East Asians by Christian missionaries and explorers at the dawn of the colonial era as European powers moved eastward.[94] Tracing the historical use of whiteness as an interpretive category in the Western Christian and Asian imaginations is well beyond the scope and competency of this book. Yet, suffice it to say that it would be intellectually dishonest to leave unexamined how the concept of whiteness (in its current racial iteration) and Asian American life intersect to this day. But the question that is missed by antiblackness advocates such as Grimes is how we should make sense of that intersection. It is too easy to suggest that the nature of that intersection centers on the Asian American preference for or willful complacency in white supremacy and its socioeconomic

---

paradigm, therefore, would be to diminish Asian Americans' capacity to "make informed political decisions and meaningfully pursue a civil rights agenda" (347). She concludes, "Asian American scholars must resist the temptation to oversimplify or underestimate the *paradigm's ability to perpetuate and refine itself by erasing histories, manipulating racial status, and dividing political alliances*" (349, emphasis added). I am sympathetic to her claims and see my project as refining and expanding on it.

94. See Jennings, *Christian Imagination*, 31–38.

vision of what constitutes a worthy existence. Whether passive or active supporters of such a white racial imagination, the alternative is to recognize how such support, rather than as a consequence of Asian American self-determination or interests, may be a function of how whiteness *imposes* itself on Asian Americans, that is, as a matter of white racial discipline. Such imposition may be overt or it can be covert, a clandestine capacity to capture our imagination and to define our daily social performances and aspirations in ways that are often far from obvious. But whether it is through specific policies and cultural attitudes and patterns of behavior that violate Asian American bodies and selfhood or a more subtle, subversive hand of racial hierarchy nudging Asian Americans to embody particular modes of being, the point is to be attentive to the ways whiteness constitutes a foreign force that bears down on Asian Americans. Such imposition recasts how the Asian American experience of race in the United States is to be understood, not from the periphery of American racial discourse but from within the very logic of that discourse, and, in so doing, controverts the typical perceptions of Asian Americans as inscrutable denizens who traverse between white America and nonwhite America, belonging to both but neither. When Asian Americans are recast in those ways, the countenance of white racism is more fully revealed.

This chapter began by expressing ambivalence about the definability of Asian American identity and now ends with a call to be less ambivalent about who we are as Asian Americans in relation to the narrative of race that is so endemic to the very fabric of life in the United States. To be more decisive and intentional about that relationship, however, is not to simply wonder whether Asian Americans are subject to white racism. Instead, it is to confront and engage the task of articulating the ways white racism defines, restrains, or, more pointedly, disciplines our very presence in the United States, that is, our self-understanding, agency, and relations with other persons, both white and nonwhite. But if the racial discipline of whiteness is so critical to what it means to be Asian American, then what are we to make of our cultural identities as Asian Americans? Should Asian American as a racialized identity necessarily displace Asian American as an ethno-cultural identity? Before we can gain a better handle on how Asian Americans are racialized, a first step is to reassess and, ultimately, move past certain perceptions of Asian Americans as having a unique Asian

American culture. To insist that there is a definable set—however wide that set may be—of cultural beliefs, attitudes, or practices that are inherent to Asian American identity, is not only conceptually problematic but tends to obscure the ways in which Asian American identity is racially disciplined. (The move to continuously widen the set of cultural values and practices that reflect Asian Americanness is indicative of the problem of Asian American identity as largely a cultural one.) Calling into question Asian American identity as mainly a cultural category is the subject of chapter 2.

2

Culture

Kimberly [a Chinese American woman] and Tyrone [an African American man] had a wonderful time during the [ballroom dance] lesson but they were both terrible dancers. Kimberly was laughing so hard, she was almost crying. "You always told me you had rhythm," she gasped.

Tyrone was marching like a soldier, trying to find the beat and failing. "I did, I swear. I don't know what's happened to me. Too much Chinese food, I think."

—*MAMBO IN CHINATOWN*[1]

A new fear I have is that I am losing my Chinese-ness. It is just flaking off me like dead skin.

And below that skin is my American-ness.

As a child, I often dreamed in Chinese, but I have not dreamed in Chinese for a long time. The steps in my logic, thus, ergo, hence, are now all in English. Oddly enough, I still count in Chinese, so I try my best to count everything that I pass.

Three bananas.

1. Kwok, *Mambo in Chinatown*, 197.

Seven bicycles.

Twelve babies strapped to twelve adults.

This way the skin stays intact.

—*CHEMISTRY*[2]

"Weird. I don't get how feng shui works."

"Common Sense," my father said. "It's just paying attention to your surroundings. It's like how Americans have a knack for laziness. No one taught them how to slack off at their jobs. No one taught them to get away with doing the least amount of work possible, and yet they're the best at it in the whole world. They're born with it. It's the same thing with feng shui for us. It's innate."

—*SOUR HEART*[3]

IN AN APRIL 1996 *Harper's Magazine* interview of the African American philosopher Cornel West and the Chicano anthropologist Jorge Klor de Alva, the interviewer, Earl Shorris, asks West whether he thinks Latinos/as are white. West responds, "I think of them as brothers and sisters, as human beings, but in terms of culture, I think of them as a particular group of voluntary immigrants who entered America and had to encounter this thoroughly absurd system of classification of positively charged whiteness, negatively charged blackness. And they don't fit either one: They're not white, they're not black."[4] Detecting some ambiguity in what West means by "in terms of culture" they are neither black nor white, Shorris asks whether he sees Latinos "in racial terms." West responds, "Well, no, it's more cultural . . . Brown, for me, is more associated with culture than race." To specify, he notes that many, though not all, Latinos/as speak Spanish (some speak indigenous languages) and "Mexicans, Cubans, Puerto Ricans, Dominicans, El Salvadorans all have very, very distinctive histories."[5] Thus,

---

2. Wang, *Chemistry*, 54.
3. Zhang, *Sour Heart*, 270–71.
4. West and Klor de Alva, "On Black-Brown Relations," 506.
5. West and Klor de Alva, "On Black-Brown Relations," 506.

in saying they are brown, West explains that Latinos/as, unlike African Americans, are not racialized: "In the eyes of the white privileged . . . they're not treated as black . . . They're not the bottom of the heap . . . When you talk about black, that becomes a kind of benchmark, because you've got these continuous generations [who have been racially marginalized], and you've got very common experiences."[6] One such common experience, he points out, is the time when his wife, an émigré of Ethiopia, who, West adds, came to the United States like Latinos/as for a better life, was hurled an epithet: "It was the first American who called her 'n****r.' That's when she started the process of Americanization and racialization."[7]

West's demarcation between race and culture as a way of articulating what it means to be Latino/a is notable for its applicability to Asian Americans. West is able to draw a relatively clean line between racial identity and cultural identity inasmuch as the experience of being black in the United States sets the terms of what it means to be racially marginalized. Unlike Latinos/as, African Americans have not only been forcibly brought to the United States but as the consequence of that original sin, African Americans are continuously formed or disciplined by social dynamics or forces—whiteness, white supremacy, privilege, racism—that dehumanizes, delegitimizes their personhood. Earlier in the interview, West's race-culture delineation sounds more ambiguous when he proposes that blackness can serve as a "springboard to raise issues of various other forms of injustice" experienced by other groups including "brown, white workers."[8] While he concedes convergence between black and brown experiences, West's starting point of the exceptionalism of black suffering in American life puts in doubt Latino/a as a racialized identity rather than strictly a cultural one. (That starting point also insulates West from having to perhaps wrestle with the possible implication that white workers are racialized persons also, since they are differentially treated like African Americans; instead, we might surmise, white workers' suffering is not a matter of race but primarily a matter of class antagonisms.) Given black exceptionalism, Latino/a life does not parallel black life in equivalent ways, or West seems to suggest; as brown, Latino/as are treated differently than whites because they are culturally different, which is not identical to being treated as a racial other in the way African Americans are. One could also say as much for Asian

6. West and Klor de Alva, "On Black-Brown Relations," 506.
7. West and Klor de Alva, "On Black-Brown Relations," 507.
8. West and Klor de Alva, "On Black-Brown Relations," 504.

American life, if we recall from the previous chapter the motivation for casting racism as specifically antiblackness.

Like Latinos/as, it is not unusual for Asian Americans to be defined in cultural terms rather than in racial terms. The following cultural construal of Asian American identity is not unusual:

> When working with individuals of Asian ancestry, educators need to understand three of the main Eastern philosophies and their impact on Asian culture: Buddhism, Confucianism, and Taoism. Within these philosophies families are highly structured, hierarchical, and paternal. Within the family systems children are taught that they must avoid bringing shame to their family and that the welfare and integrity of the family are very important. These Asian philosophies also teach principles of peace, balance, and harmony, causing some Asians to avoid confrontation or appear passive, indifferent, or indecisive. Using indirect methods of communication may be appropriate for some Asian students with strong ties to their ancestral culture.[9]

Note the emphasis on Eastern philosophies and religions, the emphasis on family relationships, and particular attitudinal principles that characterize Asian American individuals and their "Asian culture." Some Asian Americans may find this characterization familiar while others may, for sure, find this foreign if not clichéd and patronizing. But a cultural construal of Asian Americanness is not atypical, regardless of whether one finds resonance in any one particular construal or not. But if familial, ancestral, and religious customs, and, certainly, linguistic and food traditions are usual ways in which Asian American identity is commonly given definition and embodied form, then do they intimate or reveal something other than what they are? In other words, do the cultural markers of Asian American identity require or demand interpretation? That question may, to some extent, sound odd. Are not the cultural lives of Asian Americans simply what Asian Americans believe and do, by virtue of their received (and perhaps habituated) heritage or tradition? That is what the foregoing cultural description of Asian Americans clearly indicates. So, what other meanings can there be to the cultural lives of Asian Americans? In what way is eating traditional foods more than just eating those kinds of food,

9. This description of Asian Americans appears on the website of the David O. McKay School of Education at Brigham Young University, under the subheading "Diversity: Understanding and Teaching Diverse Students," https://education.byu.edu/diversity/culture/asianamerican.html.

for sustenance, for enjoyment? In what way is practicing ancestral customs more than simply honoring those customs and values? In short, is it not a given that being Asian American comes along with embodying a particular cultural modality? How else are we to construe what it means to be Asian American? Against the backdrop of West's delineation of culture and race, we might be led to believe that Asian Americans, like Latinos/as, inasmuch as Asian Americans are not black, are primarily defined by our culture, which means our ancestral customs, traditions, and values.

But is a cultural designation of identity as straightforward as it sounds? As indicated in chapter 1, I am interested in what the racialization of Asian American identity might be and what such racialization might mean for the project of understanding the fullness of white racism in American life. West's attribution of culture to Latino/a identity does not bode well for such an interest in Asian American racialization. In chapters 3 and 4, I want to map the ways in which speaking of Asian Americans as racialized are not only possible but necessary. To get there, however, it will be important to work out an alternative account of the relationship between identity and culture, more specifically, what it means be Asian American in a cultural sense; this is the task of the present chapter. Central to this alternative account is demonstrating that culture is not simply a constellation of certain kinds of values, attitudes, and practices, such as speaking a specific language, bearing "distinctive histories," as West remarks. Whether or not it was West's intention to suggest that inherent to being Latino/a are defined and obvious cultural expressions, in separating race and culture in the way that he does, he is susceptible to such a criticism. That criticism, at least with respect to Asian Americans, calls into question popular assumptions that Asian American culture is fixed and self-originating (e.g., to be Asian American is to adhere to values and practices that are distinctively or authentically Asian) in favor of a notion of Asian American culture as profoundly plural. Accounting for that plurality (and thus moving away from the veracity of cultural authenticity), however, requires attending to the ways in which the cultural lives of Asian Americans are socially constructed or, more significantly, negotiated social realities. As such, the cultural lives of Asian Americans reveal more than what Asian Americans have been habituated into doing and thinking; it is more than simply about keeping customs, honoring familial practices, or just repeating traditions because that is what has always been done. The cultural lives of Asian Americans also reveal a particular social logic; they reflect how Asian Americans grapple with the question of social existence.

Earlier in the *Harper's Magazine* interview, West asserts that black identity is a "modern construct." He elaborates: "Implicit in that category of 'black man' is American white supremacy, African slavery and then a very rich culture that *responds to these conditions* at the level of style, mannerism, orientation, experimentation, improvisation, syncopation—all of those elements that have gone into making a new people, namely black people."[10] In characterizing the cultural expressions of black identity as responses to a particular social history and ideologies, West echoes the general logic undergirding the notion of Asian American cultural expressions as negotiated social realities. Bracketing for now whether Asian Americans and African Americans are subject to the same social realities (or, if they are, whether they are subject to them in parallel ways), at the very least, what it means to be Asian American and African American must take into account how both are subject to particular social realities. As such, Asian American identity may not be as "cultural" as it may be typically perceived.

THE INAUTHENTICITY OF CULTURAL AUTHENTICITY

A lively exchange between the late chef-turned-television-personality Anthony Bourdain and the Taiwanese American restaurateur Eddie Huang is instructive of the kind of cultural assumptions often ascribed to Asian American identity and the premium that is placed on authenticity.

In the series finale of Bourdain's popular television series *No Reservations*, Bourdain and Huang find themselves at Andy Ricker's highly acclaimed (now closed) Thai restaurant Pok Pok NY, in Brooklyn, discussing the merits of Thai food cooked by a white American chef. Below is a partial transcript of that conversation:

> Bourdain: So why am I in a Thai restaurant with a Chinese dude?
> Huang: That's a good question. That's a good question.
> . . .
> Huang: I am always curious about gringo chefs doing Asian food, especially gringo chefs that win James Beard awards doing Asian food.
> Bourdain: Right, because they probably suck.
> Huang: They probably suck.

10. West and Klor de Alva, "On Black-Brown Relations," 500, emphasis added.

Bourdain: That's what you're thinking.

Huang: Yeah.

Bourdain: [You're probably thinking,] "I really would like this place to suck."

Huang: I want it to suck.

. . .

Huang: Then I ate it, and it's mind blowing![11]

Huang's declaration is revealing in its incredulity. That he ultimately finds Ricker's Thai food delicious undermines Huang's initial desire to assert cultural ownership. Is it possible for a non-Asian to cook Asian food? Yes, of course, as a description of fact; Huang is not challenging the fact that Ricker, a non-Asian man, can cook Thai food. But Huang is intimating a suspicion of the motives behind Ricker's efforts at cooking Asian food. Note Huang's assertion that he is "always curious about gringo chefs doing Asian food, *especially gringo chefs that win James Beard awards doing Asian food*" (emphasis added). Is Ricker cooking Thai food to celebrate that cuisine for its own sake or is it for his own monetary benefit or, perhaps more perniciously, for the benefit of non-Asian palettes and cultural curiosities? If the latter, then is Ricker simply another instance of a non-Asian chef "colonizing" and "fetishizing" Asian food for non-Asian consumption and, ultimately, appropriation? As the food and culture journalist Clarissa Wei remarks, "[Asian] food is still largely looked on upon from the sidelines as a mysterious cuisine of antiquity. Only certain dishes like noodles, dumplings, kebabs, and rice bowls have been normalized. The majority is still largely stigmatized because, bluntly put, white people have not decided they like it yet."[12] Huang's reference to Ricker as a James Beard award-winning chef cooking Asian food slyly alludes to those kinds of qualms.

Yet Huang's misgivings of Ricker's Thai food center on the larger question of authenticity, which amplifies his consternation over cultural appropriation as a moral problematic. A non-Asian can cook Asian food, but whether a non-Asian person can cook great, authentic Asian food is a different matter altogether. Huang suggests that authenticity is a function of the kinds of cultural traditions practiced by those whose identities are defined by those traditions. Ricker is a white person, and so by definition,

11. *No Reservations with Anthony Bourdain*, "Brooklyn," *Travel Channel*, November 5, 2012.

12. Wei, "Struggles of Writing about Chinese Food"; see also Yam, "9 Times Non-Asians Completely Screwed Up Asian Food."

he would be incapable of cooking authentic Thai food; more to the point, we should *not expect* that he would be able to cook authentic Thai food. Conversely, we should expect a Thai chef to be able to cook authentic Thai food, a sentiment that is pointedly underscored by the celebrity chef Tom Colicchio, when he faults Hung Huynh, a Vietnamese American contestant on the television reality show *Top Chef*, "for cooking that was technically dazzling but lacked explicit reference to his roots. 'You were born in Vietnam,' [Collicchio reminds Huynh]. 'I don't see any of that in your food.'"[13]

Huang does not expect to see any Thai roots expressing themselves in Ricker's food, since he is not of Thai descent, or from Thailand. Note that Huang states, rather colorfully, that he *wants* Ricker's food to be bad, which would then confirm his belief that a white person has no business cooking Thai food, especially given his many experiences of eating Asian food cooked by non-Asians gone wrong, sometimes terribly wrong, at least in his judgment.[14] On this account, one might say that a cultural practice (say, cooking) is not authentic or genuine unless it is practiced by a person belonging to a group that originated (and, therefore, "owns") that particular element of culture. That is why cultural appropriation is morally odious, because one cannot embody a particular cultural modality unless one is originally of that corresponding group identity; otherwise, one is simply a cultural imposter, exhibiting cultural disrespect. Obviously then, Thais from Thailand make the best, most authentic Thai food since it is "their" food; Thai cuisine prepared by non-Thais would be second rate, imitation at best. (This would presumably apply to other ethnicities, nationalities, or peoples, too, for instance, only white Americans from Appalachia play the kind of bluegrass music that is worth listening too, or only African Americans from the South can cook soul food properly.) But, as Huang discovers and eventually admits, Ricker has proven him wrong, or at least given him reason to reconsider.

13. Mishan, "Asian-American Cuisine's Rise."

14. Whether Huang's negative judgment of most Asian food cooked by non-Asian chefs is correct is debatable. (Is P. F. Chang's better or worse than Chinese food cooked in Chinatown? For some Asians the answer is probably yes. But for some others, the answer could very well be no.) But rather than adjudicating the merits of Huang's culinary judgment, I am more interested in the fact that Huang clearly thinks that the best, most authentic Asian food is cooked by Asians, a position supported in part by his judgment that he has had terrible Asian food cooked by non-Asian chefs. But whatever Huang's reasons, the question worth asking is whether Huang's assumptions about cultural ownership are warranted.

That Huang would even assume that cultural beliefs and practices are properly the properties of certain identities is not surprising given the kind of communities that populate much of our urban and suburban landscapes and the kind of cultural assumptions that frame our perception of the identities and experiences of those communities and its residents. In Huang's case, the New York City metropolitan area, which I also call home, continues to be divided into culturally delimited neighborhoods. The enduring reality of such borders engenders and sustains impressions and associations of what persons who live (or may have at one time lived) in such enclaves are like in terms of their daily cultural dispositions, from food, speech, and dress to religiosity and family customs, traditions, and values.[15] Thus, not uncommon in New York and New Jersey, as well as in many other metropolitan areas in North America, are assumptions (and sometimes fierce debates) about where one may find the most authentic food, or experience the most traditional celebration of a particular holiday or custom. So, for instance, go to Edison or Jersey City, New Jersey, or Jackson Heights, Queens, for authentic Indian food; for genuine Korean, where else but Fort Lee, New Jersey; or to experience the best Lunar New Year celebrations, take the 7 train to Flushing, Queens, as the conventional wisdom might go.

But the perception that members of a particular Asian American community generally embody or practice common cultural values and traditions and that only their practice of those values and traditions can be merited as authentic is, to be sure, based on a very limited engagement with that community. While such conventional associations may indeed apply to some, to the extent that they do not necessarily apply to all who identify with a particular Asian American community unveils the cultural diversity and complexity of what it means to be Asian American. A striking case in point is how the growing use of Mandarin Chinese and the correlative decline of Cantonese Chinese is challenging what it means to be Chinese American today in communities such as New York City's lower Manhattan and Flushing, Queens. Due to shifting patterns of Chinese immigration to the United States, particularly from the district of Taishan in the Pearl River Delta and Hong Kong to mainland China, primarily Fujian Province, Mandarin has been steadily displacing the Cantonese dialect. While both

15. For a sense of the character of such communities in New York City, see Fessenden and Roberts, "Then as Now." For New Jersey, see the demographic visuals compiled by the Weldon Cooper Center for Public Service at the University of Virginia, https://demographics.virginia.edu/DotMap/index.html.

Mandarin and Cantonese share the same written characters, the vast difference in pronunciation leads to a vastly different and mutually incomprehensible spoken language. Consequently, many New York City Chinese are increasingly finding their Chinese neighbors as foreign as some of their non-Chinese, English speaking neighbors. Amusingly, the *New York Times* quotes a forty-four-year-old Cantonese-speaking New Yorker who claims that when she is walking through East Broadway Avenue in New York City's Chinatown, she is now "just as lost as everyone else."[16] In short, even Asians who ostensibly share a common language (Chinese) do not necessarily, in practice, speak that language in common (since there is no single or monolithic Chinese language).

That we would be too hasty in generally associating "speaking Cantonese" as part and parcel of "being Chinese" brings into relief one way in which the notion of cultural authenticity is not as straightforward as many may assume. What is authentically Chinese depends in part on to whom you are referring—the question is, authentic to whom? While a Mandarin-speaking Chinese person may be no less Chinese than one who speaks Cantonese, what it means to be Chinese may mean one thing to the Mandarin speaker and another to the Cantonese speaker. To think otherwise would do violence to the cultural intricacies and nuances of being Chinese in actual lived experience. That also applies to the broader category of Asian American. As the sociologists Min Zhou and J. V. Gatewood observe, "What [Asian American] ethnicity means, stands for, or symbolizes differs from region to region, city to city, and town to town in the vast expanse of the United States. Being Japanese American in Hawaii or Chinese American in Monterey Park or Vietnamese American in Little Saigon is not the same as having those identity in New York, Houston, or New Orleans."[17]

But the complicated nature of cultural authenticity goes beyond the reality that Asian American identity is culturally diverse rather than monolithic. While there may be no single Asian American culture per se but rather numerous Asian American cultures (and, more accurately, numerous cultures within particular Asian American communities), the cultural beliefs and practices of particular Asian American communities are not necessarily "theirs" in some direct or simplistic way. Consider once again the misgivings Huang expresses to Bourdain about Ricker's Thai food. Huang suggests that only a Thai person can cook Thai food worth eating

16. Semple, "In Chinatown."

17. Zhou and Gatewood, "Transforming Asian America," 129.

because presumably Thai food originated from or is the invention of Thai people. (In Bourdain's narration of this segment of the episode, he notes that Ricker's Thai food draws from the cuisine that is indigenous to Thais in rural, northern Thailand.) But whether a cultural object, tradition, or practice is the invention of a particular community of persons is a more opaque question than it may seem.

Consider the emergence of a cultural practice or value as a dynamic, multivalent, or "multicultural" process. Such a process is especially underscored in the description of Latino/a and Latin American cultures as *mestizaje* or blend of ethnicities.[18] As a dynamic process of intermingling and synthesis, culture by its very nature, as the theologian Kathryn Tanner puts it, "[is not] a product of isolation; it is not a matter of a culture's being simply self-generated, pure and unmixed . . . Cultural identity becomes, instead, a hybrid, relational affair, something that lives between as much as within cultures."[19] Recognizing the relational, variegated character of culture prompts a reexamination of whether the idea of cultural authenticity is conceptually coherent. If Asian American culture—or any other culture for that matter—is built on, is an extension of, or involves some level of appropriation of elements of another culture, then defining what is culturally authentic to Asian Americans becomes confounding.

If authenticity belies the appropriative character of culture, whether we are speaking of Asian American culture or beyond, then thinking of culture as, in a way, inauthentic stands in contrast to the conceptual assumptions of contemporary forms of multicultural discourse. The moral philosopher K. Anthony Appiah describes the underlying premise of multiculturalism: "Other things being equal, people have the right to be acknowledged publicly as what they already really are. It is because someone is already authentically Jewish or gay that we deny them something in requiring them to hide this fact, to 'pass,' as we say, for something that they are not."[20] This desire for and affirmation of authenticity is a legacy of the modern (Enlightenment) aspiration for individuality, according to Charles Taylor.[21] It is an aspiration that demands a corresponding politics, "a politics that asks

18. For a sampling of the diversity of approaches to *mestizaje* in theological discourse, see Goizueta, *Caminemos con Jesús*, ch. 1; and Rodríguez's *Racism and God-Talk*, ch. 3.

19. Tanner, *Theories of Culture*, 57–58.

20. Appiah, "Culture, Identity," 92.

21. See Taylor, *Ethics of Authenticity*, chs. 2 and 3.

us to acknowledge socially and politically the authentic identity of others,"[22] or what Taylor refers to as "the politics of recognition."[23]

As Appiah points out, however, the multicultural position, one that is often assumed in so much of current popular discourse on diversity, rests on dubious premises. First, it assumes an untenable philosophical realism, the notion that there is an "essential" self to be uncovered: "Authenticity speaks of the real self buried in there, the self one has to dig out and express."[24] For Appiah, like Tanner, such essentialism belies the fluidity and contingency of culture and identity, making the question of whether there is such a thing as a real self to uncover incoherent. The analogy Appiah draws between attempts at finding "some primordially authentic culture" and "peeling an onion" is particularly provocative. Consider that the "textiles most people think of as traditional West African cloths are known as Java prints; they arrived in the 19th century with the Javanese batiks sold, and often milled, by the Dutch"; or that the "traditional garb of Herero women in Namibia derived from the attire of 19th century German missionaries." What constitutes authentic West African culture, then? Or authentic Namibian culture? "How far back must one go?" asks Appiah. Insofar as "cultures are made of continuities and changes," to suggest that this or that attire, cultural attitude, and practice define a particular ethnic and racial identity is to rarefy it and, thus, to camouflage its historical complexity.[25]

Multicultural essentialism is made further problematic by an inadequate philosophical anthropology. Appiah, borrowing from Taylor once again, observes that the popular liberal-multicultural position on authenticity assumes a monological view of the person. This is the view that a person has "a way of being that is all [her] own,"[26] apart from and sometimes "against the family, organized religion, society, the school, the state—all the forces of convention."[27] But the monological view is an unrealistic view of how identity is formed. Taylor's contrast of the monological self with that of what he terms the dialogical self is instructive on this point. Just as no one can learn a foreign language without learning from another, "people do not

22. Appiah, "Culture, Identity," 92.

23. See Taylor, "Politics of Recognition," 25–74.

24. Appiah, "Culture, Identity," 96.

25. Appiah, "Case for Contamination"; see also Appiah, *Cosmopolitanism*.

26. Appiah, "Culture, Identity," 94–95.

27. Appiah, "Culture, Identity," 95.

acquire the languages needed for self-definition on their own."[28] "Thus my discovering my own identity doesn't mean that I work it out in isolation, but that I negotiate it through dialogue, partly overt, partly internal, with others," and which "continues indefinitely."[29]

In the concluding chapter of this book, I will return to how Asian American identity complicates Taylor's notion of the dialogic self. For now, it is important to note how Taylor's dialogical conception of the person complicates the notion of cultural authenticity. It is the neglect of the historical and relational complexities of a particular culture that makes tidy typification of cultures problematic.[30] The attitude that "we are all one way; they are all another" only masks the reality of intermingling and mixture that makes cultures what they are. Consequently, "other cultures are turned into static stereotypes to produce a clear difference from one's own," when those differences may not be as hard and fast as one may wish.[31]

ASIAN AMERICAN CULTURE REIMAGINED

If the historicism and relationality of culture belies a concept of culture as self-contained and self-originating, then how is Asian American culture to be regarded? More specifically, how does culture contribute to a distinctive Asian American identity? Can Asian American culture contribute in that way? According to Tanner, while "cultural elements may cross such boundaries without jeopardizing the distinctiveness of different cultures[, what establishes the distinctive identities of cultures] is the way in which such common elements are used, how they are handled and transformed."[32] How, then, are cultural elements used, handled, and transformed in the service of establishing distinctive identities?

An important place to start is to recognize that cultural differences matter, despite commonalities. Adherents of one culture often characterize their culture in ways that maintains differences from other cultures.[33] After all, it would be hard to imagine that just because Koreans and Japanese persons (or Koreans and Chinese, or Vietnamese and Chinese, and so on)

28. Taylor, "Politics of Recognition," 32.
29. Taylor, "Politics of Recognition," 34, 33.
30. Paraphrase of Tanner, *Theories of Culture*, 55.
31. Tanner, *Theories of Culture*, 55.
32. Tanner, *Theories of Culture*, 57.
33. Tanner, *Theories of Culture*, 57.

share many cultural elements in common, Koreans and Japanese persons would be inclined to admit that many of their traditions and customs are simply variations of one another's and, therefore, their identities as Koreans and Japanese are essentially alike.[34] While cultures may share common elements, that fact does not render differences between cultures meaningless. How we talk about food is especially indicative of this propensity to insist on difference despite commonalities. Consider, for instance, a complaint expressed by David Chang, the chef-owner of the Momofuku restaurants, on the reception of Korean food by non-Koreans during the 2018 Winter Olympics in Pyeongchang, South Korea: "Among his pet peeves," reported the *New York Times*, "was how non-Koreans used Japanese names to describe Korean dishes: Hwe, sliced raw fish, is not sashimi, he said . . . ; dduk, rice cakes, can be pretty different from mochi; and kimbap, rice rolled inside seaweed with various vegetables or meats, should never, ever, be called maki. 'It's like having to explain that French and Italian food are different,' Chang explains."[35]

It may be obvious that differences between cultures matter in lived reality. Less obvious, however, is an account of why such differences are maintained, perhaps even fiercely defended. Clues can be gleaned from noticing how the assertions of cultural difference function in relation to the maintenance of distinct identities. To be more specific, if one were to claim, say, "this Korean food is our food, and this is how it is different from your food," note that the assertion of cultural difference does not simply point out differences between cultures but also recognizes differences between the identities of particular communities of persons. In other words, a sense of cultural difference often assumes or advances a sense of distinct identities; my culture is different from your culture is often taken to mean this is how my identity (or the community of persons I identity with) is different from yours. This dynamic also holds true without an explicit assertion of cultural difference between identities. So even the simple ascription of a particular cultural practice as Korean or Filipino (e.g., this is a Korean

---

34. The case of the Vietnamese bahn mi sandwich perhaps underscores the point more strikingly. As a sandwich based on the French baguette (or the Vietnamese iteration of the baguette, a legacy of French colonialism in Vietnam), the common elements between French and Vietnamese culture are on display in this one sandwich. But whether the French would claim the bahn mi's baguette as essentially the same thing as the baguette baked in a French boulangerie (which must follow certain rules and regulations set by the French state for a baguette to be properly a baguette) is debatable. See Ho, "Banh mi."

35. Keh, "Olympic Challenge."

custom; this is the way Koreans do it; that attitude or behavior is so Filipino, and so on) suggests implicitly a measure of distinctiveness on a cultural scale, even if there is some level of recognition that there are shared cultural elements between identities. Otherwise, the assertion of Koreanness or some other identity is a meaningless assertion, an assertion without a difference so to speak.

At least three caveats are worth noting. First, cultural difference in the service of identity differentiation may serve relatively benign yet admirable goals such as the preservation of a particular heritage. For instance, preservation in the sense of handing down a way of life to succeeding generations or keeping "alive" a way of life that is receding, whether due to globalizing market or political forces, generations of conflict and war, or, simply, the aging and dying of senior members of a community. In other words, asserting and maintaining an identity through cultural differentiation need not mean drawing boundaries between persons simply for the sake of drawing boundaries as an end in itself. It also need not be for more muscular reasons such as propping up and advancing those boundaries for the sake of maintaining some notion of cultural purity or for the purpose of "conversion," which is to say, the desire to expand the number of members of a particular community.

Second, the use of culture as a way of asserting or affirming the distinctiveness of a particular identity applies to a wide range of identities, including religious and national identities. Efforts at delineating a sense of religious identity often involve identifying not only doctrinal but also cultural elements that differentiate it from other religions partly because certain religions are closely knit to cultural identities (e.g., Arab/Sunni Islam, Persian/Shi'i Islam, Greek/Eastern Orthodox, Dutch/Reformed or Calvinist). This also applies to nationalities, in that culture is often bound tightly to a nation state (e.g., France, Russia, Ghana, India, the United Kingdom, and Canada),[36] or because the nation state model necessitates the

36. Recently in the UK, the British minister of education has proposed that the General Certificate of Secondary Education English Exam focus more on British literary authors and eliminate a number of novels from American authors. See Erlanger, "Goodbye, Steinbeck." In India, note how the Flag Foundation of India articulates its strategy for the promotion of Indian patriotism and national unity through appreciation of the Tiranga or flag of India: "One of the primary objectives of the Foundation [of India] is to instill in citizens of India, a sense of pride in Tiranga. In order to spread the symbolism of the Tiranga, the Flag Foundation uses all available mediums such as music, art, photography, cultural programmes, festivals, seminars and workshops." See the homepage of the Flag Foundation of India, http://www.naveenjindal.com/meetnaveen/flag-foundation-india.

intentional cultivation of a common culture to engender a sense of cohesion and unity to what is often a political amalgamation of multiple cultural groups (for instance, the United States in its cultivation of a civic culture). Religions and nationalities also employ other non-cultural realities to secure a sense of national selfhood and identity, such as force or military prowess, territorial or geographic integrity, and sometimes expansion. At any rate, the larger point to be had is that communities, including nations and religions, possess a variety of tools to secure and maintain the longevity of their identities, and one of the primary tools is the assertion and maintenance of cultural differentiation.

Third, while culture may be a primary or, at least, readily accessible tool for identity differentiation and self-definition, that does not mean that the mere adherence to certain cultural practices will necessarily merit membership into a corresponding group identity, even if the community generally understands itself primarily within that cultural framework. A passage from Amy Chua's *Battle Hymn of the Tiger Mother* illustrates the kind of problem I refer to here. The following is a lively account of Chua's trip to China with her daughters, Sophia and Lulu:

> Sophia and Lulu were model children. In public, they were polite, interesting, helpful, and well spoken. They were A students, and Sophia was two years ahead of her classmates in math. They were fluent in Mandarin. And everyone marveled at their classical music playing. In short, they were just like Chinese kids.
>
> Except not quite. We took our first trip to China with the girls in 1999. Sophia and Lulu both have brown hair, brown eyes, and Asianesque features; they both speak Chinese. Sophia eats all kinds of organs and organisms—duck webs, pig ears, sea slugs—another critical aspect of Chinese identity. Yet everywhere we went in China, including cosmopolitan Shanghai, my daughters drew curious local crowds, who stared, giggled, and pointed at the "two little foreigners who speak Chinese." At the Chengdu Panda Breeding Center in Sichuan, while we were taking pictures of newborn giant pandas—pink squirming, larvalike creatures that rarely

---

aspx. In Canada, something as prosaic as poutine, French fries doused with gravy and dotted with cheese curds, has become a flash point in what it means to be Quebecois: "'Poutine is Quebecois; it is not Canadian,' said Zak Rosentzveig, 25, a poutine-obsessed economist from Montreal . . . 'Calling poutine "Canadian" makes me feel very uncomfortable because Quebec has a distinct culture and history from the rest of Canada, and poutine is a strong symbol of that" (Bilefsky, "Calling Poutine 'Canadian'").

survive—the Chinese tourists were taking pictures of Sophia and Lulu.[37]

Whatever one may think of Chua's account of the so-called Chinese model of parenting, the above passage alerts us to, in a striking, lively way, basic realities of the relationship between culture and identity. While there may be some sense of what it means to be Chinese in terms of cultural practice across Chinese communities (in this case, in the United States and mainland China), not all Chinese communities will regard all practitioners of what is understood as Chinese culture as "authentically" Chinese. While cultural practice to some large degree must be manifest, some will also require or, at the very least, will reflexively assume other measures of identity. In the case of Chua's two daughters' reception in mainland China, the measure of skin color or tone and other morphological features (they looked too "white" or "American" as biracial children of Chinese and Jewish descent) mitigated what Chua suggests is their perfection in Chinese cultural behavior.[38] At any rate, while culture may not be the singular differentiator of identities, without culture, identity differentiation or self-definition is hard to imagine. Perhaps this is why those in mainline China were so fascinated with the Chua daughters: how could these women who looked, from their perspective, so foreign act so familiar?

Inasmuch as culture is an integral means in which identity differentiation and self-definition is made visible and manifest, it is not difficult to see, as Appiah insightfully reminds us, why, when it comes to ethnicity and culture, "it is so easy to conflate them." He continues:

> Ethnic identities characteristically have cultural distinctions as one of their primary marks . . . Ethnic identities are created in family and community life. These—along with mass-mediated culture, the school, and the college—are, for most of us, the central sites of the social transmission of culture. Distinct practices, ideas,

37. Chua, *Battle Hymn of the Tiger Mother*, 56.

38. The Chua daughters' experience is not unusual for mixed-race Asian Americans, as the historian Paul R. Spickard observes. He relays the experience of Cindy Cordes, "a woman of Caucasian and Filipino ancestry raised in Hawaii." She recounts, "I have a *hapa* [multiple-identity] mentality. I look white but I don't identity with white culture. I grew up with a Filipino mother in an Asian household. We ate Asian food, had Filipino relationships, Filipino holidays, with Filipino values of family." "But then," according to Spickard, "she went to Columbia University and found that other Asian Americans 'look at me as white.' When she went to a meeting of an Asian American student group, 'They asked me, "Why are you here?"'" (Spickard, "What Must I Be?," 394–95).

norms go with each ethnicity in part because people want to be ethnically distinct: because many people want the sense of solidarity that comes from being unlike others. With ethnicity in modern society, it is often the distinct identity that comes first, the cultural distinction that is created and maintained because of it—not the other way around. The distinctive common cultures of ethnic and religious identities matter not simply because of their contents but also as markers of those identities.[39]

Whether ethnic identities are cultural identities is not in question. Asian American identity is not culture-less. What is in question is the ordering of identity and culture, that is, whether both are necessarily bound together or whether one precedes the other. For Appiah, the ordering more often than not falls toward the latter, a prevailing phenomenon especially, as he suggests, in modern society given concerns over preserving difference in the face of globalization and other homogenizing trends. From this perspective, cultural difference or distinctiveness is less a conceptually coherent idea in itself and more a feature that is "added" to culture (or, more precisely, given more weight to it) in the effort to secure borders between identities. In the effort to define who we are as a people (or who we are as Asian Americans, or Korean Americans, Vietnamese Americans, and so on), the typical route taken is to identify with certain attitudes and customs that are "indigenous" or "original" (i.e., authentic) to Koreans or Vietnamese, or to identify with how one's parents or prior generations have embraced traditions so-conceived. Claims to cultural authenticity offer a strategy for reinforcing the desire for ethnic difference. There is a certain stability and solidity to one's ethnic identity and sense of self when a culture can be claimed as genuinely belonging to that identity. Otherwise, a sense of meaningfulness in claiming and living that identity diminishes. Recalling Huang's dialogue with Bourdain about Ricker's ability to cook Thai food can be instructive on this point. Inasmuch as Ricker cooks good Asian food, his skill destabilizes common, conventional expectations of what it means to be Asian: e.g., Asians cook Asian food, among doing other "Asian things," and to the extent that Asians cook Asian food, they are most capable of cooking it well. But alas, Huang finds a white person doing what is not necessarily expected of a white person: cooking good or, as Huang finally attests, "mind-blowing" Asian food. What then does it mean to be

39. Appiah, "Race, Culture, Identity," 89.

Asian if a non-Asian person can do Asian things as well as if not better than an Asian person?

ASIAN AMERICAN IDENTITY AS AN EXERCISE
IN SELECTIVE CULTURAL PERFORMANCE

To further emphasize the idea that cultural expectations are often enlisted as a central means of giving identities distinct form and definition, Appiah proposes the metaphor of identity as a kind of script.[40] Just as the dialogue of a script gives the script its shape, so too the cultural expectations that typically delineate an identity's particularities. In other words, it is the desire for a distinctive script that comes first, and the dialogue that follows in support of that desire; or, it is culture that supports the goal of affirming the distinctiveness of a particular identity.

The script metaphor illumines the liabilities of strong identities. If being of a particular identity is akin to following some script, then Appiah wonders whether certain kinds of identities can end up too constraining, limiting life possibilities and stifling cultural creativity.[41] (Note the inherently restrictive quality of scripts in this account; scripts delineate modes of being that bring with them certain expectations for their characters/actors.) To demand "respect for people *as blacks*," for instance, "[requires] that there be some scripts that go with being African-American."[42] It is for that reason Appiah thinks "we need to go on to the next necessary step, which is to ask whether the identities constructed in this way are ones we can all be happy with in the longer run."[43] I am not unsympathetic to such a question. Common cultural expectations especially for Asian Americans are cautionary indicators: in addition to the rising rate of suicide among Korean adults, consider instances of Asian American teenage suicides, often attributed, in part, to sometimes overwhelming academic expectations.[44]

40. Appiah, "Race, Culture, Identity," 97.

41. Appiah, "Race, Culture, Identity," 99.

42. Appiah, "Race, Culture, Identity," 99 (emphasis original).

43. Appiah, "Race, Culture, Identity," 98–99.

44. For instance, at Cornell, from 1996 to 2004, 9 out of 16 student suicides were Asian / Asian American (Arenson, "Worried Colleges"). A more recent article reports the alarming rise of suicides among adult Koreans in the United States, particularly in the New York-New Jersey region. Reasons for this uptick are disputed. However, one growing opinion among Korea experts calls attention to the kinds of pressures placed on many Korean immigrant families due to certain expectations of success that are not necessarily

However, identities conceived of as scripts need not only draw our attention to the potentially restrictive qualities of certain kinds of identities. Identities as scripts is also useful in illumining the *inherent degree of cultural creation and choice* that goes into embracing and embodying a particular identity. For instance, consider Appiah's account of contemporary black identity as emergent from the Black Power movement:

> An African American after the Black Power movement takes the old script of self-hatred, the script in which he or she is a n****r, and works, in community with others, to construct a series of positive black life scripts. In these life scripts, being a Negro is recoded as being black: and this requires, among other things, refusing to assimilate to white norms of speech and behavior.[45]

For Appiah, contemporary black identity is a function of African American agency. Black identity, as any script itself, is a creation that draws from multiple sources to make visible or manifest a particular way of life, in this case, a certain existence that disavows "white norms of speech and behavior." So too with Asian American identity. As the sociologist Min Zhou explains, "The term 'Asian American' was coined by the late historian and activist Yuji Ichioka during the ethnic consciousness movements of the late 1960s. To adopt this identity is to reject the Western imposed label of 'Oriental,'"[46] In both cases, black and Asian American identities are creations and, thus, a function of choice, but not in some absolute sense, just as literary scripts are not simply created *ex nihilo* from the author's mind. Black identity as well as Asian American identity (and, importantly, what it means to be those identities at the cultural level) emerges in response to past and present social circumstances or experiences (e.g., racism, economic and political marginalization). And it is from this response to a specific social reality and history that such identities are given definition through, among other means, selective cultural retrieval and construction. Asian American is not simply a reiteration of a particular Asian culture, just as black identity is not

---

"traditionally Korean." These expectations have emerged and taken hold among many recent Korean immigrants due to Korea's own rapid industrial-capitalist transformation and corresponding values of materialism as primary parameters of success. In one highly reported suicide of a Korean couple on September 11, 2009, the couple left the following short letter to the daughter they were leaving behind: "I love you, my daughter. I'm sorry to leave you alone. It would've been much better if you had a wealthier father." "Along with the note, they left $40 in cash for her" (Semple, "Surge in Suicides").

45. Semple, "Surge in Suicides," 98.

46. Zhou, "Are Asian Americans Becoming White?," 354.

a mere repetition of some African culture; the cultural landscapes of both identities are more complicated than that.

Amerasian adoptees, particularly of Korean ancestry, provide an especially focused view into such complexity. Korean Amerasian adoptees, according to the sociologist Paul R. Spickard, tend to express more interest in Korean customs and traditions than non-adoptee Korean Americans and Amerasians. Reasons vary, but, as Spickard suggests, those who are adopted into white, non-Asian households and communities (e.g., rural Minnesota, where there is a particularly high concentration of such adoptees), tend to express a desire "to connect with their Korean background."[47] Such a desire would seem to underscore the earlier point that the embrace of a particular identity through culture is responsive to social circumstance. Particularly curious, however, are the kinds of practices, traditions, and customs that are taken as Korean or, at the very least, exemplifying Korean identity for many adoptees of Korean ancestry: tae kwon do, Korean drumming, Korean fan dancing, and the like.[48] To be sure, Korean cultural practices, as is the case with cultures generally speaking, are wide-ranging. But inasmuch as these few practices (often practices associated with Korean royal court life) are considered gateways to better appreciating Korean and Korean American identity, the attention given to these practices rather than other perhaps more obscure practices raises interesting questions about the extent to which the identity is culturally constructed in a *selective* manner in response to specific social dynamics.[49]

47. Spickard, "What Must I Be?," 401. The high concentration of Korean American adoptees in Minnesota has spurred a robust newspaper that caters specifically to them. See *Korean Quarterly*, http://www.koreanquarterly.org/Home.html.

48. See, for instance, the website to Camp Friendship, NJ, https://www.campfriendshipnj.org/Korea/, a summer camp in Stirling, NJ, at the Shrine of St. Joseph. This camp is dedicated to introducing Korean adoptees to Korean culture as a way of better understanding and appreciating their ethnic heritage. (The tagline for the camp is "A Korean Culture Camp.") A camp for Chinese adoptees is also sponsored by the organization.

49. Such selective cultural focus is not exclusive to Korean Americans. Consider the experiences of many Chinese immigrants to the United States. As the writer Bonnie Tsui recollects on her Chinese American upbringing, "Family friends sent their kids to Chinese school when I was growing up—weekend classes in Chinatown that emphasized language and crafts and songs. It was the familiar effort to "stay Chinese" in a larger society that doesn't make it easy to be different" (Tsui, *American Chinatown*, 3). Beyond Asian Americans of East Asian descent, consider the popularity of Hindu Heritage Summer Camp in Macedon, NY. According to a recent profile on the camp, its attraction stems from the interest of Indian immigrants to the United States in strengthening their children's identity as Indians "in a polyglot nation with an enticingly secular popular

Another example, but this one in the realm of Asian American food-ways, reinforces further the idea that social circumstance or experience often informs the selective cultural construction of identity differentiation and self-understanding. In the opening to her article on the history of Filipino food in the mid-twentieth century, the historian Dawn Bohulano Mabalon recounts a formative event in her father's ethnic consciousness:

> My father Ernesto Tirona Mabalon arrived in Stockton, Califor-
> nia, in 1963 to be reunited with his father, Pablo "Amblo" Maba-
> lon, who had left their hometown of Numancia, Aklan, for the
> United States in 1929. My *lolo* (grandfather) Ambo ran a popular
> Filipino American diner, the Lafayette Lunch Counter, in the heart
> of Stockton's Little Manila. Almost immediately after he arrives,
> my *tatay* (father) was "itching to have dried fish" and craved his
> favorite variety, called *tuyo*. When my lolo stepped out one after-
> noon, my father threw some *tuyo* on the restaurant's hot grill. The
> reek of the fried, fermented fish wafted down Lafayette Street. Lolo
> rushed back to find angry patrons [most of whom were Filipino
> Americans] and warned tatay never to fry *tuyo* again. After he ate,
> tatay lambasted the customers. "I said, *Mabaho pala kayo!*" (You're
> the ones who stink!), he remembered.
>
> After this *tuyo* debacle, ["Tatay"] swore that "wherever I am, I
> will always eat dried fish, the old dependable."[50]

For the author of the article from which I have been citing, Tatay's *tuyo* story raises questions about the history of Filipino food both in the Philippines and in the United States, such as: was *tuyo* a food staple for Filipinos before migration and afterwards? While an interesting historical question, I am more interested in how this story pushes us to consider the kind of dynamics that shape the cultural choices Asian Americans make to give definition and differentiation to their respective ethnic identities. In other words, what are the social forces that inform the choices of Asian Americans to adhere to or celebrate this tradition over that? Or, what are the social

---

culture." As such, the camp's "approach is built around a set of hybrid rituals," a blending of Hindu customs and so-called American customs. For instance, a common morning activity is gathering "in a circle [of] about 150 children and counselors burst[ing] into 'Rise and Shine,' an American Christian song about Noah's Ark—a story that also happens to have a Hindu parallel in the myth of Manu, who helps to save humanity from a great flood." In the evenings, campers may reenact "the Hindu festival of Holi, which observes the coming of spring, with an Indian-American version of color war." See Freedman, "Building on U.S. Tradition."

50. Mabalon, "As American as Jackrabbit Adobo," 147.

forces that contribute to Asian American re-appropriation, recreation, or re-imagination of certain cultural forms? In some cases, why do Asian Americans prefer or desire to preserve, to the extent possible, as much of their ancestral homeland customs?

For Tatay, before coming to the United States, eating *tuyo* was part and parcel of everyday life; taken for granted, in other words. It is only when he arrives in the United States that it takes on a different status, becoming a way of asserting what he thinks it means to be a particular kind of person. More specifically, the decision to "always eat dried fish" is now marked as part and parcel of his identity as Filipino and, thus, not as one who has succumbed, he suggests, to a way of life in the United States that questions its propriety. Tatay, therefore, devotes himself specifically to a cultural dimension of Filipino life as a means of reasserting and preserving a particular Filipino identity in response to specific socioeconomic and sociopolitical forces that may discount that particular identity. Revealing is Tatay's continued tirade against his fellow Filipinos in Stockton, California, who complain of the smell of fried, fermented fish in his father's diner:

> I said: When you left the country [the Philippines] you were eating dried fish, were you not? This is what made you what you are! Dried fish! Because you are here [in America], you hate the smell of dried fish? You did not come to this country if you were eating steak in the Philippines![51]

For Tatay, the eating of *tuyo*, despite its odious smell, is an act of rejecting a kind of cultural imperialism, the perception that to fit in American life requires softening the edges of one's own cultural practices. Eating *tuyo* also serves to affirm a rural way of life that presumably many of his fellow Filipino émigrés are attempting to escape in hopes of a more affluent lifestyle in the United States. Interestingly, the social forces that inform Tatay's insistence on eating *tuyo*, and thus on the preservation of a particular Filipino identity, are not all that different from the desire of many Hawaiians in the 1980s and 1990s to advocate for what they called regional Hawaiian cuisine: rural, local, and drawing from indigenous Hawaiian communities rather than the cooking philosophies and tastes of continental or European cuisine.[52]

51. Mabalon, "As American as Jackrabbit Adobo," 147.
52. Yamashita, "Significance of Hawai'i Regional Cuisine," 117.

THE SOCIAL LOGIC OF ASIAN AMERICAN IDENTITY

Tatay's *tuyo* story draws attention less on the question of cultural authenticity and more on the question of the reality of cultural construction. After all, how authentically Filipino is eating *tuyo*? For Tatay, the point is not about authenticity per se, but about resisting the marginalization of a particular identity and way of life. That social logic is operative throughout Asian American foodways. As the literary and food studies scholar Wenying Xu remarks, "There is nothing natural or culturally predetermined about Asian Americans' vital relationship with food."[53] Asian Americans' relationship with food, such as Tatay's *tuyo* story, calls specific attention to the social contexts from which Asian Americans (or any other identity for that matter) culturally construct their identity. Those contexts or circumstances shape the cultural choices Asian Americans make to give definition and differentiation to their respective identities. How we think about Asian American identity, therefore, must move beyond narrow claims to cultural originality or authenticity. The cultural markers of Asian American identity are not inherent to who they are. Who Asian Americans are culturally is complicated and colored by the social experiences that inform the choice for and embrace (and sometimes re-imagination or outright rejection and subversion) of certain, select cultural forms by Asian Americans.

The relationship between identity and social experience is brought to the fore in what the political theorist Iris Marion Young calls "social perspective."[54] Drawing from the work of sociologists Pierre Bourdieu, Young reminds us that persons are situated in social contexts that are prior to themselves. These are prior social contexts insofar as they are conditions to which we have been "thrown" into, thus "positioning" us in particular ways in society. That notion of being thrown into a particular social reality is critical for Young, underscoring the extent to which our identities are social responses; it is from this thrown-ness or positionality that we "become ourselves," individually and collectively.[55] Attentiveness to how persons construe themselves, therefore, does not necessarily offer a window into

53. Xu, *Eating Identities*, 12.

54. Young, "Difference as a Resource," 383–406.

55. More specifically, "We are unique individuals, with our own identities created from the way we have taken up the histories, cultural constructs, language, and social relations of hierarchy and subordination that condition our lives" (Young, "Difference as a Resource," 392).

some genuine or unique sense of self.[56] Rather, such attentiveness provides perspective on the kinds of "constraints, dilemmas, tensions, and indeed possibilities that are specific"[57] to particular individuals or groups given how they are subject to the ways society's institutions, structures, and ideologies distribute power, privilege, opportunity, resources, and expectations. In that way, defining who one is, is not unlike a process of constant *negotiation* of the social forces and dynamics that she inescapably experiences, whether explicitly or implicitly. The kinds of cultural lives Asian Americans lead or embody, then, are not simply value neutral modes of being and, in turn, trivial (or morally irrelevant) features of Asian American identity, but rather are critical arenas through which they define, assert, or make sense of themselves given their social realities.

But not *every* cultural value or tradition that Asian Americans practice or embody is intentionally constructed in response to or as a negotiation of a given social context. It would be a mistake to socially instrumentalize all aspects of Asian American cultural identity; that would be descriptively reductive. Instead, to say that the cultural markers of Asian Americans are constructed is to call attention to the dynamics operative in the ways in which Asian Americans emphasize certain traditions or practices or reimagine them. Eating *mandoo* (Korean style dumplings) for a Korean American may be something he or she has done since childhood without much reflection. Or, making *mandoo* with "non traditional" ingredients may be a function more of cultural-culinary adaptation rather than some attempt at responding to particular social circumstances. But in addition to our long held cultural habits, in many cases, as Tatay's *tuyo* story suggests, Asian Americans also pick and choose certain customs, traditions, and values, that is, elevate, reimagine, or forsake them in one way or another, as particular ways of making sense of their identities within the context of particular social realities that they find themselves in or encounter. Our cultural existence, in other words, is not simply a matter of having been habituated into repeating or being what it means to be Asian American as determined by ancestral heritage or familial customs. Eating *tuyo* or, more broadly, eating a particular "traditional" food, more so than as a matter of cultural convention, can take on the dimension of self-definition as a way of responding to or negotiating with particular social pressures.

56. Young, "Difference as a Resource," 395.
57. Young, "Difference as a Resource," 392.

As strategies for negotiating their social circumstances, the cultural lives of Asian Americans are not simply mediations of them. Consider how the theologian Roberto Goizueta writes about the mediating nature of Latino/a culture.[58] In reference to US Hispanic popular religiosity, Goizueta elaborates, "rather than superseding the ethical-political; the aesthetic dimension of human action is mediated by the ethical-political; it is encountered and lived out within ethical-political action, as the deepest meaning and significance of the ethical-political."[59] The concept of mediation in that citation, as well as in the following passage, suggests a too direct, cause-and-effect, or predictable relationship between culture and social experience:

> It is no coincidence that the extent to which a particular Latino community continues to participate in traditional, popular forms of religion is closely related to that community's level of economic and political integration into U.S. society: in Latin America as in the United States, the religion of the upper classes is often virtually indistinguishable from liberal Catholicism. The religiosity of middle and upper class U.S. Hispanics often exhibits the characteristics of what Mark Francis called Euro-American devotionalism. Thus popular Catholicism is not only a cultural but also a class phenomenon.[60]

The concept of negotiation (that culture is a strategy of negotiating socio-economic, political realities) rather than mediation suggests with greater precision a relationship between culture and social experience that involves a greater degree of selectivity and judgment. Consider one more time Tatay's insistence on eating *tuyo*. Not only does he eat it, but, as we saw earlier, flaunts that act, not without thought, but as an act of judgment of the social situation he finds himself in, which leads him to embrace *tuyo* in defiance of that social situation (which in this case is the sense of foreignness among white Californians). Other members of his Filipino community, however, have shied away from eating *tuyo*, as a part of a larger attempt to fit into mainstream American life. In either case, cultural choices are made, and each choice is indicative of a judgment of particular social factors or experiences. It is that sense of choice or judgment that I am attempting to capture with the notion that Asian American cultural choices are more akin to strategies of negotiating social realities more so than a mediation of

58. Goizueta, *Caminemos con Jesús*, 127, emphasis original.
59. Goizueta, *Caminemos con Jesús*, 128.
60. Goizueta, *Caminemos con Jesús*, 128.

those circumstances. In short, the cultural lives of Asian Americans are not reflective of a particular political and economic dynamic in some obvious way. Eating *tuyo* is neither a working-class phenomenon nor an upper-class one; it is more complicated than that.

ASIAN AMERICAN IDENTITY: CULTURALLY INCOHERENT, SOCIALLY COHERENT

If the cultural lives of Asian Americans reflect a deep social logic, then we have good reason to cast suspicion on cultural claims to authenticity; there is no culturally authentic way of being Asian. Discerning Asian American identity requires being attentive to how Asian Americans constitute, construct, or selectively perform their cultural selves in response to particular social experiences or circumstances. The social logic that underlines that cultural construction accounts for, in part, the immense cultural variability of Asian American life and identity; there is no cultural given-ness to being Asian American but only the cultures that individual Asian Americans choose to have and selectively perform. For some Asian Americans (perhaps primarily, but not exclusively, among first generation Asian immigrants to the United States), being Asian American demands "concerted effort[s] to preserve [ancestral homeland cultures],"[61] while for others, it may be more appropriative, reimaging or refashioning only particular dimensions of ancestral homeland cultures, as perhaps in Tatay's *tuyo* story. Other Asian Americans still may move even further, beyond such selective and creative appropriation and toward a kind of cultural ambivalence wherein they regard their ancestral homeland cultures, in whole or in part, as a "leisure-time activity" rather than formative features of one's identity.[62] These are only broad typological ways in which Asian Americans culturally construct themselves, and doing justice to the immense cultural variability of Asian Americans would require that we discern how these typologies are more specifically manifested or lived daily within various Asian American communities and by Asian American individuals.

Whatever the range and depth may be of that cultural variability, acknowledging that there is indeed tremendous cultural diversity is key to destabilizing possible if not real misperceptions of what it means to be Asian American. What it means to be Asian American cannot simply be

61. Zhou and Gatewood, "Transforming Asian America," 129.
62. Zhou and Gatewood, "Transforming Asian America," 129.

neatly contained within certain defined cultural parameters. While deeply embedded popular cultural attitudes may assume certain values, practices, and events as inherently Asian American (while others are, say, Italian American or African American, even though all persons can appreciate and celebrate "their" respective cultures), these familiar cultural markers hardly capture or define the fullness and plurality of Asian American identity. One person's way of being Asian American may not be necessarily the same as another's. That is a truism of sorts. (After all, no one is a clone of another, whether Asian or non-Asian.) But that seemingly obvious intuition is worth punctuating only if to remind us of a larger conceptual point about racial identities that is easily missed given the persistence of how popular culture shapes and maintains our perceptions of persons. Asian American identity does not necessarily pertain to a distinct and hermeneutically sealed cultural style and form of life. There is no authentic, normative Asian American culture.

To insist on cultural normativity risks what the African American studies scholar Henry Louis Gates Jr. refers to as cultural geneticism, which, in effect, reinscribes a concept of race that is defined biologically but under the guise of culture. Jazz and hip-hop are inherently "black things," whereas kung fu and taekwondo are "Asian," so too feng shui, as the last epigraph to this chapter posits. Or, as the first epigraph intimates, African Americans have rhythm, whereas Asian Americans do not. Along the same lines of that cultural logic, but even more perniciously, Asian Americans have an aptitude for math and computer science, unlike African Americans who are better at basketball and football.[63] To resist a normative cultural construal of identity is to underscore that familiar vernacular comments such as "that is typical of Asian Americans" (or "African American") disregard a deeper complexity to racial identity. So, an Asian American jazz artist unsettles any preconceived notion of being Asian American.[64] (So too a non-Asian American chef who is exceptionally skilled in cooking Thai food, as we

63. The burden of that cultural logic may explain, in part, the intense interest that Asian Americans have had for the Taiwanese American basketball player Jeremy Lin of the Atlanta Hawks. See Kang, "Lives of Others."

64. See, for instance, Zeng, "Yes, We Play Jazz Too." Note the inference in the title of this article as if many non-Asians (and maybe Asian Americans too) would find the association of Asian American and jazz artist as incongruous, unexpected. Why? Presumably because jazz is not an Asian art form, but typically regarded as belonging to African Americans. But the fact that many Asian Americans are not only jazz artists but exceptional ones at that raises tough questions about the relationship between culture and racial identity.

saw earlier.) Such cultural mixing may appear incongruous and perhaps even, to a degree, fraudulent, if and only if racial identities are culturally demarcated with rigidity, that is, if cultures are owned by particular identities. It is difficult to imagine how that sense of cultural ownership does not take on an air of biological designation, in some sense. Cultural ownership has a way of tying a certain culture to persons who are grouped according to particular physical and morphological characteristics and geographic provenance.[65]

The notion that Asian American identity corresponds to an inherent Asian American culture (that it owns a particular culture, that a particular culture "naturally" belongs to an Asian American community of persons that shares a similar appearance and geographic history) is poignantly depicted in an erstwhile Starburst candy advertisement. A Korean man wearing a Scottish kilt declares to his son, who is also wearing a kilt while eating Starbursts, "Look at this! One contradiction eating another! . . . You're Scotch-Korean. You don't make a wee bit of sense! And neither does Starburst! Starburst is a solid, yet juicy, like a liquid!"[66] But that is only a contradiction (being Scotch-Korean, not Starbursts themselves) if being Korean means by definition doing certain things that are marked as normatively "Korean." Wearing kilts is apparently not one of them, among other Scottish customs, since that is what Scots do. But that begs the question, what if a Scottish man does not wear customary clothing, is he less of a Scot than one who does? Similarly, is an Asian American sporting a kilt somehow less Asian American than one who does not? To discern what kind of culture Asian Americans "have" or should have is to wade through the treacherous waters of ethno-racial stereotyping, as well as to stoke the flames of *intra* ethno-racial tyrannies.[67] As Young observes, "Any attempt to

65. This is, argues Appiah, what W. E. B. Du Bois was unable to avoid even though he insisted on a concept of race that was cultural and sociohistorical rather than biological or "scientific." To claim that what defined a race is its particular culture in effect makes race a "metonym for culture . . . at the price of biologizing what *is* culture" (Appiah, "Uncompleted Argument," 135). While Du Bois, according to Appiah, sought to "deny that the cultural capacities of the black-skinned, curly-haired members of human kind were inferior to those of the white-skinned, straighter-haired ones," that denial of inferiority presumed, and perhaps even conceptually required, that those cultural capacities were "an inherited racial essence" (Appiah, "Uncompleted Argument," 127).

66. Transcription of the commercial is taken from https://www.commarts.com/project/15095/starburst.

67. For instance, consider the questions of racial exclusivity that are emerging in South Korea, as well as among Korean immigrants in the United States. With the rapid

describe just what differentiates a social group from others and to define a common identity of its members tends to normalize some life experiences and sets up group borders that wrongly exclude," thereby "setting up rigid inside-outside distinctions among groups" that are inherently, conceptually artificial.[68]

Eschewing cultural normativity to Asian American identity underscores the realities that Asian Americans hail from a diversity of nationalities and ancestral origins, origins which themselves contain cultural multitudes. (So just as there is no normative Asian American culture, there is no normative Korean culture, Chinese culture, Thai culture, and so on.) It also underscores the realities of cultural intermingling that takes place especially in cosmopolitan contexts. As the author Bonnie Tsui rightly claims, "White or black or Asian America isn't monolithic and never was . . . Everyone's story can be parsed ever more minutely: Haitian-Hawaiian, Mexican-Salvadorean, Cuban-Chinese. And when you start mixing up stories, as many [families have], . . . [race is] intensely individual."[69] Such observations, however, cannot fully account for or explain the deep cultural diversity of Asian American life; what is descriptively true does not necessarily lend insight into the rationale for that description. A more adequate account of the cultural diversity of Asian American life requires moving beyond axiomatic statements about the descriptive realities of diversity and entails a critical recognition that the cultural diversity of Asian Americans also reflects a larger dynamic informing and shaping how Asian Americans define who they are. More specifically, how Asian Americans culturally construct and selectively imagine and perform themselves reflect the various ways in which Asian Americans negotiate (attempt to make sense of) the social circumstances within which they are situated. The cultural lives of Asian Americans, therefore, are not merely a reflection of who they are and what they do as a matter of course. Rather, their cultural lives also reflect the myriad ways in which Asian Americans define themselves within existing social logics.

---

increase of marriages between Korean men and Southeast Asian women (e.g., India, Malaysia) in South Korea, questions of what it means to be Korean—for instance, whether a Korean can forfeit some genuine sense of Koreanness if he or she does not follow what are considered "traditional" familial patterns and customs—have been brought into public discussion more explicitly and frequently. Choe, "South Koreans Struggle with Race."

68. Young, "Difference as a Resource," 389, 387.

69. Tsui, "Choose Your Own Identity."

And yet, to the extent that the cultural lives of Asian Americans are a function of those social logics, the reality of those social logics indicate a way of talking about what it means to be Asian American that cuts across the diversity of Asian American communities while also preserving the genuine differences among Asian Americans. Yes, Asian American culture can only be spoken of in the plural, but that pluralism also reveals a commonality of experience. Not a cultural experience but *a social one*. Inasmuch as their cultural differences reflect underlying strategies for making sense of the social forces or circumstances within which Asian Americans are situated, the cultural differences of Asian Americans reveal a common social task that confronts all Asian Americans, how to respond to the question of social existence. As we will see in the following chapters, while that response can move either in the direction of resistance or conformity to the prevailing social forces that Asian Americans, individually and collectively, confront, resistance may be a more formidable direction than conformity.

3

Racism

Typically fourth grade was too young for even *pre*-sex education sex education, but a woman with spiky blond tips and big pins all over her blazer informed us at a mandatory assembly that we had been targeted as a high-risk school and measures had to be taken to ensure for the future. She spoke to us spitefully, as if we were awful, terrible children, and used the words "at risk" several times without going into detail. What were we at risk for?

After I told my mother about the assembly, she started to fret that there were too few white kids in my school. Am I at risk? I asked her. It's a sign, she said . . .

—*SOUR HEART*[1]

The other kids thought I was strange of course. I didn't fit in . . .
[But somehow], Mrs. LaGuardia had mistaken me for one of the white kids, the ones who had housekeepers waiting at home, ready with an afternoon snack.

—*GIRL IN TRANSLATION*[2]

IF WHAT IT MEANS to be Asian American requires being attentive to the ways in which Asian Americans constitute their cultural selves in response

1. Zhang, *Sour Heart*, 54–55.
2. Jean Kwok, *Girl in Translation*, 58, 98.

to particular social experiences or circumstances, then what are those circumstances? In this chapter, I want to consider the extent to which race or the social experiences of racism is *formative* for Asian American identity. In emphasizing formative, we finally arrive at the question of Asian American identity as a *racialized* identity. Accordingly, the focal question of this chapter is not whether racism is socially relevant for Asian Americans; I take that as a given. But what is not a given is the nature of that discrimination, that is, how it has played in Asian American self-understanding, or its role in the cultural construction and performance of who we are as Asian Americans. Consider how two Asian Americans have addressed the question of racism and Asian American identity.

First, the journalist and author Jay Caspian Kang, who observes, "'Asian-American' is a mostly meaningless term. Nobody grows up speaking Asian-American, nobody sits down to Asian-American food with their Asian-American parents and nobody goes on pilgrimages back to their motherland of Asian-America [because there is no such country] . . . We share stereotypes, mostly—tiger moms, music lessons and the unexamined march toward success, however it's defined . . . Discrimination is what really binds Asian-Americans together."[3] Kang echoes at least two main features of what I have been emphasizing with respect to Asian American identity: that there is no set cultural reality to that identity and whatever cultural identity (or identities) Asian Americans embody, that embodiment is a function of Asian American responses to specific social realities. In other words, what defines and animates Asian American identity is the social logic that underlies its cultural construction. For Kang, that social logic is primarily responding to racism against Asian Americans.

Second, compare Kang's assessment of Asian American identity's rootedness in racial discrimination with the food critic Ligaya Mishan's observations about the identity of Asian American chefs, restaurateurs, and food trendsetters. "There's . . . no one cultural touchstone or trauma that binds Asian immigrants," she writes, "no event on a national scale that has brought us together."[4] While Mishan is not dismissive of the reality of discrimination against Asian Americans, her comment displays ambivalence as to its role in defining Asian American life. If there is indeed no one historical moment of discrimination that necessarily informs what it means to be Asian American (such as chattel slavery for African Americans), then

3. Kang, "What a Fraternity Hazing Death Revealed."
4. Mishan, "Asian-American Cuisine's Rise."

in what way can (and should) racial discrimination be regarded as the primary social driver of what it means to be Asian American? Mishan suggests that a singular focus on racial discrimination against Asian Americans is too tidy, perhaps reductive, which can too easily mask the complex reality and promising future of Asian Americans as interculturally conscious, or embodying cultural hybridity.

In what follows, I want to adjudicate the two kinds of approaches to the relationship between racism and Asian American identity that Kang's and Mishan's comments reflect by first mapping and assessing what Asian American hybridity means. The meaning of hybridity within an Asian American frame is multivalent. Chapter 2 alluded to the cultural identities of Asian Americans as hybrid (without using the term explicitly) inasmuch as Asian Americans, responding to particular social dynamics or realities, selectively appropriate or re-create their Asian ancestral values or traditions. In this chapter, I am particularly interested in a complementary but distinct approach to hybridity, that is, an approach that employs hybridity or interculturality as an interpretative frame for how Asian Americans *are* responding to and, more significantly, *should* respond to the social realities of racial discrimination. This account of hybridity is distinct insofar as it does not necessarily begin with the premise that Asian Americans are by definition intercultural, though that is the case to an important degree, again, as chapter 2 argued. The emphasis, rather, is on interculturality as a strategy of liberation and innovation in the face of the realities of racial discrimination against Asian Americans. But does such an account of and advocacy for hybridity sufficiently understand the nature of the discriminatory pressures Asian Americans are subject to? And does it offer a sufficient response to such discriminatory dynamics? In focusing on these questions, I hope to circle back affirmatively to Kang's observation about the binding nature of racial discrimination for Asian American identity. While Kang's account of racial discrimination in Asian American life is limited, the emphasis on its centrality and persistence in Asian American life is not. Hybridity fails to attend to that persistence, and it does so because it fails to understand the subtly subversive ways in which white racism operates on Asian American life. Asian Americans are not simply other, if by other is meant the intractable perception that Asian Americans are perpetual immigrants or foreigners (or just exotic) and, thus, culturally, socially, and perhaps even ontologically different. But such otherness of Asian Americans is only one important part of the way in which Asian Americans are racialized. It is how our otherness is configured within the social visions and demands of whiteness that the turn to hybridity too easily obscures.

RACIAL DISCRIMINATION AS THE BINDING SOCIAL NARRATIVE? CONSIDERING HYBRIDITY

One way in which hybridity is understood within an Asian American context is as a description of how Asian Americans are responding to their social situatedness, which is to say their status as other in American society. Mishan's account of hybridity in Asian American life is one striking case in point. Asian Americans, she suggests, are increasingly turning to an intercultural, borderless understanding of themselves in light of the fact that Asian Americans belong to neither Asia nor America. Mishan writes,

> Among the children of immigrants, Asians in America seem most caught in a state of limbo: no longer beholden to their parents' countries of origin but still grasping for a role in the American narrative. There is a unique foreignness that persists, despite the presence of Asians on American soil for more than two centuries; none of us, no matter how bald our America [*sic*] accent, has gone through life without being asked, "Where are you from? I mean, originally?" But while this can lead to alienation, it can also have a liberating effect. When you are raised in two cultures at once—when people see in you two heritages at odds, unresolved, in abeyance—you learn to shift at will between them. You may never feel like you quite belong in either, but neither are you fully constrained.[5]

Note that Mishan does not dismiss the reality of discrimination for Asian Americans. Asian Americans are foreign and the persistence of that perception of Asian Americans as different, not of America—that nagging, inescapable question "'Where are you from . . . originally?'"—has an alienating effect. But that sense of difference and alienation also applies to their ancestral cultures inasmuch as they are geographically removed from Asia. Thus, neither of America nor Asia, a sense of borderlessness is profoundly felt, especially among, as Mishan notes, "children of immigrants."

The sociologists Min Zhou and J. V. Gatewood parse this description of native-born (or American-born) Asian Americans as borderless with greater sociological precision. "The immigrant generation," they observe,

5. Mishan, "Asian-American Cuisine's Rise."

"generally reaffirms its ethnic identity on the basis of homeland cultures and life experiences not only through ethnic practices but also through memories of its lived experiences in the homeland or during the process of movement." As an example, they highlight Southeast Asian refugees who "share the common experience of having lived through internal power struggles in their home countries, the horrors of war, and the ordeal of exile and death."[6] Note the contrast between "native-born Asian Americans and those who arrived in the United States as infants or as school-age children." Native-born Asian Americans "usually do not seize on traditional cultural symbols . . . Rather, they tend to build their identities largely on the basis of mediating *interpretative memories* of homeland cultures in which they have never personally lived, and their own diverse life experiences in the United States."[7] Those life experiences are exclusionary in nature and often more formative than memories of their parents' homeland culture: "Often, however, actual experiences in American society outweigh memories. Transplanted cultural heritage is no longer the requirement or the defining characteristic of ethnicity for the native born. Rather, the emergence and persistence of ethnicity depends on the structural conditions of the host society and the position that the immigrant groups occupy in that social structure."[8] As distanced from their ancestral cultures and also distanced from mainstream American culture, post-immigrant Asian Americans occupy multiple cultural worlds, which has led to an Asian American culture that "is neither mainstream American nor clearly associated with the immigrant generation. It is a hybrid form."[9]

It is important to note that Zhou and Gatewood employ the term hybridity for Asian Americans of post-immigrant generations who are *not only* Asian multiracial (e.g., persons who are of multi-Asian ancestry and persons who are racially mixed, Asian and non-Asian[10]). Hybridity *also* describes how native-born Asian Americans are negotiating their cultural

6. Zhou and Gatewood, "Transforming Asian America," 128.

7. Zhou and Gatewood, "Transforming Asian America," 129, emphasis original.

8. Zhou and Gatewood, "Transforming Asian America," 129.

9. Zhou and Gatewood, "Transforming Asian America," 128.

10. According to Pew, 4 percent of the multiracial population is Asian-white and 70 percent of white-Asian persons identity also as multiracial. See Pew, "Multiracial in America." Research on the role mixed-race Asians are playing in Asian American identity formation has steadily increased since 2000. For a fuller accounting of this growing body of study, see, for instance, Schlund-Vials and Wu, "Rethinking Embodiment," 201.

in-betweenness.[11] Yet, as the post-colonial feminist theologian Kwok Pui-Lan reminds us, cultural hybridity or multiple cultural belongings is not the singular province of the children of Asian American immigrants; it is not, in a manner of speaking, merely a youth or generational phenomenon but one that has a long historical lineage. Consider Asian Christianity, which she claims is rooted in experiences of interreligious encounter, dialogue, and exchange. Taking the Chinese Protestant experience as a point of departure, Kwok argues that Asian Christianity never emerged simply as a branch of Western Christianity *in* Asia, but it emerged as it dialogued with various Asian beliefs, practices, and meanings, whether Buddhist, Daoist, Confucian, or more localized, popular religious and nonreligious cultural forms. Hence, the introduction to an "inter-spiritual world" when reading Asian translations of the Bible, "whether one is conscious of this or not," argues Kwok. "In the Chinese Protestant Bible, the prologue in the Gospel of John begins this way: 'In the beginning was the *dao*, and the *dao* was with God, and the *dao* was God.' The Chinese Bible also uses many Buddhist terms, including those for heaven and hell."[12] In Asian Christianity, therefore, one sees what Kwok refers to as the hybridity of Western Christian and Asian cultural forms, though I think a more illustrative image is that of Western Christian forms cohabitating with Asian cultural forms, with both cohabitating partners not simply existing side-by-side but mutually challenging, expanding, and revising each other's self-understandings. That idea of cohabitation is taken up as a model for Asian Catholicism when, according to the theologian Peter C. Phan, SJ, the Synod of Asian Bishops called on the Asian Catholic Church to "discover their own identity" in light of the promulgation of *Gaudium et spes* in 1965.[13] The Synod of Asian Bishops held that such discovery can only take place through a tripartite dialogue between the Asian church and the various sociocultural and religious traditions of Asian nations and peoples. "This dialogal model is the

---

11. In this book, as I note in the current and following paragraphs in greater detail, I do not take hybridity simply as pertaining to racially mixed persons, but also Asians or Asian Americans of single ancestry who, nevertheless, engage in multiple cultural transit, intermixing cultural practices and forms resulting in a new synthesis of those practices and forms.

12. Kwok, "Conversation," 46–47.

13. Phan, "'Reception' or 'Subversion' of Vatican II," 48. See also Phan's notion of the "Church not in but of Asia" in Phan, *Christianity with an Asian Face*, 171–83.

new Asian way of being Church, promoting mutual understanding, harmony and collaboration," proclaimed the Asian Catholic Bishops.[14]

Kwok's observations of Asian religiosity as inherently intercultural, interreligious, and interspiritual is meant to complicate perceptions of Asians as cultural monoliths. Being Asian belies culturally static or essentialist conceptions and instead punctuates its inherent inclusivity. Asian American magnifies such hybridity in its very definition: it is neither Asian nor American but a belonging to both, traversing from and dialoguing with two worlds. However, while Mishan, as we saw earlier, sees the hybrid turn among Asian Americans as a response to the social distance engendered by a persistent otherness that Asian Americans feel with respect to their reception in both Asia and America, it is less clear that for Kwok Asian interculturality is a response to social experiences of alienation and distance.[15] In that way, Kwok's vision of Asian hybridity does not neatly align with Mishan's (and maybe even Phan's) conception of Asian Americans as hybrid, that is, intercultural. Yet, what they do share is an account of hybridity that is inflected with a kind of racial hopefulness and optimism. Hybridity, whether with respect to Asians or Asian Americans, permits a substantial level of freedom to define what it means to be Asian or Asian American. That freedom is not only a freedom from stifling racial conventions and stereotypical perceptions but as such it is a freedom for cultural innovation.

Recall Mishan's earlier assessment of Asian Americans as intercultural and borderless, which has allowed Asian Americans, for instance, working in the food industry to "[take] freely from both sides [Asian and American] to forge something new."[16] She is not referring to the phenomenon of fusion cuisine, since fusion implies two definite entities when mixed or mashed together still retain their distinctive forms. That belies what she thinks is the reality of Asian American life and its emergent cuisine, that is, originality, the birth of something creative, new, and different:

> The acute awareness of borders (culinary as well as cultural) that both enclose and exclude, allows, paradoxically, a claim to borderlessness, taking freely from both sides to forge something new. For Asian-American chefs, this seesaw between the obligations of

14. Phan, "'Reception' or 'Subversion' of Vatican II," 42.

15. Zhou and Gatewood sound more like Mishan when they argue that the hybridity of native-born Asian Americans "has come to assume tremendous significance . . . as a viable means of resistance and compromise within the existing power structure [in the US]" (Zhou and Gatewood, "Transforming Asian America" 128).

16. Mishan, "Asian-American Cuisine's Rise."

inheritance and the thrill of go-it-aloneness, between respecting your ancestors and lighting out for the hills, manifests in dishes that arguably could come only from minds fluent in two ways of life.[17]

That sense of possibility and newness is infused throughout Phan's approach to Asian American theology: "Asian American theology, as implied by its dual character, is neither purely Asian nor purely American. An offspring of the marriage of two widely divergent cultural and religious heritages, it bears all the marks of *mestizo*, a mixture of the two traditions."[18] The language of mixture, however, can be ambiguous. Is Asian American theology simply a sum of its different, distinct parts or is it something more than that? His reference to Asian Americans as being "in a betwixt-and-between situation" is suggestive of a more radical understanding of what it means to traverse between Asian and American. He elaborates:

> This betwixt-and-between predicament, while a source of much soul-searching and suffering, can be an incentive and resource for a *creative rethinking* of both cultural traditions, the native and the foreign. Being in-between is, paradoxically, being *neither* this *nor* that but also being *both* this *and* that. Immigrants belong fully to neither their native culture nor to the host culture. By the same token, however, they belong to both, though not fully. And because they dwell in the interstices between the two cultures, they are in a position to see more clearly and to appreciate more objectively, both as insiders and outsiders (emically and etically), the strengths as well as the weaknesses of both cultures; as a result, they are better equipped to contribute to the emergence of a new, enriched culture. Hence, to be in-between as an immigrant is to be *neither*-this-*nor*-that, to be *both*-this-*and*-that, and to be *beyond*-this-and-that.[19]

It is critical to note that for Phan the possibilities of a "new, enriched culture" for Asian Americans are implications of the immigrant status of Asian Americans. Asian Americans occupy the in-between space of Asian and American—we are neither this nor that—because of the Asian American experience of migration and distance. As persons who are no longer of their homeland yet newcomers to US shores (and thus outsiders in a sense), the

---

17. Mishan, "Asian-American Cuisine's Rise."
18. Phan, "Christianity with an Asian Face," xiii.
19. Phan, "Christianity with an Asian Face," 9, first emphasis added.

notion of in-betweenness is, to a degree, inherent to being Asian American. Inhabiting a twofold distance necessitates for Asian Americans blazing their own path, appropriating from both Asian and American worlds but in a way that is not of both worlds. To be in between worlds is to take those two worlds toward a new synthesis.

The theologian Sang Hyun Lee conceptualizes the possibilities of such Asian American innovation as emerging from Asian American liminality. While liminality is meant to capture the situation of in-betweenness that Phan articulates, Lee's turn to liminality functions to highlight how Asian American in-betweenness is a consequence of racial discrimination against Asian Americans more so than simply being migrants and immigrants. In doing so, Lee, while not explicitly, calls attention to the ways in which being an immigrant and being marginal are not mutually exclusive experiences, but often go hand-in-hand. For Lee, Asian Americans, both older and newer generations, are pushed to a liminal space because as Asian Americans we are not of Asia and not of America, especially due to the kind of racially marginalizing realities Asian Americans confront. As such, liminality—our in-betweenness—signals Asian Americans existence on the peripheries.[20]

There is some ambiguity in whether Lee thinks the liminal situation of Asian Americans is an effect of not only American discrimination but also a kind of discrimination that Asian Americans experience from their ancestral homelands and cultures. Consider for instance, the following: "When persons, like Asian Americans, are pushed to the liminal and peripheral places by two worlds (Asia and America), their liminality means their being in the space between two worlds and at the same time at the peripheries, edges, or margins of both worlds. Asian Americans find themselves not fully accepted by, or fully belonging to, either the American world or the Asian."[21] Later, he will reiterate a similar point by stating, Asian Americans "are liminal or 'out of structure,' both in the sense of not fully belonging to America and also in the sense of not belonging to their ancestral place back in Asia. They are at the edge of America, and also between America and Asia."[22] Are Asian Americans marginalized by Asia because of geographic and generational separation or are they not fully accepted by Asia because Asia actively rejects Asian Americans as those who have forsaken their homelands for a new one? Lee is unclear. But whatever the case may

20. Lee, *From a Liminal Place*, 4.

21. Lee, *From a Liminal Place*, 5.

22. Lee, *From a Liminal Place*, 7.

be, Lee's point is to underscore the proposition that Asian Americans occupy a liminal space—a space of in-betweenness—due to, at the very least, a resistance on the part of mainstream American society to embrace Asian Americans as full and equal citizens.

While such racist marginalization may lead to a "powerless and demoralizing space,"[23] for Lee, our liminality or in-betweenness is a condition of inherent possibilities; in other words, Asian Americans are put in a situation where they have no choice but to innovate, to create and recreate what it means to be Asian American, lest Asian Americans are to merely exist, to be without a sense of identity and self. Being Asian American, then, would indeed be a lonely condition.[24] But as Lee notes, in his reference to the anthropologist Victor Turner's use of the term liminality, *limen* is "the Latin word for 'threshold,'" which connotes the sense of being on the edge of a new frontier.[25] Accordingly, Asian Americans, because of their liminality, are positioned to be explorers rather than simply persons who are forced into constraining and disempowering identity scripts.

For Lee, to explore or innovate what it means to be Asian American, rather than simply falling back on preconceived notions of Asian Americanness, is to indicate resistance to racism against Asian Americans. Drawing from the post-colonial theorist Homi Bhabha, Lee thinks Asian Americans, in their liminality, *ought* to embrace a "third space" where Asian Americans can embody hybrid modes of being.[26] Hybridity moves beyond the in-betweenness that Asian Americans experience due to their distance from their ancestral homeland and, especially important, the discrimination they feel from their new, adopted society. To move beyond, or to "construct a hybrid Asian American identity in American society is, first of all, to resist the essentialized idea either of America or Asia. The Eurocentric idea of America has been essentialized—that is, made into a permanent truth."[27] He then states,

> The term *American* includes Native Americans, African Americans, Hispanic Americans, English Americans, Italian Americans, and many others. To construct an Asian American identity is to

23. Lee, *From a Liminal Place*, 4.

24. This is Kang's passing characterization of Asian Americans in his "What a Fraternity Hazing Death Revealed."

25. Lee, *From a Liminal Place*, 4.

26. Lee, *From a Liminal Place*, 112.

27. Lee, *From a Liminal Place*, 112–13.

embrace all these different kinds of Americans in our own conception of ourselves. The cultures and histories of the peoples of all the different ancestral background cannot be, in a mechanical way, the material content of what constitutes the Asian American identity. But none of those peoples can be excluded from the meaning of an Asian American identity. What this means is that Asian American identity could appropriate as our own some aspect of the cultures of all the peoples who belong to America, and that Asian American identity must be permanently open.[28]

RACIAL DISCRIMINATION REDUX? CHALLENGING THE LOGIC AND HOPEFULNESS OF HYBRIDITY

It is interesting that the Asian American turn to interculturalism, liminality, or hybridity is motivated by not only a desire to provide a more accurate description of what Asian American life is like (e.g., it is not simply what pop culture may perceive it to be, oftentimes playing off of stereotypes), but also a desire to resist Asian American experiences of discrimination, marginalization, and otherness. In other words, calling attention to the hybridity of Asian American life provides an opportunity for Asian American empowerment, the possibility of creating for ourselves ways of being that do not conform to any preconceived or determined ways of being. In that way, the turn to a hybrid account of Asian American life amounts to a desire to supplant and move beyond the narrative of otherness that often frames and undermines Asian American agency. (And part of that strategy entails bringing to greater light the ways in which Asian Americans thwart commonly held perceptions and conventions in their intercultural modalities.) If Asian Americans are neither fully included in Asia nor America, then Asian Americans are free to innovate their own sense of self, what it means to be Asian, American, or both. Perhaps that prospect is what Mishan, as we saw earlier, finds so exciting about the kind of inventiveness that is taking hold in contemporary Asian American foodways. That inventiveness, she notes, "[reflects] a new cockiness in a population that has historically kept quiet and encouraged to lay low."[29]

Inasmuch as such inventiveness challenges the unfamiliar view of Asian Americans as demure, docile, and insular, the Asian American turn to hybridity is noteworthy—an achievement even. Nevertheless, despite those

28. Lee, *From a Liminal Place*, 113.
29. Mishan, "Asian-American Cuisine's Rise."

instances of innovative success, do Asian American advocates of hybridity underestimate the challenges that confront the innovation or creativity that they envision as possible (or in some cases already emerging) from the so-called borderless situation of Asian Americans? To ask the question in a slightly different way, are Asian American advocates of hybridity too optimistic in their estimations of what Asian American hybridity or liminality can effect, that is, are they too uncritically dismissive (or simply neglectful) of the ways in which Asian Americans are subject to the realities of racism in the United States (or to its racial pitfalls)? In asking the question, I am not necessarily casting suspicion on the intercultural character of Asian Americans as descriptive fact. The reality of Asian Americans as hybrid depends on how hybridity is defined. In a way, the cultural lives of Asian American could be considered hybrid inasmuch as the kind of cultural lives Asian Americans embody are, as I argued in chapter 2, selective appropriations or re-creations of Asian ancestral traditions. As the sociologist Russell Jeung, in referring to the observation made famous by the comparative literature scholar Lisa Lowe, points out, "Asian American culture is a hybridized construct, where members consciously and unconsciously reject or select aspects of their ethnic heritage and upbringing. They then include these aspects with their American values and tastes."[30]

So, Asian Americans can be considered hybrid, existing in a liminal space, in a certain kind of way. However, it is one thing to claim that Asian Americans embody an intercultural identity of some sort, and another to claim that such interculturality offers a constructive resistance and response to the racism that confronts Asian Americans. To the extent that Asian Americans are *racialized* and *not simply discriminated against* speaks to the complexity of the racial realities that Asian Americans are situated in. The distinction between being racialized versus experiencing *incidences* of racial discrimination aims to call attention to the extent to which Asian American agency is confined in such a manner that intercultural innovation and creativity, despite some instantiations of that dynamic, is more a theoretic or notional possibility than a practical one. That complicates the advocacy for hybridity as a sufficient response to the kind of racial-discriminatory dynamics or pressures to which Asian Americans are subject. To better illumine the kind of racialization that Asian Americans undergo, it will be helpful to first consider at least three ways in which racism confines

30. Jeung, "Creating an Asian American Christian Subculture," 309–10; cf. Lowe, *Immigrant Acts.*

Asian American life. The first provides a more general accounting of such racial confinement and the second and third a more particular, Asian American–specific accounting.

(1) Recall Lee's proposal that Asian American identity should be "permanently open" given the hybrid or liminal space that Asian Americans oc cupy in society. Such openness means that "Asian American identity could appropriate as our own some aspect of the cultures of all the peoples who belong to America." His use of the term appropriate, however, raises hard questions about perhaps the inherent risks of cultural innovation. In calling for appropriation, I do not think Lee is suggesting that Asian Americans innovate their self-understanding in ways that disrespect cultural beliefs and practices of non-Asian Americans[31] or to innovate in ways that ignorantly "appropriates" cultural forms without regard for or reckoning with their possible problematic historical context.[32] But at what point does such innovation that incorporates (appropriates) "cultures of all the peoples who belong to America" threaten a trivialization or misuse of those cultures, even if one's intent is to celebrate those cultures, learn from them, engage them as a way of challenging and transforming one's own assumptions and sense of self?

While the lines of intercultural exchange and cultural appropriation can be difficult to demarcate with some objective firmness, that does not necessarily mean that the kind of cultural innovation that Asian American hybridity and liminality can encourage will inevitably fall into the problem of cultural appropriation. But that the aspirations of cultural innovation is so fraught with the threat of cultural appropriation calls attention to how the entrenched realities of race and, more specifically, white racism, whether in the form of colonialism or various forms of social marginalization, intersect with and stunt the cultural possibilities of Asian American borderlessness. As such, is it realistic to think that the kind of cultural innovations that are called for from such borderlessness can be a promising, effective, or realistic means of resisting (moving beyond) racial discrimination?

(2) While liminality, hybridity, and, ultimately, cultural innovation may undercut preconceived racial notions, attitudes, and identities,

31. For instance, consider the controversy over Rachel Dolezal who was criticized for appropriating and thus trivializing what it means to be black in a predominantly white society. See Weaver, "Rachel Dolezal Is Back."

32. An interesting example of such historical ignorance is the singing of the song "My Old Kentucky Home" at the Kentucky Derby. See Bever and Robinson, "My Old Kentucky Home." Consider also Tucci, "When K-Pop Culturally Appropriates."

it may also perpetuate and continue to be tangled up by them. Accordingly, the philosopher Linda Alcoff notes that, "within the context of racially based organized systems of oppression, [it seems clear that] racial identity will continue to be a salient internal and external component of identity."[33] Compare that assessment with the religious ethicist Susannah Heschel's insistence on the tenacity of racism, its "tenacious hold on the imagination."[34] That tenacity or persistence of racism against Asian Americans is supported by a long history of cultural marginalization as well as structural marginalization, that is, in American economic and political life. Case in point, governmental acts of discrimination such as the infamous 1944 Supreme Court case *Korematsu v. United States*, when Franklin D. Roosevelt's Executive Order 9066 to intern Japanese Americans was given judicial affirmation. That "yellow peril" mentality was in many respects a continuation of the kind of suspicions that Asian Americans elicited since the nineteenth century, most prominently expressed in the Chinese Exclusion Act of 1882. Before ultimately being signed into law by Chester A. Arthur, the Irish immigrant Denis Kearney, who founded the Workingmen's Party of California, described Chinese immigrants in the following way to persuade the law's passage:

> These cheap slaves fill every place. Their dress is scant and cheap. Their food is rice from China. They hedge twenty in a room, ten by ten. They are whipped curs, abject in docility, mean, contemptible and obedient in all things. We [white Americans] are men, and propose to live like men in this free land, without the contamination of slave labor, or die like men, if need be, in asserting the rights of our race, our country, and our families. California must be all American or all Chinese. We are resolved that it shall be American, and are prepared to make it so.[35]

Striking is the description of Chinese immigrants' temperament and appearance, which intersect and diverge with how black persons have been described. As the philosopher Cornel West remarks, black persons, resulting from Ham's failure to cover his father Noah's nakedness as outlined in the Hebrew Bible, are marked as rejecting authority and practicing unruly

---

33. Alcoff, "Mestizo Identity," 155.

34. Heschel, "Slippery Yet Tenacious."

35. Kearney and Knight, "Appeal from California," cited from http://historymatters. gmu.edu/d/5046; cf. Greenberger, "Cheap Slaves."

behavior.[36] Compare that with the Chinese who are the converse: docile and obedient. Yet their submissiveness is not attributed as positives but convicts them as whipped, abject, and contemptible beings. However, the Chinese do parallel black bodies in terms of the manner of their appearance and capabilities and are judged accordingly. Once again, as West points out, black bodies are ugly, culturally deficient, and intellectually inferior.[37] Compare that with Kearney's observation that the Chinese's style of clothing is less than desirable, and their food, rice from China, if not paltry, is certainly strange and not relatable, perhaps confirming the uncivilized nature of the Chinese. So we might say that just as black bodies were observed, measured, ordered, and compared according to visible physical characteristics of human bodies in light of Greco-Roman aesthetic standards, so too the Chinese.[38]

Labor and political leaders such as Kearney were not the only ones to degrade and reject the Chinese. Even the clergy, both Catholic and Protestant, supported the Chinese Exclusion Act with the same kind of suspicious, exclusionary sentiments expressed by Kearney. As the theologian Jeannine Hill Fletcher notes, the Jesuit Catholic priest James Bouchard "insisted that the 'immoral, vicious, pagan Chinese' were driving 'good, honest [Christian] souls' into professions of ill refute when they took their jobs."[39] On the Protestant side, the Reverend Otis Gibson, while reluctant to endorse Fr. Bouchard's invectives and called for the repeal of legislation that harmed the Chinese, believed that "[white] Christian men and women must multiply their efforts to uplift and Christianize these people.' To be

36. West, "Race and Social Theory," 263.

37. West, "Race and Social Theory," 263.

38. This is a rewording of a sentence from West, "Race and Social Theory," 263; cf. Pat Chew, who observes, "Like African Americans, Asian Americans' skin color and other facial features physically distinguish them . . . As Justice Sutherland noted in United States v. Bhagat Singh [decided in 1923] 'It cannot be doubted that the children born in this country born of Hindu parents would retain indefinitely the clear evidence of their ancestry,'" cited from Kim, "Are Asians Black?," 345.

39. Fletcher, *Sin of White Supremacy*, 57. She cites Bouchard, "Chinaman or White Man." Consider also a similar judgment by the Honorable George C. Perkins of California in the US Senate: "The Chinese are an undesirable class of people. This is the unprejudiced argument of people who know them, after years of experience . . . We would be much better off if they had never come among us, or if they would now go back again" (Fletcher, *Sin of White Supremacy*, 66). Fletcher cites Lee, "Immigrants and Immigration Law," 87.

American was to be Christian, and if the Chinese could be Christianized, they might assimilate into a White Christian nation."[40]

The legacy of Kearney's discriminatory advocacy—the call to not only marginalize Asians from participating in American society and institutions but to exclude them from arriving in the United States altogether—continued well into the twentieth century, notably with the 1924 Johnson-Reed Act, which "intended to 'preserve the ideal of American homogeneity' by stemming the 'rising tide' of unwanted immigrants from Southern Europe, Eastern Europe, and Asia."[41] This act reduced the quota for non-Northern and Western European immigrants from 3 to 2 percent, while banning immigration from Asia entirely.[42] Despite the relief that the landmark 1965 Immigration and Nationality Act provided from such exclusionary immigration policies, for Asian Americans, such exclusionary attitudes continue to be sustained and put into practice through a variety of more subtle and covert ways, for instance, in microaggressions and the stereotypical regard of Asian Americans as peculiar or exotic at best and perpetual foreigners at worst. (Though it is important to recall that immigration policies have not entirely left Asian Americans alone; as noted in chapter 1, the threat of deportation looms large for the many Asian Americans who are undocumented.) As we saw earlier, while Mishan relays the ubiquitous experience of Asian Americans being asked about their "true" origins, she also sounds dismissive of the extent to which such micro-aggressive stereotyping, that dogged regard for Asian Americans as essentially non-American, impacts Asian Americans emotionally and psychologically. However, in summarizing a study on the everyday prejudice and discrimination experienced by Asian Americans, the psychologist Anthony Ong remarks, "Our finding suggest that exposure to day-to-day racial microaggressons is common and that seemingly innocuous statements, such as being asked 'Where were you born?' or being told 'You speak good English' can have an adverse effect on Asian-Americans, in part, because such statements often mask an implied message that you are not a true American."[43] Michael Guo, a *New York Times* editor, provides a striking illustration of the everyday persistence of

40. Fletcher, *Sin of White Supremacy*, 57–58. She cites Gibson, *Chinaman or White Man*, 9, 13.

41. Schlund-Vials and Wu, "Rethinking Embodiment," 197.

42. Schlund-Vials and Wu, "Rethinking Embodiment," 198.

43. Cited from Booker, "Asian-Americans." See also Ong et al., "Racial Microaggressions," 188–89. Cf. Sue et al., "Racial Microaggressions," 72–81.

Asian American otherness (or not being a true American) when he recalls the time that a non-Asian woman, frustrated that Guo and his baby stroller constricted the flow of traffic on an Upper East Side New York City sidewalk, yelled at him and his family to "go back to China."[44]

The literature and food studies scholar Wenying Xu helps us to see further how that sense of otherness has seeped into the cultural imagination of mainstream American life. She calls attention to the use of Asian American food traditions to maintain and reinforce the foreignness of Asian Americans and, therefore, essential difference between Asian Americans and "genuine" Americans. Her powerful narration of how such difference is established through the stereotyping of Asian American foodways is worth an extended consideration:

> "They eat rats." "They eat dogs and cats." They eat monkey brains."
> "They eat snakes and grasshoppers." "They eat slugs." I could go on
> reiterating the many dietary accusations against Asians, for these
> sensational tidbits litter news reports, literature, scholarly studies,
> cartoons, TV shows, movies, and everyday conversations. Even
> though there is a certain degree of truth in some of these accusa-
> tions, they are not made to simply offer facts about Asian food-
> ways. Rather, these tales are told with the intention of defaming,
> of othering, and of abjecting Asians in America. American media's
> representation of Asian Americans is irrevocably associated with
> "the food of their ethnic ancestries," as Jennifer Ho points out. "In-
> deed, it is fair to say that Asian Americans are almost invariably
> portrayed through foodways in television and film" (11). As re-
> cently as December 2005, such dietary othering was alive and well
> on television. In *Curb Your Enthusiasm*, episode number 49, Larry
> David's Korean American bookie is suspected of having stolen and
> killed Jeff's German Shepherd, Oscar, for food. It also happens that
> this jolly, entrepreneurial Korean American man supplies flowers
> for a fancy wedding on the beach. Along with flowers he brings a
> meat dish, which the wedding guests find exceptionally delicious.
> When Larry (mis)informs the wedding crowd about the source of
> the meat, mass vomiting breaks out, everyone spitting, choking,
> and writhing on the beach. This episode's comicalness, though sa-
> tirical of Larry's ignorance and misjudgment, depends upon racist
> stereotyping of Asian foodways.[45]

44. Guo, "Open Letter."

45. Xu, *Eating Identities*, 8. While dog-eating is an outlier practice in Asia, the extent to which American popular culture (and increasingly US legislative actions) is fixated on it is indicative of how Asians and Asian Americans are received as foreign and, more

The racial stereotyping of Asian American foodways as strange and foreign extends to not only so-called "traditional" foods but also, rather notably, *hybridized* creations, what the Asian American food studies scholar Robert Ji-Song Ku aptly refers to as dubious Asian American foods, that is, foods that are familiar as Asian of a sort but also not American in the American-as-apple-pie sort of way (think, for instance, kung pao chicken, California rolls, or SPAM). In referring to them as dubious foods, Ku reminds us that even hybridized creations, insofar as they are deemed either inauthentic, not the "real thing," or just off-putting or revolting, while perhaps innovative in their own ways, do not escape the racializing forces that subject so much of American life. The lesson to be drawn here from the dubious nature of hybridized Asian American foods for the question of Asian American identity is that hybridity does not necessarily guarantee racial resistance and transcendence but can operate in the exact opposite way by condemning, and, thus, further "othering," Asian Americans for their lack of "authentic" identity. Ku's argument, below, then offers a word of caution if not a sobering assessment of hybridity and its racial consequences:

> The privileging of authenticity serves as reproof not merely of so-called dubious Asian foods but also of Asian *peoples* . . . In the United States the burden, if not blame, of Asian inauthenticity falls most heavily on the shoulders of Asian Americans, who are construed as human analogs of inauthentic cultural products. Discursively positioned neither as truly "Asian" nor truly "American," they are read as doubly dubious. The Asian presence in the United States is commonly seen as watered down, counterfeit, inauthentic—at least when measured against a largely authentic Asia. [In that way] dubious Asian foods . . . share a special fellowship with Asian Americans.[46]

(3) It is in view of this legacy of marginalization and exclusion that we need to assess the prospects for moving from Asian American in-betweenness to cultural innovation. That assessment necessarily brings us back to Kang's observation that was noted at the outset of this chapter: "Discrimination is what really binds Asian-Americans together." For Kang, the observation is meant to recall the contemporary origins of Asian American identity, the search for which was taken up by Asian American

---

demeaningly, barbaric, despite the popularity of Asian American cuisines more generally. See Ho, "Do You Eat Dog?"

46. Ku, *Dubious Gastronomy*, 9.

studies programs, especially in California and then also in East Coast Ivy League schools, that proliferated in the 1970s.[47] The project of defining Asian American identity was motivated by the legacy of discrimination against Asian Americans and came to a head in 1982 when Vincent Chin, "who worked in an automotive engineering firm in Detroit, was beaten to death by assailants who blamed Japanese competition for the downturn in the American auto market." According to Kang, the sentencing of Chin's assailants to probation and a $3,000 fine galvanized Asian American protest marches "in cities across the country, giving rise to a new Pan-Asian unity forged by the realization that if Chin, the son of Chinese immigrants, could be killed because of Japanese auto imports, the concept of an 'Asian-American' identity had consequences." Subsequently, "a rhetoric took hold that argued for a collective identity" in the wake of Chin's murder, coupled with the increasing disaffection and alienation of Asian American students on college campuses with affirmative action policies of the eighties, claiming that a quota system was being employed by many elite colleges to limit Asian American student entrance (a claim that persists among some Asian Americans, such as those who have applied to Harvard, as discussed in chapter 1). That rhetoric for a collective Asian American identity moved in tandem with the emergence of Asian American social organizations, most prominently Asian American college fraternities, according to Kang.[48]

Asian American college fraternities, however, are not the only arena one can turn to witness the social pressures toward cultural familiarity and bonding and away from intercultural exchange and innovation among Asian Americans. Compare college campuses with the dynamics operative in Asian American church life. Drawing from Jeung's study of the role of panethnicity in Asian American churches in northern California, the sociologist Sharon Kim observes the extent to which experiences of being racial minorities, among other experiences (e.g., children of immigrants, legacy of Confucian values) play in the strong reliance on and preference for pan-Asian connectedness. The following quote from a member of a pan-Asian American church is telling of this desire for collective Asian identification:

> There's something about being an Asian American in this country.
> For example, I'd be at a big party and there would be another Asian

47. Cf. Schlund-Vials, *Flashpoints for Asian American Studies*; Wu and Song, *Asian American Studies*; Ono, *Companion to Asian American Studies*; Wu and Chen, *Asian American Studies Now*; Chen, *Routledge Handbook of Asian American Studies*.
48. Kang, "What a Fraternity Hazing Death Revealed."

person in the room. By the time the night is over, I'd be talking and socializing with that person only. I don't know how that is. It's strange but we feel more comfortable with each other maybe because we grew up in a similar way, as racial minorities with Asian immigrant parents. It doesn't really matter what part of the country you grew up in. I could meet up with a person who grew up in Texas and still we'd have much in common because most likely we've had similar experiences. There's just more to talk about because we can relate better.[49]

Such preference for and comfort with Asian identification stands in some tension with the kind of hybrid hopes that Lee articulates with respect to Asian American liminality, as we saw earlier.

That tension is perhaps also discernible in the arena of interracial dating in multiracial Asian American churches. On the one hand, the kind of cultural inclusion or intercultural exchange that Lee advocates for as a function of Asian American liminality is on vivid display at many multiracial Asian American churches. As a pastor of one such church is quoted

49. Kim, *Faith of Our Own Book*, 143. Compare this passage with the following views that Russell Jeung relays in his study of Grace Community Covenant Church, a pan-Asian church in Silicon Valley, CA. The church's pastor, Steve Wong, describes the church as serving a population of Asian Americans who are in a purported liminal space, where they feel neither fitting in a predominantly white church nor in an Asian church serving primarily immigrant Asians: "I'm a third-generation Asian American: But I'm often the victim of mistaken identity. Caucasians are surprised that I don't speak Chinese, they expect me to have the same emotional ties to my Asian heritage as they do . . . There are a lot of Asian Americans like me. The immigrant Asian community expects us to be more Asian. The Caucasian majority expects us to be either more Asian or blend into the Caucasian American culture. Neither category fits us, *so we're overlooked by many American institutions, including the church*" (Jeung, "Creating an Asian American Christian Subculture," 292, emphasis original). Pastor Wong thus sees Grace Church as meeting the needs of that in-between Asian American population. Yet, upon closer inspection of how congregants think about their church, it becomes clearer that the church is not necessarily a space for cultural, religious innovation per se, but a space for solidarity and connectedness among Asian Americans who share / can identify with a common set of experiences of otherness and distance. Note one congregant's comments: "One of the big things is connecting, a sense of community. And knowing a sense of belonging. For people who are Asian American, what you see again and again is that there is a feeling of connecting with people who understand your experience" (Jeung, "Creating an Asian American Christian Subculture," 300). And then Pastor Wong finally notes, "Being in an Asian American church helps people with things like that [finding a place where others can identity with your experience of otherness]. And you can talk about things like food, and nobody's going to look at you funny when you say you like thousand-year-old eggs. (Laughter)" (Jeung, "Creating an Asian American Christian Subculture," 307).

as saying by Kim, "We have a gospel choir in our church that looks and sounds a lot like African American gospel choirs. A few weeks ago, we sang a Swahili song in our worship service. We've also sung Spanish songs."[50] On the other hand, according to Kim, that kind of intercultural inclusion does not necessarily translate over to the area of social life. Kim observes: "A large percentage of the members of these churches are singles in their twenties and early thirties who are very interested in finding future mates among fellow church members. While all the Asian singles that I spoke with seem to accept the idea of interracial marriage in theory, it is quite another matter for them to state that they themselves were willing to marry outside of their race."[51]

The extent to which Asian Americans are open to interracial dating and marriage is, to be sure, not a necessary benchmark of whether Asian Americans are pushing the boundaries of their hybrid or liminal position (nor should it be). But Asian American attitudes and practices with respect to interracial dating offers a useful vantage point into the social context that frames and, more specifically, constrains the possibilities of innovation and, ultimately, liberation that hybridity and liminality are seen as enabling. As Kim observes, while attitudes about dating and marriage are formed by personal preference, they are also, she claims, formed by "perceived constraints," by which she means perceived racial constraints. In that sense, attitudes about interracial relationships are more than simply emblematic of a desire for cultural rootedness or a sense of in-group belonging motived by a sense of intrinsic shared values, as sociologists who promote the primoridialist view of Asian panethnic organizational formation might say. Nor do such attitudes about interracial relationships indicate the instrumentalist view of Asian panethnicity, or the sociological view that the turn toward collective Asian identification, in-group belonging, and coalition building is a function of Asian Americans mobilizing within racial categories created by the state for power and favorable resource allocation.[52] Instead, such attitudes about interracial relationship offers an important case study on how "external" racial attitudes or prevailing racial norms and stereotypes inform and direct how Asian Americans engage or relate to one another

50. Kim, *Faith of Our Own Book*, 147.

51. Kim, *Faith of Our Own Book*, 151.

52. For a discussion of the primordialist versus instrumentalist approaches to Asian American identity, see Jeung, "Creating an Asian American Christian Subculture," 289–90, 306–7. See also Omi and Winant, *Racial Formation*, and Min and Kim, *Struggle for Ethnic Identity*.

as well as in relation to non-Asian Americans. For some Asian American men in multiracial Asian American churches, Kim points out, their "preference for dating Korean women is shaped by the fact in the United States, the media portrayal of Asian men has not been favorable and has negatively impacted their level of desirability."[53] Such an example of racialized gender stereotyping—specifically, their persistence in popular culture and sustained impact on Asian American self-perception—suggest that racial discrimination that Asian Americans experience cannot be wholly cast off or escaped through hybridity or cultural innovation, if such hybridized innovation is realistically possible to begin with.

RACIAL DISCRIMINATION BY LESS OBVIOUS MEANS: HYBRIDITY AND THE APPEAL OF WHITENESS

To claim, as Kang does, that Asian American life is rooted in a political consciousness of racial discrimination—our collective othering by mainstream white society—certainly helps to explain the logic of Asian American solidarity, whether in academic spheres (e.g., Asian American fraternities), the economic spheres (e.g., Asian American business alliances and associations), Asian American churches, or perhaps even everyday practices of eating and socializing together among Asian American peers. Inasmuch as that logic, manifest across sectors of Asian American life, reflects resistance to the kinds of discriminatory pressures Asian Americans bear, it is difficult to see how that logic of Asian American solidarity does not stand in tension with the kind of optimism that is often placed on the supposed interculturality of Asian American life.

Yet, it is also important to acknowledge that not all Asian Americans think of themselves, or choose to be Asian American, with a kind of solidaristic "band together to resist and insulate ourselves from discrimination" reference point. As Kang observes, despite those numerous instances in which Asian Americans express and embody forms of cultural rootedness and in-group belonging, for many Asian Americans today, their sense of ethno-racial solidarity or attachment "is cartoonish and blurry."[54] The blurring of what it means to be for and with Asian Americans is growing more pronounced as "traditional," tightly-knit immigrant Asian American communities or enclaves are fraying with the increasing mobility of second

53. Kim, *Faith of Our Own Book*, 152. See also Choi, "Gender and Sexuality," 19–40.
54. Kang, "What a Fraternity Hazing Death Revealed."

and third generation Asian Americans.[55] The impact that such mobility is having on what it means to be Asian American and to be Asian American together (i.e., in solidarity with one another) reminds us, to some extent, of the applicability of religious ethicist Victor Anderson's provocative assessment of descriptions of black experience for Asian American experience. He questions taking the narrative of "suffering, rebellion, and survival" as "categorically descriptive of black experience." Such description "trivializes the nature of oppression many blacks genuinely experience by the absurdity that any one who is black is also oppressed." His reservation is not meant to deny the reality of racial discrimination. However, it acknowledges the "plurality of world views held by African Americans" inasmuch as they "occupy varying social positions of class, gender, sex, and ethnicity."[56] Whether black male identity, therefore, is congruent with black female identity, or whether the experiences of working class African Americans are identical to affluent African Americans is more nuanced and ambiguous than it may appear.

That plurality and possible incongruity also applies to all communities, including Asian Americans. For Asian Americans, that pluralism of experience raises the question of whether the narrative of discrimination that has been framed by particular historical moments of indignity, insecurity, and exclusion—such as the death of Vincent Shin, the 1991 Koreatown riots in Los Angeles in the wake of the Rodney King verdict, the internment of Japanese Americans, the Chinese Exclusion Act, and so on—captures how racism is experienced by Asian Americans. This is not to ask whether racism is a formative experience for Asian Americans. But it is to ask whether there is a risk of overstating the influence of those historical instances of racism and, as such, whether the nature of the racism experienced by Asian Americans and the way it informs and shapes Asian American life

55. The Vietnamese American community in the greater New Orleans area is an interesting case in point. As the *New York Times* reports, "Now, 43 years after the fall of Saigon and almost 13 years after Katrina, the Vietnamese enclave within Village de l'Est is changing, in some ways drastically . . . Some of the strongest ties that once bound people together here—particularly the reliance on a shared language and religion—are beginning to fray within the younger generations, many of whom are no longer fluent in Vietnamese and, following a general trend, are less invested in the Roman Catholic Church. Greater access to education, and the subsequent job prospects that such access provides, are also driving younger Vietnamese-Americans increasingly farther from New Orleans East—especially in light of a dearth of local economic opportunity" (Hiltner, "Vietnamese Forged a Community").

56. Anderson, *Beyond Ontological Blackness*, 103.

is as straightforward as the narrative of marginalization and exclusion suggests. In many respects it is straightforward, insofar as Asian Americans in many instances have responded to the legacy of racial marginalization and exclusion—that is, the sustained efforts at "othering" Asian Americans as non-Americans—through collective mobilization. But it is also not as straightforward insofar as Asian Americans have responded to the legacy of discrimination in ways that are not overtly solidaristic or communal. In claiming as much, I do not want to backtrack now on the intractableness of racism in Asian American life. I do, however, want to raise awareness of a more elusive way in which racial discrimination operates and quite possibly underwrites Asian American life, which raises even more questions about the viability of Asian American hybridity as a mode of resistance to the marginalizing, exclusionary legacy of whiteness in Asian American life.

To map out this more elusive influence of racism in Asian American life, it may be helpful to first consider an additional perspective about interracial dating that Kim highlights in her study of second-generation Asian American churches. As Kim notes, if Asian singles are willing to date or marry outside of their race, "they implicitly were referring to marrying whites and, in some cases, Latinos." Kim relays the perspective of Kathy, a second-generation Asian American student at UCLA, who stated that

> her parents would adamantly disapprove of her marrying or dating an African American man. "My parents have always told me ever since I was really young that they want me to marry a Korean man. During high school, I only dated white guys and that bothered them but they eventually got used to it. If it was a black guy . . . well that would be another story altogether. They'd probably kill me or disown me. Korean is best. White is tolerable. Black is forbidden.[57]

The judgment that white is tolerable and black is forbidden is perhaps unremarkable in light of the larger social suspicion and entrenched racism against African Americans. What is striking, however, is the extent to which that suspicion is manifest among Asian Americans as well.

Given that this—white is tolerable, black is forbidden—is the attitude of Kathy's parents, perhaps this attitude constitutes a generational divide. Millennial attitudes about race may suggest as much; according to the 2017 GenForward Survey, Asian American attitudes on race are not necessarily at odds with those of African American millennials but more so with white

57. Kim, *Faith of Our Own Book*, 152.

Americans.[58] But these statistics must also be taken with other studies that show a significant divergence between Asian Americans and non-Asian Americans of color, a consequence, in part, of geographic segregation. "Asian Americans and Blacks, in particular, appear to lack the extensive contact and shared experiences that facilitate coalition building," report the political scientists Claire Jean Kim and Taeku Lee.[59] To attribute such an attitude (white is tolerable, black is forbidden) to simply generational differences, therefore, too simplistically dismisses the significant racial dynamics at play across Asian American life and, therefore, unduly insulates Asian Americans (especially, in this case, younger, more recent generations of Asian Americans, e.g., second-generation Asian Americans and beyond) from a difficult racial spectrum that begins with an attitude that white is tolerable and moves successively to more explicit partiality for whiteness and even identification as white.

In regard to the more explicit identification with whiteness, consider the author Bonnie Tsui's consternations over her biracial, Asian-white child who insists that he is white, not Chinese. "It never occurred to me that my sons could possibly identify *only* as white. I'm forced to think more carefully about what it is that actually makes me uncomfortable with that idea," she laments.[60] Part of that discomfort has to do with the kind of hopefulness she sees in the idea of racial hybridity or fluidity, of which her son, as biracial, is a living example. But it is a hopefulness that is at least strained by his almost matter-of-fact, reflexive identification as someone who is white and not Chinese. That reflexive identification as white, coming especially from a biracial person, suggests "that a simplistic promotion of [racial] fluidity will not suffice," at least when it comes to destabilizing and undermining conventional racial identities, perceptions, and assumptions and spurring innovative modes of being.[61]

One way of accounting for such matter-of-fact, reflexive identification as white is as a consequence of Asian American economic gains and educational achievements. These achievements have garnered increased sociological scrutiny as contributing factors to Asian American identification as white, and if not identification as white then at the very least a sense that Asian Americans are adjacent to and, thus, more alike or akin to white

58. Cohen et al., "'Woke' Generation?"
59. Kim and Lee, "Interracial Politics," 545.
60. Tsui, "Choose Your Own Identity."
61. Alcoff, "Mestizo Identity," 153.

Americans (i.e., an identification *with* whiteness).[62] A 2017 Pew Research Center study reports that the median household income of Asian Americans as a group is $73,060, which is at least $20,000 above all US households. And while that high household income does not necessarily coincide with Asian Americans having the highest homeownership rate (57% vs. 63% for the US public overall), Asian Americans have a lower poverty percentage compared to the general US population (12.1% vs. 15.1%). With respect to education, 51% of Asian Americans ages twenty-five and older have a bachelor's degree, which is 21% higher than all similarly aged Americans.[63] While these statistics masks some of the educational and income complexities and disparities that exist among various Asian American communities, a matter that I will turn to briefly later, the general, aggregate picture is one of Asian Americans as a group that has experienced significant upward mobility, especially into middle and upper middle class communities.

Yet, why might such upward mobility necessarily coincide with identification with whiteness, or even identification as white? Such a question is all the more curious when posited next to the issue of hair bleaching among Asian American women. The trend, according to the *New York Times*, dates back to the 1960s, when Japanese celebrities who "have been changing their hair color . . . to emulate manga and anime characters, [but since 2015/2016] on the heels of the ombré ['silver granny hairstyle'] trend, [salons in the United States] began to see a spike in Asian clients looking to go full platinum."[64] Why? Partly due to the increased visibility of Asian American fashion bloggers and models such as Irene Kim, Yoon Ahn, Vanessa Hong, Tina Leung, and Margaret Zhang. But perhaps more interesting is the thesis that it is a form of rebellion against conventional norms of Asian female behavior and aesthetics:

> For those who [go full platinum], it may serve, symbolically, as an act of rebellion against the Asian good-girl trope, an extension of the "model minority" stereotype—conservative, quiet, and hard-working. And since "Asian hair" has a history of being exoticized, often accompanied with descriptors like "long, silky smooth and

62. Zhou, "Are Asian Americans Becoming White?," 354–59. As noted in the introduction to this book, my reference to adjacency is taken from Kang's reference to Asian Americans as "adjacent whites." See Kang, "How Should Asian Americans Feel."

63. López et al., "Key Facts about Asian Americans."

64. Chang, "Why So Many." On the ombré trend, see *Style & Design*, https://www.stylendesigns.com/grannyhair-ombre-hair-color-trends/.

jet black," flipping it completely on its head becomes a way of taking back ownership and of reclaiming identity.[65]

But if it is in part taken as a way of reclaiming identity as Asian American,
then why do so in a manner that mirrors Western beauty ideals of blondness? That question remains even if, as the Japanese studies scholar Laura
Miller suggests, bleached hair is less about emulating "white Americans,
but rather Asian celebrities such as Moga Mogami or Hyo-yeon Kim."[66] Yet
of all the hair options one can emulate, why are Asian American women,
and women in Asia, turning increasingly to bleached hair rather than, for
instance, dreadlocks or Afro hairstyles, in other words, cultural cues from
nonwhite persons? It is one thing to suggest that hair bleaching is an out-
let for creativity and hybridity of colors and styles, and another to confine
that creativity and hybridity within aesthetic style cues that are markedly
white-Western.

The desire to take cues primarily if not exclusively from white-Western
norms and ideals raises questions of whether Asian American identification with whiteness (or as white) is simply an economic and education-
driven outcome. That question necessarily brings us to confront a more
challenging reality. That reality emerges when the relationship between
Asian Americans and whiteness is approached more structurally, by which
I mean through an analysis of how the insider-outsider dynamic of American society necessarily disposes Asian Americans to whiteness. Consider
once again racial hybridity as the state of occupying an interracial, intercultural space. Alcoff observes that while racial hybridity can be positive,
for example, in the ability of a mixed-race person to potentially serve as
a mediator between diverse forms of life,[67] the capacity for such border
crossings can also lead to alternative outcomes. Alcoff offers Malinche, the
Nahua woman who served as a go-between for the Spanish conquistadores
and the Aztec Empire, and Pocahontas as cases in point. "Thus, such figures
as Malinche and Pocahontas are often reviled for their cooperation with

65. Chang, "Why So Many."

66. Chang, "Why So Many."

67. "The mixed person is a traveler often within her own home or neighborhood,
translating and negotiating the diversity of meanings, practices, and forms of life. This
vision provides a positive alternative to the mixed-race person's usual representation as
lack or as the tragically alienated figure" (Alcoff, "Mestizo Identity," 158).

dominant communities and their love for specific individuals from those communities," she writes.[68]

The idea of cooperation with dominant communities offers an important frame through which to account for the spectrum of white is tolerable to explicit partiality for and identification with whiteness. Such cooperation in modern American society can take multiple forms, not the least of which is the assimilation or acculturation into one community or culture over another. Referencing the sociologist Peter McLaren, the theologian Jonathan Y. Tan remarks, "In reality, 'whiteness' is the norm in contemporary US society, and minorities are compelled to go through the process of *engabachamiento* (whitening) in order to succeed in life."[69] Tsui's son's reflexive identification as white may be one example of that kind of acculturation and perhaps why Tsui is somewhat ambivalent about it, since she worries whether her son's reflexive identification as white will shade him from the realities of racial discrimination. The following reflection is telling: "It's not that I want my sons to experience discrimination, but if they do choose to identify as white, there is something about being a racial minority in America that I would want them to know. As a child, I most wanted to fit in . . . In the experience of being an 'other,' there's a valuable lesson in consciousness."[70] The following admission from the chef and restaurateur David Chang indicates more explicitly the normative pressures that bear down on Asian Americans in the direction of such acculturation into whiteness. When asked if he ever regretted growing up Korean, he responds, "I was always like, 'Man, I wish I was just white,' because of acceptance and culture, but also acceptance of the food, because there was so much more to explain. If you hung out with a lot of white people, you tried not to eat Chinese food or Korean food around white people."[71] The promise of acculturation, as Tan notes, is to bring those who are on the margins within the fold of the mainstream, specifically the white mainstream. Such a promise is captured in what sociologists call, according to Tan, "the 'straight line' assimilation theory of immigration," which suggests that "a newly arrived immigrant first goes through a period of acculturation

68. Alcoff, "Mestizo Identity," 158–59.

69. Tan, *Introducing Asian American Theologies*, 46.

70. Tsui, "Choose Your Own Identity."

71. *Ugly Delicious*, "Fried Rice," season 1, episode 7, starting at 26:19. Chang's interlocutor in this exchange, who is Chinese American, responds similarly when Chang asks in return, "Did you ever grow up thinking Why am I Chinese?" She responds, "Of course!"

or cultural adaptation (that is, 'cultural assimilation'), and once this acculturation is complete, that immigrant would be accepted unconditionally by
the dominant white American majority as 'one of us.'"[72] Tan then goes on
to observe:

> Most Asian Americans have no problems with "cultural assimi-
> lation," namely, the *acculturation* into white American cultural
> norms, so as to enable them to achieve the American dream in a
> "white" American society. In particular, Asian Americans who are
> born in the United States grow up being surrounded by and encul-
> turated into the same sociocultural world as their white American
> counterparts. Asian American newspapers and magazines are full
> of advertisements of accent-losing programs ("Learn to speak like
> an American *without* an accent!") and plastic surgery to "correct"
> their Asian physiognomic features (e.g., eye slants) to more ac-
> ceptable (read "superior") white American equivalents.[73]

The relative ease with which Asian Americans are able to culturally
assimilate into what are perceived as white American cultural norms is
helped by the extent to which Asian Americans have been able to move into
white, middle-class, suburban neighborhoods. This is where race meets the
economic aspirations of Asian Americans. Consequently, as the sociologist
Min Zhou points out, "Asian Americans are the most acculturated non-
European group in the United States." He elaborates:

> Many children of Asian ancestry have lived their entire childhood
> in white communities, made friends with mostly white peers, and
> grown up speaking only English . . . By the second generation,
> most have lost fluency in their parent's native languages. [The so-
> ciologist] David Lopez finds that in Los Angeles, more than three-
> quarters of second-generation Asian Americans (as opposed to
> about one-quarter of second-generation Mexicans) speak only
> English at home.[74]

It is important to consider, however, how acculturation into whiteness is
not simply an outgrowth of economic or financial aspirations. That would
make acculturation too benign of a phenomenon, giving insufficient attention to the force of acculturation's logic. That logic is one of belonging and
acceptance wherein society, inasmuch as it is rooted in a white ideal, sets

72. Tan, *Introducing Asian American Theologies*, 41.
73. Tan, *Introducing Asian American Theologies*, 41–42.
74. Zhou, "Are Asians Becoming White?," 354.

the terms of that belonging by way of assimilation. Asian Americans have in effect one choice if they wish to belong, to either assimilate into whiteness or to remain Asian, which would mean to remain as other, different. Implicit in that choice is the cultural superiority of Anglo-European visions of the good and the kind of social advantages, privileges, and power that coincides with such a vision.[75] Given the nature of that choice, then, it is not difficult to imagine the allure of whiteness as the means through which one measures material successes but also the means through which one gains a sense of equality. There is, in short, a structural bias toward whiteness, which engenders a desire for it as one's aspiration, the alternative being social alienation.[76] It is, therefore, important that Asian Americans are clear when expressing a desire to be accepted in the mainstream of American society and not to be perceived as other. To desire Americanness can mean to simply be accepted for who Asian Americans are, however Asian Americans define themselves. Such a desire is of course a desire to belong and to be accepted by other Americans. But what the logic of acculturation or assimilationist discourse demands is the prioritization of being acceptable to not any community of Americans but specifically a community of Americans that exemplify the norm and ideal of whiteness. As such, Asian Americans do well to be critically self-aware and reflective as to what it means to want acceptance as American and not other; to want to be American is to want to be white or, at the very least, to be fully embraced by white Americans. The following recollection by Sang Hyun Lee is a striking reminder of the subtle but deeply rooted influence of that racialized desire:

> One day in class, an African American student raised his hand and asked, "Dr. Lee, what do you mean by the term *American* whenever you use the term *Asian American*? Are you sure you don't mean 'white American' by the word *American*?" I just jumped out of my chair. It did not take me long to realize for the first time that I always had in mind "Asian-white American" whenever I used the term *Asian American* . . . I confessed to the student and the class

---

75. Zhou, "Are Asians Becoming White?," 354.

76. Cf. Alcoff, "Mestizo Identity," 155: "Universalist pretensions often produce alienation in those whose identities are not dominant. When such false universalisms become influential in oppressed communities, the result is that, for example, nonwhite peoples internalize the perspective of white identity. In *The Bluest Eye*, Toni Morrison dramatically captures this phenomenon for the young black child who wants blond hair and blue eyes."

that I had been living with the idea of white Americans as the "real Americans." And that I would never do it again.[77]

RACIALIZATION AND COMPLICITY

Calling attention to how Asian Americans are subject to the assimilationist pressures toward whiteness punctuates the racial obstacles as well as incentives that deter the kind of innovation that Asian American advocates of hybridity hope for. I do not want to suggest, however, that hybrid innovation is out of reach for Asian Americans, or to deny that such innovations are wholly absent in Asian American life. Yet it would be a mistake to downplay the intractableness of racial discrimination in Asian American life. Avoiding that mistake requires in part recognizing not only the persistence of overt discrimination against Asian Americans, but also to be alert to the ways white assimilationist discourse and pressures in American society are basically a means of *racializing* Asian Americans. To be sure, Asian Americans are already racialized insofar as they are publicly recognized as Asian Americans, distinguishing us from other non-Asian persons of color. But the racialization of Asian Americans through assimilation moves further as it seeks to render Asian Americans as more than Asian Americans, or beyond persons of color, and into whiteness. Consideration of two interrelated problems that befall Asian Americans as consequences of such acculturation into whiteness signals the especially sinister and tragic character of Asian American racialization.

(1) The first is how assimilationist discourse draws Asian Americans into a false sense of equality. As Tan points out, while the United States touts the virtue of a color-blind society, the reality is that whiteness is the standard through which participation in society is measured. This is in part the allure of assimilationist discourse. However, "a difference is maintained." "In other words, Asians are at best, 'white but not quite.'"[78] Such a claim recalls our earlier discussion on the ways in which Asian Americans bear the legacy of exclusion and stereotyping; we are perpetual outsiders, which stands in constant tension with the demands of acculturation. But simply reasserting the reality of our outsider, almost white but not quite, status insufficiently attends to and muddles how Asian Americans may

77. Lee, *From a Liminal Place*, 113, emphasis original.

78. Tan, citing McLaren, *Introducing Asian American Theologies*, 46.

be complicit in the perpetuation of our almost white but not quite status. Our relationship with the model minority classification is a striking case in point.

Asian Americans are of course familiar with the model minority attribution, one that signifies a celebration of the work ethic of Asian Americans, economic and educational achievements, and the alleged giftedness for science, engineering, and math. But what is perhaps less familiar is the way that conferral and acceptance of the model minority status of Asian Americans masks a more complicated reality. Certainly, Asian Americans have benefited from significant economic and educational gains, as we saw earlier. But, as a Pew study shows, Asian Americans are hardly "model minorities" when we are examined at the more "local" level. Once we move beyond a myopic view of Asian Americans as only East Asians (Chinese, Koreans, Taiwanese, Japanese) but also including Southeast Asians and South and Central Asians, then a fuller account of Asian success (or lack thereof) emerges.[79] And given that non-East Asian Americans account for at least 45 percent of Asian Americans, it would be inaccurate to claim that the economic diversity of Asian Americans is pertinent to only a small number or percentage of Asian Americans.[80]

Part of the problem with the conferral and acceptance of Asian Americans as model minorities is not simply that it unduly generalizes the socioeconomic situations of Asian Americans but it does so not by honest ignorance but as a broader strategy to maintain a sense of Asian American ascendency into the mainstream; we are no longer outsiders but insiders, and very accomplished insiders at that. In that way, the conferral and acceptance of Asian Americans as model minorities not only masks the fullness of our socioeconomic reality, it also masks the limitations of our participatory capacities in society. As model minorities, Asian Americans are truncated or abbreviated Americans; we are allowed to be here in the United States but not fully present; we are not "here" in the same way white

79. For instance, as Pew reports, "The U.S. Asian population overall does well on measures of economic well-being compared with the U.S. population as a whole, but this varies widely among Asian subgroups . . . Four groups have household incomes well below the median household income for all Americans: Bangladeshi (http://www.pewsocialtrends.org/fact-sheet/asian-americans-bangladeshis-in-the-u-s) ($49,000), Hmong ($48,000), Nepalese ($43,500) and Burmese ($36,000)" (López et al., "Key Facts).

80. Recall from chapter 1 the kind of dismissive characterization of Asian American economic inequality among many Southeast and Central Asian American communities in Grimes, "Black Exceptionalism," 54.

Americans are "here." This moves beyond simply feelings of alienation and social isolation or loneliness in our status as perpetual foreigners, although those are irrefutably relevant here. Being recognized as model minorities is not necessarily a conferral of equal status but more akin to being tolerated. Tolerability does not require full equality of recognition. After all, as *model* minorities, we are still model *minorities*, not merely in numbers but in terms of status and worth. In that respect, the assimilation of Asian Americans into whiteness moves in a markedly different trajectory than it has for other immigrant populations such as Irish, German, and Italian Americans. As the journalist Serena Dai reminds us in reference to the regard for Chinese food in the United States, "Italians are white . . . the truth is, Italians have very much assimilated into the culture. [But] there's still that block for Chinese-Americans because we're not white."[81] And recall the incident with Guo, the *New York Times* editor who was told to go back to China. Guo's own reaction to the incident is notable for pinpointing the paradoxical status of Asian Americans. He writes:

> Walking home later, a pang of sadness welled up inside me. You had a nice rain coat. Your iPhone was a 6 Plus. You could have been a fellow parent in one of my daughters' schools. You seemed, well, normal. But you had these feelings in you, and, the reality is, so do a lot of people in this country right now. Maybe you don't know this, but the insults you hurled at my family get to the heart of the Asian-American experience. It's this persistent sense of otherness that a lot of us struggle with everyday. That no matter what we do, how successful we are, what friends we make, we don't belong. We're foreign. We're not American . . . My parents fled mainland China for Taiwan ahead of the Communist takeover.

81. *Ugly Delicious*, season 1, episode 7, "Fried Rice." See also Tuan, *Forever Foreigners or Honorary Whites*. A controversial segment on a Food Network show that was filmed in 2012 exemplifies vividly the not-quite-American status of Asian American food. Dee Drummond, a white cook and food blogger in the Midwest, pretends to serve Asian-style chicken wings ("Asian hot wings") to her family, who are described as chicken wing fanatics. Her husband and children react in shock as one of them asks, "Where are the real wings?" Another declares, "I don't trust 'em." Drummond reveals that she is pulling a prank and says, "I'm just kidding guys, I wouldn't do that to you." She then serves a tray of more "traditional" buffalo-style wings and one of her children responds in relief, "Now those are some wings." While the Asian hot wings are an iteration of the buffalo style wings, note that they are regarded as not real. For historical accounts of how "new immigrants" from Europe (early to mid-twentieth century) were eventually racialized as white and thus mainstream American, see Jacobson, *Whiteness of a Different Color*, and Roediger, *Working toward Whiteness*.

They came to the United States for graduate school. They raised two children, both of whom went to Harvard. I work at the *The New York Times*. Model minority, indeed. Yet somehow I still often feel like an outsider.[82]

On the one hand, Asian Americans are often regarded as "Americans," typically through the lens of the model minority category. Being ascribed the status of model minority is meant to be an honorific that recognizes the work ethic and educational and economic advancements of Asian Americans. On the other hand, Asian Americans, despite the honorific, continue to embody a fundamental foreignness to mainstream white American society. Whether our status as model minorities contributes to a kind of racial ignorance of this paradox is one challenge that befalls Asian Americans; it is this very ignorance that the assimilationist discourse of whiteness aims to achieve. And at the heart of this discourse is the model minority myth, which functions to reassure Asian Americans that we are Americans—because of what we have been able to achieve—in return for Asian Americans' quiet submission to the discipline of whiteness, the prevailing norms, attitudes, and values of American society, despite our persisting otherness. The model minority myth, then, alienates Asian Americans from themselves, blocking the possibility of self-knowledge, as Alcoff might say.[83]

So long as the model minority attribution sticks (not simply because we are numerically in the minority), then Asian Americans are "privileged" only to a degree, as the limited numbers of Asian Americans in corporate, political, and educational leadership roles indicate.[84] That limitation perhaps underscores Alcoff's contention that an operating premise of assimilationist discourse in modernity is that nonwhite peoples are intrinsically fixed in nature, while white peoples, paradoxically, are capable of fluidity in their hospitality to the integration of "the other."[85] Thus, when it comes to

---

82. Guo, "Open Letter."

83. Alcoff, "Mestizo Identity," 156.

84. Consider, for instance, Chou and Feagin, *Myth of the Model Minority*.

85. Drawing from Homi Bhabha's notion of "fixity," Alcoff proposes, "The fluidity of cultural identity promoted by the assimilationist discourse actually was used to bolster Northern European-Americans' claims to cultural superiority: Their (supposed) 'fluidity' was contrasted with and presented as a higher cultural achievement than the (supposed) fixity and rigidity of colonized cultures. Here, fixity symbolized inferiority and flexibility symbolized superiority (although of course, in reality, the designation of 'fixity' meant simply the inability or unwillingness to conform to the Northern European norm. This paradox of the meaning of fixity explains how it was possible that . . . WASPS

Asian American assimilation into whiteness, the force of their fixed nature can only accommodate a limited form of whiteness, the model minority. It is not difficult to see, then, how popular conventions on cultural authenticity, as discussed in chapter 2, can solidify such perceptions of the "fixity" of Asian Americans (or any nonwhite persons), whereas white persons are inherently culturally flexible and adaptable or, essentially, sophisticated. If there is a culturally authentic way of being Asian American—often implied in referring to Asians as "ethnic"—then such authenticity indicates their inability to fully assimilate (to be someone who they are not; the impossibility of making an orange an apple) or it also indicates the violence of full assimilation. Accepting Asian Americans as model minorities limits such cultural violence. It amounts to white Americans having their cake and eating it too; being assimilationist, yet respectful of diversity. Whether that is a premise in assimilationist discourse and, thus, what underwrites the "almost whiteness" of Asian Americans is an interesting question. It certainly underscores the larger question of what assimilation actually means for Asian Americans and the implications of what it means to be assimilated into only the ideal of the model minority. It is worth noting how the notion that Asian Americans can only be assimilated to a certain degree—as model minorities and nothing more—harkens back to claims made in the late nineteenth and early twentieth centuries that Asians, Chinese in particular, are unwilling to be Americans, if not actually innately incapable of being assimilated at all. As the *Century* magazine published in 1905, "These Orientals have a civilization older than ours, hostile to ours, exclusive, and repellent. They do not come here to throw their lot with us. They abhor assimilation, and they have no desire to be absorbed. They mean to remain alien; they insist upon being taken back when they are dead; and we do well to keep them out while they are alive."[86]

To be a model minority is to live in the lie of that ideal; it is to embody and to be disciplined by its false promises. In that respect, the benefits of rendering Asian Americans as model minorities—as assimilated whites of a sort—accrues more to those who are conferring the status rather than the ones who may be accepting of that status. As Zhou observes, in noting the ambivalence that some Asian Americans feel about being conferred

---

could be fluid, tolerant, and evolving, but the natives could not. The fluidity of identity that one might think would break down hierarchies was used to justify them. Given this, a prima facie danger exists in drawing assimilationist rhetoric, as it was espoused in the United States, to reconfigure relations of domination" (Alcoff, "Mestizo Identity," 146).

86. Cited from Song, "Asian American Literature," 3.

the privilege of whiteness, "Whiteness has more to do with the beliefs of white America than with the actual situation of Asian Americans. Speaking perfect English, effortlessly adopting mainstream cultural values, and even intermarrying members of the dominant group may help reduce this 'otherness' at the individual level but have little effect on the group as a whole. New stereotypes can emerge and un-whiten Asian Americans anytime and anywhere, no matter how 'successful' and 'assimilated' they have become."[87]

(2) While acceptance of the conferral of Asian Americans as model minorities raises the prospect of our complicity in our own racial marginalization, that same dynamic raises the prospect of how Asian Americans are drawn into the discriminatory aims of assimilationist discourse against non-Asian persons of color. I do not want to suggest that this form of complicity, as well as the one just discussed above, is inevitable, or that Asian Americans who are swept up in the acculturative dynamics of American society are complicit in white racism plain and simple, without qualification. Instead, it should alert us to the ways in which Asian Americans are configured and socially oriented within a racially divisive matrix.

We can for starters map this racial configuration anecdotally, for instance, in a 2014 incident at the University of Michigan where a fraternity, "whose members were mostly Asian and white," planned on hosting a party inviting "rappers, twerkers, gangsters" and others "back to da hood again."[88] One question to be drawn from this example is how the conferral and acceptance of whiteness by way of the model minority myth facilitates Asian American reinscriptions of racially discriminatory patterns of behavior and speech, or what I have elsewhere referred to as the phenomenon of Asian American whiteness.[89] Part of that reinscription is the ignorance of the history of racism: specifically, how certain forms of speech and idioms are racially loaded and fraught. Such ignorance feeds into the perception that Asian Americans and non-Asian Americans of color are indeed different even though that difference is more presumed than actual. As Claire Jean Kim and Taeku Lee note, "Studies show that . . . while roughly 40 percept of Asian Americans report having personally experienced discrimination, few Americans (Asian Americans included) believe that Asian Americans as a group face special obstacles. This data suggests that Asian Americans, on the one hand, and Blacks and Latinos, on the other, may not readily

---

87. Zhou, "Are Asian Americans Becoming White?," 359.

88. Vega, "Colorblind Notion Aside."

89. Choi, "Racial Identity and Solidarity," 131–52.

identify with each other or perceive common interests, despite their shared experience of racial discrimination in the United States."[90]

Who benefits from that racial divide? Consider that the divide between Asian Americans and non-Asians of color is suggestive of what Asian American studies scholar Kandice Chuh observes is the "potency of model minority discourse" in "both inducing identification with the exceptionalism that is Asian difference and affirming the unquestionable value of majoritarian U.S. culture and politics."[91] The perception that Asian Americans are different from non-Asian persons of color and are more alike to the white mainstream, Chuh adds, serves the critical purpose of "sustaining political economic structures" built on the rise of global capitalism and the US's economic interests in that rise post-World War II. With the liberalization of immigration from Asian countries with the 1965 Immigration and Nationality Act,[92] the emergence of the US led global capitalist regime pivoted on the "modernization of Asia"[93] and, on the domestic front, the "figure of the model minority." Given the pivot to Asia, Asian American buy-in to that pivot was aided by the discourse of the model minority, or what Chuh refers to as model minoritarianism, by which she means the idea of Asian and, by association, Asian American ascendency and importance to the new global order, unlike those who are non-Asian American persons of color, brown and black.[94] Asian American identification with the figure of the model minority, then, was critical to the maintenance of

90. Kim and Lee, "Interracial Politics," 545.

91. Chuh, "Asians Are the New . . . What?," 231.

92. For the complex link between more favorable immigration policies toward Asians and the cultivation of the model minority myth, see Schlund-Vials and Wu, "Rethinking Embodiment," 199–200.

93. "While excluded from the Marshall Plan's distribution of postwar financial aid, Asian countries nonetheless received just under $6 Billion from the United States, with China and India as foremost recipients. These Cold War efforts to establish U.S. hegemony in Asia played out through collaborations between specific Asian entities and the U.S. government. Asia—or, at least, some specific parts of it, which came to function as a metonym for the whole—in effect functioned as a U.S. investment in its own future" (Chuh, "Asians Are the New . . . What?," 227–28). See also Lee, "Cold War Construction," 469–84. Lee describes how this focus on Asia commenced in part with the United States' commitment to the redevelopment of Japan in order to secure US interests in the Pacific and Asia after World War II.

94. "By contrasts . . . U.S. foreign policy actively refused investment in Africa during the same period, and . . . concretized into the architecture of post war hegemonic U.S. culture and politics the idea of black pathology, factors that contributed to the traction of model minority discourse" (Chuh, "Asian Americans Are the New . . . What?," 228).

the emerging global capitalist regime; it required "Asian American subjects who are drawn to capital—who, in effect, have enthusiastically identified as the model minority."[95]

The need for Asian Americans to identify with the model minority myth represents an important *shift* in the racially marginalizing logic of white majoritarian culture and politics. Historically speaking, the late nineteenth- and early twentieth-century immigration laws barring Asian entry into the United States on nativist fears that Asians were inassimilable because they were nonwhite "coincided with Jim Crow segregation" and other raced-based restrictions in US law.[96] But note how the *parallel* tracks of discrimination felt by both Asian Americans and African Americans *intersect* and *depend* on one another in a critical way with the passage of the 1965 Immigration and Nationality Act and the subsequent turn in US foreign and economic policy toward the Pacific hemisphere, which required for its success the recasting of Asian Americans as model minorities rather than other or not-white. That recasting "problematically placed Asian Americans in an antithetical position vis-à-vis African Americans" and other non-Asian minorities. The recasting of Asian Americans as model minorities provided a means of measuring the meritoriousness of African Americans and other non-Asian minorities for participation in the emerging geopolitical and economic order led by the United States.[97]

The conscripting of Asian Americans for the emerging global capitalist order had a domestic counterpart. The American studies scholar Robert G. Lee points out that with the ascendency of American liberalism in the 1950s and late 1960s, "with its universalist claims on science and progress," liberalism "required an adherence to a doctrine of racial equality" that would serve as an additional testament to what the United States stood for in the Cold War era and how it would facilitate global economic and political modernization in a post–World War II world. Deemed the theory of ethnic assimilation to "replace the invidious category of race," this strategy would provide a "nonradical solution to the 'Negro problem,'" as Gunnar Myrdal famously and influentially called it in his 1944 Carnegie Council report, *An American Dilemma: The Negro Problem and Modern Democracy*. It would be non-radical in the sense of promoting an orderly, politically uncontroversial, and individually oriented assimilation. The strategy of ethnic

95. Chuh, "Asian Americans Are the New . . . What?," 222.
96. Schlund-Vials and Wu, "Rethinking Embodiment," 198.
97. Schlund-Vials and Wu, "Rethinking Embodiment," 199–200.

assimilation, therefore, would "develop the Negro" while "contain[ing] black demands for the systematic and structural dismantling of racial discrimination." Such demands would require policies, at least on the face of it, that uncomfortably and unacceptably resembled Communism's collective, state-directed, and anti-individualistic solutions to social, economic, and political issues. As Lee puts it, the theory behind ethnic assimilation "articulated a vision of the color-blind society but evaded a critique of the historical category of race altogether. Ethnicity theory offered a promise of equality that could be achieved, not through political organization and community empowerment, but only through individual effort, cultural assimilation, and political accommodation." Lee then explains, "The representation of Asian American communities as self-contained, safe, and politically acquiescent became a powerful example of the success of the American Creed in resolving the problems of race." It did not turn out that way, however. With the 1955 lynching of Emmett Till, an African American teenager, and the US Supreme Court declaring unconstitutional "separate but equal" educational arrangements as another flash point shortly before that, "a strategy of 'massive resistance' to racial equality, especially in the South," undermined the aims of ethnic assimilation.[98] Rather than becoming "models" of ethnic assimilation that would inspire emulation among African Americans, Asian Americans as model minorities became a witness to what African Americans are purportedly not and could not be.

Asian American identification as model minority obscures the winners and losers of acculturation into whiteness. That is not to suggest that being a model minority lacks discernible social privileges. But how should those privileges be accounted for so long as the perpetuation of model minority discourse serves the values of majoritarian US culture and its interests in global capital and geopolitical ascendancy? These economic and political interests rely on the values of self-motivated industriousness, disciplined work ethic, and technical skill and knowledge, all of which persons of color are often perceived (falsely) to be challenged at achieving, except for Asian Americans. Asian American acquiescence to the model minority myth, then, strongly suggests a kind of complicity. But complicity inasmuch as Asian Americans, in submitting to the model minority myth, have fallen into the trap of whiteness's hold on power and privilege.

The manipulation of Asian Americans into that kind of complicity (complicity in white racism's hold on political and economic privilege and

98. Lee, "Cold War Construction," 481.

employment of racial marginalization to bolster that hold) is depicted jar-
ringly in the movie *Get Out*, a 2017 horror film steeped in social commen-
tary. One blog post's description of the surprising insertion of an Asian
character in a movie that is purportedly about white racism against African
Americans (and not about Asian Americans per se) captures the logic of
that manipulation well:

> *Get Out*, from writer-director Jordan Peele, uses the horror genre
> to express the very real fears and subtleties of racism against black
> people in America. For a majority of the film, Chris, the protago-
> nist, is the only black character surrounded by white people when
> he is brought upstate to visit his girlfriend Rose's parents. How-
> ever there is one exception to the black and white makeup of *Get
> Out*: an Asian man seen briefly during one of the film's more tense
> moments. As the only non-black person of color in the film, he
> certainly stands out . . .
>
> The Asian man only appears in two scenes and has only one
> line, but his presence makes a big impression . . . The charac-
> ter—unnamed in the film but identified in the credits as Hiroki
> Tanaka—is one of the guests at the majority-white cocktail party
> thrown by Rose's parents that doubles as a modern slave auction.
> It's a spooky scene in which Chris is paraded around to middle-
> aged white people, all of whom ask him oddly pointed questions
> about his race. One woman reaches up to feel his bicep and asks
> Rose about his prowess in bed; a retired golf player inspects his
> build and casually mentions that he met Tiger Woods. And then
> there's the Asian man, who asks Chris if he thinks being African-
> American in America has more disadvantages or advantages.[99]

The question, posed by the only nonblack character of the film, encapsulates one striking way in which the manipulative discourse of Asian Americans as model minorities operates. To be rendered as model minority is to
align Asian Americans with white America. But that alignment is based on
an affirmation of difference from those who are not model minorities. That
difference demarcates lines of privilege in society, to be a model minority
is preferable to being identified with those who are not, namely, in this
instance, African Americans. Hence the leading question of whether it is
advantageous or not to be African American; obviously, it is less advantageous. And given that the racial lines of privilege are established in such a

99. Truffaut-Wong, "Why the Asian Character."

manner, it is not difficult to embrace being a model minority and thus not black.

The manipulation of Asian Americans into whiteness based on that stark sense of difference from those without privilege (African Americans), however, works both ways and is perhaps one of the significant inadequacies of the film in its attempt to depict the realities of racism in the United States. The insistence on the difference between Asian Americans (insofar as they are model minorities) and African Americans (who are not model minorities and, thus, continually shut out of the mainstream of American society), not only pushes Asian Americans to align with and perhaps even defend the interests of white society (since it is now seen as our interests), but it also fuels and sustains African American perceptions that they are indeed *different* from Asian Americans. Recent reformulations of white racism as specifically and especially antiblackness, as discussed in chapter 1, underlines that perceived divide and intrinsic difference between Asian Americans and non-Asian Americans of color, and raises the question of whether that insistence on difference plays into the hands of the assimilationist discourse of white racism.

In chapter 1, I proposed the prospect of white racism instantiating racial marginalization through mutually reinforcing or interlocking strategies. That prospect is aided by the manipulation of Asian Americans into whiteness, which is not an insulated logic, but one that is part and parcel of white racism's violence against and suppression of African Americans. The effectiveness of the latter is dependent to a high degree on the effectiveness of the former. The push to align Asian Americans with the interests of white society effectively serves to isolate African Americans from other persons of color, namely, Asian Americans. Such isolation does not simply sow divisions and thus thwart collective action, but it also removes the potency of the complaint of African American victimhood and correlative demands for structural and systemic political and economic transformation. Insisting on whiteness as singularly a form of antiblackness, especially if that is specified as discounting the veracity and depth of anti-Asianness because Asian Americans are white, adjacent to white, or sympathetic to whiteness, takes on the work of white racism in ways that are not necessarily obvious but nevertheless consequential. Complicity in the sustaining of white racism, therefore, is as much an African American problem as it is an Asian American one. The invisibility of such complicity is an accomplishment of white racism's work on Asian Americans. Thus approaching whiteness as antiblackness can too easily promote a call for racial justice that does not take seriously the racialized realities of Asian Americans, which only then feed into the susceptibility of Asian Americans to the manipulation into whiteness and their purported difference from African Americans and racial resentment of them. That then fuels further African American perceptions of Asian Americans as other. Trapped in a vicious cycle of perpetuating difference and resentment, the seeds of racial discontent are sown and bearing (rotten) fruit.

Efforts at adopting and practicing a hybrid identity can be regarded as one way of resisting such complicity in white racism's logics, at least on the part of Asian Americans. My aim in this chapter is not to be dismissive of such efforts. Yet, that turn to and advocacy for hybridity, for the kind of cultural innovation that it can afford, requires being alert to the ways in which Asian Americans are dissuaded from hybridity and innovation and retreat into preconceived, conventional, maybe even stereotypical, notions of themselves as Asian Americans. But, more significantly, it requires being vigilant to the ways in which the structure of our social and cultural desires are framed by the promises (albeit false) of white assimilationist discourse, one that pivots on the myth of the social advantages of Asian American difference. Sharpened attunement to the manipulative hand of such assimilationist discourse, therefore, clarifies what it means to be Asian Americans as racialized persons in contemporary society.

4

Agency

This film has the right to be about these people, and Asian American characters have the right be whoever the hell they want to be.

—ROGER EBERT, COMMENTING ON THE FILM *BETTER LUCK TO-MORROW*, BY ASIAN AMERICAN DIRECTOR JUSTIN LIN[1]

What she saw when she looked at me must have been my yellowness, my slightly smaller eyes . . . in America it was all or nothing when it came to race. You were either white or you weren't.

—*THE SYMPATHIZER*[2]

CHAPTER 3 PROPOSED THAT Asian American advocacy for a hybrid construal of Asian American self-understanding requires a more sober consideration of the extent to which Asian Americans are subjected to the assimilationist discourse of whiteness. That subjection identifies the basic contours of the racial formation of Asian American identity, a racial formation that risks at least a twofold account of Asian American complicity. First, a complicity in perpetuating the false image of Asian American

1. As cited by Fang, "Globalization, Masculinity," 79.
2. Nguyen, *Sympathizer*, 127.

equality, and, second, a complicity in perpetuating whiteness by upholding difference with non-Asian persons of color through the model minority myth. Such complicity is neither inevitable nor does it describe the totality of contemporary Asian American attitudes and practices. At the same time, the ongoing threat of such complicity casts a wide and deep shadow over Asian American life, raising the question about the prospects for Asian American self-determination and, thus, the extent to which being Asian American is racialized or reflects a racially formed identity. This question is not solely about whether the prospects for the kind of hybrid innovation discussed in the previous chapter are ultimately hopeless for Asian Americans, but rather it is a question that seeks a fuller accounting of what it means for Asian Americans to be self-determinative persons and, therefore, the kind of social and moral choices Asian Americans are afforded within American society.

In this chapter, I turn to contemporary Asian American fiction to further unpack the implications of Asian American racialization. What does the racial formation of Asian Americans say about the nature of Asian Americans as social and moral agents? Undoubtedly, my turn to Asian American literature is limited both in scope and in the themes Asian American fiction covers. The novels featured below, while mostly of the "popular" fiction genre, are neither representative of contemporary Asian American fiction as a whole nor representative of those that might be called "canonical," if such a canon of Asian American literature exists at all. Whether Asian American fiction can be represented in some collective manner is an open question given the diversity of interests that inform this literary category.[3] It would also be misleading, therefore, to suggest that the novels I turn to in this chapter explicitly deal with the issue of Asian American identity, no less what Asian American identity implies about Asian American agency; that is not the case, at least not in a singular way. Thus, there is some reluctance to refer to the novels in this chapter as Asian American novels as if they work with explicitly Asian American themes (or, correlatively, as if their authors had specifically set out to write so-called Asian American novels). It may be more appropriate to simply note that I focus on a select number of contemporary novels written by authors who identify as Asian Americans and feature characters whose identities, as is

3. See Nguyen, *Race and Resistance*. Nguyen argues that Asian American literature has historically encompassed thematic diversity, especially when it comes to race; themes of resistance and accommodation to race are both prevalent throughout Asian American literature. See also Song, "Asian American Literature," 3–15.

the case in real life, are multivalent. But to the extent that these authors do write about characters who, among other identities, identify as Asian American, these novels necessarily grapple with the social implications of that racial marker, and the authors narrate such struggles in ways that are revealing of our question here, the question of Asian American self-determination. In short, my aim is not to provide a sweeping assessment or interpretation of contemporary Asian American fiction, but instead, more modestly, I turn to select novels, all published since 2003 except for one published in 1995, as points of departure for reflecting on the question of Asian American identity and its implications for Asian American agency. In that way, I turn to, for lack of a better phrase, "Asian American fiction" as a cultural medium (or source) through which critical self-assessment about our agency as Asian Americans can be facilitated. Perhaps another more apt way of putting the matter is that Asian American fiction is approached as a kind of mirror, to borrow a metaphor from, among others, Augustine, and a mirror that supports self-critical awareness that is less abstract and engages the imaginative, affective, and experiential dimensions of reflective thought.

There are at least two proposals to be made with this turn to contemporary Asian American fiction. First, far from providing a unitary perspective on what it means to be Asian American, recent Asian American fiction offers diverse representations of Asian Americans. That diversity ranges from characters who identify as Asian American, but not in conventional and obvious ways, to those who are explicitly narrated as Asian American stereotypically. That diversity of representation offers readers of these novels a concrete, particularized panorama of the range of identity choices that are available for Asian Americans. Yet that diversity, paradoxically, also pushes us to consider the socially delimited nature of the characters' identities as Asian American and, correlatively, what is and is not possible for Asian Americans. As each of the novels considered below depict characters who struggle with who they are, these characters embody particular conceptions of Asian Americanness in ways that are not necessarily self-determinative but rather as a means of social survival or belonging within the confines of white cultural and social hegemony.

Adopting identities as a means of social survival or inclusion is strikingly evocative of the concept of racial "passing," which brings us to the second and more important reason for turning to Asian American fiction. The theologian Brian Bantum describes passing, historically speaking, as pertaining to the "practice of a person of African descent who could be perceived as white 'passing' themselves off as white and thus 'pass' into white society."[4] This historical definition of passing is not applicable to Asian American life in a duplicate way. However, to the extent that the novels considered in this chapter depict characters who are in one sense or another either enticed or compelled to embody certain kinds of identities so as to endure and in some cases even prosper in a society that they experience as either hostile or ambivalent toward them, these novels provide a critical medium though which to reflect on the salience of passing for Asian American life. A focus on passing necessarily attunes us to the racial and, thus, the sociopolitical dimensions of Asian American agency. Inasmuch as the practice and concept of passing, as I will discuss below, is about the kinds of identities or, more precisely, *bodies* we decide to inhabit in response to racialized hierarchies of value and relationships, a focus on passing within an Asian American context reconfigures how we talk about Asian American agency and prospects for self-determination away from talking about what the possibilities of Asian American agency are to what Asian Americans are necessarily and tragically limited to.

PRELIMINARIES: ASIAN AMERICAN FICTION AND PASSING AS RACIAL CONSTRAINT

The idea of passing—that one could indeed pass from one racial modality to another even though that "new" identity is not "original" to the person—has gained some renewed attention in popular media thanks to the likes of Rachel Dolezal (a white woman from Washington state who identified as black). Such instances, however, have also trivialized the gravity of what passing has meant, historically speaking. Historically, the practice of passing was hardly a recreational exercise or a consequence of one's desire to express one's "true" racial identity. Instead, as Bantum reminds us, passing was motivated by the tragic necessity of a person of African descent to *perform* into a particular, white racialized world.[5] In characterizing passing as a racial performance, Bantum's aim is to underscore the idea that racial identity is a fundamentally constructed reality while also making sense of the lived reality of racial and cultural ideals. That a person of African descent could pass as white undermines the very idea of ontologically fixed

4. Bantum, *Redeeming Mulatto*, 46.
5. Bantum, *Redeeming Mulatto*, 16.

and racially pure identities, and yet being black or white is experienced as a felt, disciplined commitment to a predefined set of social and cultural practices reflective of a particular racial vision. That experiential character of race underscores passing as not simply a mental state or a certain kind of attitudinal orientation but, more deeply, an embodied act, the actual day-to-day living of a particular identity. In short, passing indicates the kind of bodies we ultimately inhabit.

However, insofar as persons of African descent who could pass as white found themselves *needing* to pass as white, passing as racial performance "reveal[s] the intense pressure of racial life and hope in America" and the kind of "inherent trap" that a racialized society lays before persons.[6] In "an intractably racialized world," in order to be a person, one must conform or follow "a certain form of life" based on one's "pigmentation."[7] In other words, "personhood is understood only within the confines of a particular people" and in the enactment (or performance) of what society perceives it to mean to be a part of such a community.[8] This is not unlike, as we saw in chapter 1, K. Anthony Appiah's idea of racial identity as a kind of script one follows, but a script that is not necessarily of one's own choosing but one that is oftentimes imposed on persons by the prevailing racial visions and stereotypes of society. Inasmuch as racial identities are imposed—that we find ourselves socially pressured to inhabit or perform a particular racial identity—the performative reality of racial identities is fundamentally a tragic one. While that tragic reality, according to Bantum, is magnified for interracial, black-white persons (or "the mulatto body"), that tragic reality—of being required to be black or pass as white—binds "all bodies in the modern world."[9]

By "all bodies" Bantum presumably also means the inclusion of Asian American bodies and not just black and white bodies and mixed-race mulatto bodies. But to *what extent* is the claim that the tragedy of passing binds "all bodies" applicable to Asian American bodies? More specifically, to what extent do Asian Americans find themselves *needing* to pass from one racial identity or body to another? Lastly, if passing is indeed a phenomenon that Asian Americans find themselves participating in, *what are Asian Americans passing into?*

6. Bantum, *Redeeming Mulatto*, 46, 42.

7. Bantum, *Redeeming Mulatto*, 82.

8. Bantum, *Redeeming Mulatto*, 71.

9. Bantum, *Redeeming Mulatto*, 16, 15.

Consider first Bantum's emphasis, as we noted above, on the normative pressures that a racialized society exerts on persons toward a particular racial identity. Passing serves as a striking case study of how such pressures necessarily curb the possibilities of self-determination or self-definition. That idea of racial constraint converges with and finds expression in sporadic depictions of Asian Americans who are frustrated by racialized perceptions of who they are as Asian Americans in a number of contemporary (post 1990s) Asian American novels. While those depictions of frustration do not typically anchor the primary thematic or narrative interests of many Asian American novelists, to the extent that such depictions of frustration appear in characters who are identified as Asian American, these novelists show a willingness to acknowledge the consequences of that racial marker (Asian American) when narratively appropriate.

For instance, in Susan Choi's novel *American Woman* (2003), a story based on the 1974 Patty Hearst kidnapping by the Symbionese Liberation Army, we find its protagonist the twenty-five-year-old Jenny Yamada in one pointed scene exasperated by the stereotypical perceptions of her as Asian and, specifically, Japanese from her cohorts-in-crime and Marxist revolution. Juan, Jenny's "revolutionary" trainer of sorts, goads Jenny into taking a greater leadership role in enlisting other Japanese Americans in the fight against the oppressive American government. His pitch appeals to Jenny's purported racial origins and the kind of advantaged perspective that being racially marginalized offers. "You owe your people your leadership," says Juan. "You can't go denying your race. You don't just owe the revolution in general, you owe your people in particular."[10] And then he concludes, "All I'm saying . . . is your skin is a privilege. Your Third World Perspective's a privilege."[11] In response, Jenny, clearly irritated, insists, "Just because I'm a Japanese woman, you can't define me in terms of just that . . . Stop saying I'm from the Third World when I'm from California."[12] Yet, Juan, failing to catch her point, continues with his stereotypical perceptions of Jenny's Asianness while practicing their shooting skills in preparation for the revolution. "'Joining us?' Juan asks Jenny genially. 'You must be a good shot. Oriental people always have exceptional aim. They're inherently good marksmen, they're good at precision sports like pool and golf, they're good

---

10. Choi, *American Woman*, 139.

11. Choi, *American Woman*, 140.

12. Choi, *American Woman*, 139–40.

archers.'"[13] Now beyond exasperated, Jenny responds to Juan coldly with "I've never touched a gun in my life."[14]

The frustration over the tension between being able to define oneself and being defined by others receives more studied attention in Chang-rae Lee's novel *Native Speaker* (1995). The novel chronicles the life of Henry Park, a Korean American who wrestles with his own past in the midst of a marital crisis. At one point in the novel, he recalls a childhood memory of his parents' efforts to be inconspicuous in their affluent suburban neighborhood of Ardsley, in Westchester County, New York. Henry recollects:

> I know [my father] never felt fully comfortable in his fine house in Ardsley. Though he was sometimes forward and forceful with some of his neighbors, he mostly operated as if the town were just barely tolerating our presence. The only time he'd come out in public was because of me. He would steal late and unnoticed into the gym where I was playing kiddie basketball and stand by the far side of the bleachers with a rolled-up newspaper in his hand, tapping it nervously against his thigh as he watched the action, craning to see me shoot the ball but never shouting or urging like the other fathers and mothers did.
>
> My mother, too, was even worse, and she would gladly ruin a birthday cake rather than bearing the tiniest of shames in asking her next-door neighbor and friend for the needed egg she'd run out of, the child's pinch of baking powder.
>
> I remember thinking of her, *What's she afraid of,* what could be so bad that we had to be that careful of what people thought of us, as if we ought to mince delicately about in pained feet through our immaculate neighborhood, we silent partners bordering WASPs and Jews, never rubbing them except with a smile, as if everything with us were always all right, in our great sham of propriety, as if nothing could touch us or wreak anger or sadness upon us.[15]

Henry remembers his parents' efforts to "fit in" in Ardsley with frustrating disapproval. His frustration gestures to a sense of stifled being and what amounts to a shameful deception, the longing to belong or the desire to be seen as "normal," if being normal means simply keeping up with appearances.[16] For Henry's parents, that also means, paradoxically, blending

13. Choi, *American Woman*, 188–89.

14. Choi, *American Woman*, 189.

15. Lee, *Native Speaker*, 52, emphasis original.

16. Shortly after the passage just cited, Henry notes that his parents' efforts to fit in was also, in a way, an extension of how his father approached his grocery store on

in with their non-Asian neighbors to a point where they, in essence, have become invisible to them.

Henry's frustration projects an image of Asian Americans who are always at unease. Jenny in Choi's *American Woman* provides at least one reason why that apprehension is warranted. Her exchanges with Juan are indicative of Asian Americans always at risk of being defined by limiting or trivialized perceptions of who they are as persons. In the case of Henry's parents, their fear is rooted in being defined as an outsider, different from their non-Asian neighbors. But what is interesting is the way in which Jenny and Henry's parents respond to those fears. In Jenny's case, she constantly attempts to undermine Juan's stereotypes with counterfactuals (e.g., I am not from the third world, I am from California; I am not a good marksmen because I am Asian, I have never held a gun), whereas in Park's parents' case, they do all that they can to not draw attention to themselves. In both cases, their sense of self is always in response to either an actual (in Jenny's case) or potential (in Henry's parents' case) experience of alienation. (I characterize Park's parents as experiencing potential alienation inasmuch as they strain for normalcy not because of any actual event that alienates but rather for a desire to avert alienation given their nonwhite identity.)

To the extent that both Choi and Lee depict characters that, frustratingly, must account for how others perceive them, these characters begin to provide a sense of how Asian Americans are not immune from the same kind of racial pressures that motivate the phenomenon of passing. Just as some persons of African descent, especially mixed-race African Americans, find the need to pass as white or be black, Choi and Lee depict characters who find the need to embody a particular identity and persona in response to racial perceptions of them. That sense of necessity undermines, to a degree, their capacity or freedom for self-determination. Is the identity and persona they project in response to racial perceptions of them those that they genuinely desire? Could they have "appeared" and responded differently? Reflecting on Henry's and Jenny's situations in relation to passing forces such questions, for the practice of passing is fundamentally a response to the kind of social constraints on self-definition or

---

Madison Avenue in Manhattan. Henry recounts how frustrating it was to be pulled into his father's desires to make his store more appealing to its Upper East Side customers: "My father, thinking that it might be good for business, urged me to show them how well I spoke English, to make a display of it, to casually recite 'some Shakespeare words.'" Henry's response: "Mostly, though, I threw all my frustration into building those perfect, truncated pyramids of fruit" (Lee, *Native Speaker*, 53, 54).

self-determination of a racialized society. Henry is perhaps less ambiguous in this regard than Jenny. Recall that Henry refers to his parents' efforts to be normal as a sham. To call it a sham suggests that a more acceptable or honest, at least in Henry's judgment, alternative is possible. But could they have reasonably opted for an alternative to the so-called sham other than moving out of their Ardsley neighborhood? If not, then would it be more accurate to characterize their efforts at "normalcy" a form of passing, that is, the need to perform a particular way of being as a matter of survival? But even with Jenny, given the persistence of Juan's stereotypical construal of her Asianness, it is perhaps easy to sympathize with not only her exasperations but also her tit-for-tat, sometimes sardonic corrections of Juan. Did she have a choice to do otherwise? Would it have been more reasonable for her to simply accept, quietly and acquiescently, Juan's definitions of her? What kind of choices did she really have?

EITHER "WHITE" OR "ASIAN" AND NOTHING IN BETWEEN (OR BEYOND)

We can broaden the foregoing question to include Asian Americans more generally. What kind of choices do Asian Americans really have? Toward the end of *Native Speaker*, Henry declares,

> This is a city of words.
>
> We live here. In the street the shouting is in a language we hardly know. The strangest chorale. We pass by the throngs of mongers, carefully nodding and heeding the signs. Everyone sounds angry and theatrical. Completely out of time. They want you to buy something, or hawk what you have, or else shove off. The constant cry is that you belong here, or you make yourself belong, or you must go.[17]

This characterization of what the "city" demands serves as an apt metaphor of the kind of racial demands that Asian Americans face.[18] Either be a racial outsider or insider. Whichever choice you make, it is a choice that must be made.

This *need* to embody a particular identity is magnified and given a more explicit racial context in a number of more recent novels by Asian

17. Lee, *Native Speaker*, 344.

18. Patricia P. Chu's attention to the foregoing passage from *Native Speaker* facilitated the formulation of this claim. See Chu, *Assimilating Asians*, 1–23.

American authors (post-2003). Noteworthy in these novels is how their Asian American characters not only reiterate the kind of racial constraints that both Jenny and Henry struggle with (the constant need to negotiate racial stereotypes or the unease of not belonging), but also indicate the difficulty of transcending those constraints and what that intractability implies for their characters' identities as Asian American. Rather than transcending those racial constraints, these novels depict how Asian American characters exist within those confines, moving from one racial modality to another. That movement from one racial modality to another is described in different ways, sometimes as a matter of survival, in other instances as promising liberation, but in the end, all of the following novels depict Asian American characters who are presented with only *limited* racial modalities. Furthermore, these racial modalities are not necessarily identities they create for themselves, but often are ones made available to them and, in one form or another, imposed on them by prevailing racial ideals and stereotypes. To the extent that these are often the only identities these characters are able to choose from—and choose they must if they are to survive or, as some see it, gain a sense of belonging—these newer novels help us to imagine further how Asian Americans construct their identities and gain a sense of self or agency essentially within the general logic of passing.

Passing as White
(Patricia Park and Gene Luen Yang)

It should not be surprising that one racial modality that Asian Americans are subject to is whiteness. In chapter 2, I discussed the ways Asian Americans are subject to the assimilating discourse of whiteness. The challenges that such pressures create for Asian Americans in terms of their identity are common concerns in twentieth-century Asian American literature.[19] Reflections on those challenges continue to be the topics of concern in recent Asian American fiction, such as in the novels by Patricia Park and Gene Luen Yang, with a decidedly strong emphasis on whiteness as an identity of personal and social desire. While they diverge somewhat on their characterizations of such desire (Yang is wary of it, Park less so), they are both bound by the depiction of what whiteness promises.

19. See Chu, *Assimilating Asians*, though once again, Nguyen, in his *Race and Resistance*, reminds us that concerns over strategizing resistance against such racial pressures are not the only concerns of twentieth-century Asian American literature.

(1) A Korean American adaptation of Charlotte Brontë's *Jane Eyre* set in New York City, post-9/11, Park's *Re Jane* (2015) tells the story of a college-bound student named Jane Re, the daughter of a Korean woman and a white American tourist; in other words, a mixed-race child or *honhyol* in Korean. Abandoned by her father, and then with the passing of her Korean mother, Jane ends up in the United States under the care of her uncle Sang who owns a grocery store in Flushing, Queens.

Jane eventually finds herself entangled with a married man, Ed Farley. As Jane's romantic travails unfold, Park weaves in a secondary narrative of racial identity and belonging, perhaps unavoidable given Jane's *honhyol* status. From the start of the novel, Jane struggles to define her identity on her own terms, constantly contending with her uncle's and aunt's insistence that she is, despite her biological provenance, Korean. At one point she finds the need to remind her uncle, "I'm half American."[20] But her insistence is often taken as gestures of ingratitude to and disrespect for her extended family who has so graciously taken her in. A respectful attitude would be one that reflects a greater commitment to her Korean lineage, a point reinforced when her grandfather Myungsun Re (or, more traditionally, Re Myungsun, with surname first) visits her uncle's family. During one evening dinner, Jane's grandfather remarks, "*But you look more Korean now. How fortunate . . . A Korean person should look Korean.*"[21]

To be sure, such a normative assertion betrays the performative nature of race, which recalls Bantum's essential point about the nature of passing. Jane is neither Korean nor white, but is expected to be like her mother. The expectation is not that Jane should be, like her mother, a mom herself or whatever characteristics that define motherhood; the expectation is that she be Korean. The pressure to perform as Korean is a matter of preference and respect to her Korean caretakers (and ostensibly her mother's lineage). In this way, Park's novel reveals how the myth of racial purity is not simply a white desire but also a desire for nonwhites. Jane lives in a world in which being Korean is the ideal; the fact that Jane is multiracial is beside the point.

Park, however, paints a more complex picture of Korean racial attitudes. When Jane is told by her grandfather that a Korean person should look Korean, Park, interestingly, conveys to the reader that such an attitude belongs to the world of Jane's uncle's generation and generations prior, not necessarily to Jane's millennial generation of Koreans and Asian

20. Park, *Re Jane*, 41.
21. Park, *Re Jane*, 113, emphasis original.

Americans. That point is made subtly toward the middle of the novel when Jane, after having precipitated Ed Farley's divorce, finds her way to South Korea, living with other relatives in the hope of regaining her sense of self. While in Korea, she is once again faced with her uncomfortable status as *honhyol*. "When I was younger, *I tried to pass*. It would have been easier to lie [about my white, American father]," Jane recounts.[22] But as it turns out, her newfound Korean friends give her reason to embrace her *honhyol* status (to pass in the other direction, to pass as white), not because being inter-racial offered new, unconventional modes of self-understanding. Instead, it meant that as *honhyol*, Jane was desirably "whiter." As Jane's friend Monica (a name adopted out of her love for the nineties television sitcom *Friends*) assures Jane, "I'm so jealous! . . . *Honhyol* has the white skin, big eyes, big nose, small chin, long legs . . . You're so lucky."[23]

That declaration captures assumptions that most of the Korean and Korean American characters in Park's novel hold. American is synonymous with white; Park provides confirmation toward the end of the novel when Jane's uncle declares about Carroll Gardens in Brooklyn, "That neighbor-hood, change a lot. More American people." Jane then notes, "I knew what he meant. American like Beth [Ed Farley's wife]. Not American like Ed [who is Jewish] or Nina [Jane's Latina friend]. And certainly not black."[24] The identification of American with white buttresses Monica's jealousy of Jane's *honhyol*-ness; to be Korean and white is to be more white than Ko-rean. After returning to New York, even Jane's Latina friend Nina admits, "*Honhyol* celebrities like you are all the rage now . . . You half-Asian girls are the new California blonds."[25]

At the beginning of the novel we find Jane recoiling from the insis-tence that she be Korean. As the novel concludes, we find a rather differ-ent Jane, one who is more at ease. That sense of contentment, however, is hastened by her emergence as *honhyol*, which no longer connotes racial impurity but racial desire; her *honhyol* status now signals the racial ideal of whiteness. No longer seeing her *honhyol* status as a liability, the Jane who is depicted at the end of the novel is one who is ultimately embraced for her whiteness and is encouraged by her friends, both Korean and non-Korean, to embrace her whiteness without shame. Jane begins to embody that status

22. Park, *Re Jane*, 187, emphasis added.
23. Park, *Re Jane*, 187.
24. Park, *Re Jane*, 237.
25. Park, *Re Jane*, 336.

because others have affirmed it for her as the preferred, most desirable, status and she responds in kind. Questioning the desirableness of the white aesthetic (admiration of Jane's *honhyol*-ness is largely that she looks white and what that white aesthetic evokes—"California cool") is not a primary concern for Jane. What matters in the end is that Jane's transmutation from *honhyol*-Korean to *honhyol*-white is what enables her to finally find the kind of freedom and purpose that she lacked before. As free, she is no longer beholden, burdened by the kind of expectations that are associated with being Asian, Korean. It is, in short, the kind of freedom that Jenny, in another Asian American novel, *Sour Heart* (2015), can only hope for:

> But now I wanted to be free. I wanted to be free to be selfish and self-destructive and indulgent like the white girls at the high school my parents worked so hard to get me into, and once they did, once we moved into a neighborhood where no one hung out on the streets, where everyone was the same pasty shade of consumptive blotchy paleness, all it did was make me want to get away from my family. I envied white kids whose relationships with their parents were so abysmal that they could never disappoint them. I wanted white parents who didn't care where I went or what I did, parents who encouraged me to leave home instead of guilting me into staying their kid forever.[26]

(2) Whiteness as an ideal, an identity to be desired, is iterated in Gene Luen Yang's graphic novel *American Born Chinese* (2006). But whereas whiteness, embracing and celebrating whiteness, is more about finding freedom and purpose for Jane, whiteness for Jin Wang, the main protagonist of Yang's graphic novel, is about the desire to fit in, to befriend non-Asians. The novel begins with Jin arriving as a new third grader at Mayflower Elementary School, where he is one of only two Asian Americans, the other being Suzy Nakamura, who is Japanese American. But he stays clear of her once the white students begin to joke that Jin and Suzy are arranged to be married when they both turn thirteen. That sense of being an outsider is magnified for Jin when his lunches are the object of ridicule—what kind of kid eats dumplings for lunch? Nonwhite kids, of course, and to drive that point further, one of Jin's classmates, upon learning that Jin is eating dumplings, demands in disgust, "Stay away from my dog."[27]

26. Zhang, *Sour Heart*, 154–55.

27. Yang, *American Born Chinese*, 32.

Jin, as he moves from being an adolescent to a teenager, begins to notice a white girl by the name of Amelia Harris. "Even though we'd been in school together since the third grade, I never noticed Amelia Harris until one humid afternoon in Mr. Kirk's seventh grade class," he says. "Life was never quite the same again."[28] Indeed it was not, given his infatuation with her, leading him to find ways of seizing her attention. Eventually, he thinks that the more he looks like Greg, a white classmate who sits next to Amelia in science class, the greater the chances of befriending Amelia. That eventually leads him to style his hair into wavy locks like Greg's. But as Amelia and Jin become more acquainted, Greg confronts Jin and slyly encourages him to stay away from Amelia, purportedly for her own good. "It's just that she's a good friend and I want to make sure she makes good choices. We're almost in high school. She has to start paying attention to who she hangs out with," explains Greg. Then he finishes his pitch by being more up front, "I just don't know if you're right for her, okay? That's all."[29]

Feeling alienated, later that evening Jin begins to recall the Sundays he would spend with his mother visiting the Chinese herbalist just around the corner from his childhood home. While his mother would consult the herbalist, Jin would wait for her in the front room with the herbalist's wife, who would often stand there calculating bills on her abacus. Jin then recalls the one Sunday when the herbalist's wife asked, "So little friend, what do you plan to become when you grow up?" Jin, as any young boy might respond, said he wanted to be a transformer. Not knowing exactly what he meant, the herbalist's wife shares with Jin what she characterized as a secret, "It's easy to become anything you wish . . . so long as you're willing to forfeit your soul."[30] Jin's reaction is one of complete befuddlement; he does not think much about her so-called secret and continues to play with the Optimus Prime transformer he had brought with him to the herbalist's shop. But now, a teenager, wanting to be Amelia's boyfriend, he wishes to transform, and the herbalist's wife, appearing in his dream, acknowledges his wish and says, "So little friend, you've done it."[31] The next morning Jin wakes to find himself no longer Jin, at least in appearance, but looking just like the tall, athletic, blond-haired, good-looking, and most popular boy in school. Jin looks in the mirror and approvingly renames himself Danny.

28. Yang, *American Born Chinese*, 87.

29. Yang, *American Born Chinese*, 179, 180.

30. Yang, *American Born Chinese*, 29.

31. Yang, *American Born Chinese*, 193.

What is interesting in this transformation is the herbalist's wife's assertion that Jin, in transforming, has "done it," which recalls the central message of the little secret she had shared with Jin when he was a boy. To transform, you have to be willing to give up your soul. Yang, in depicting a Chinese American boy who wishes to be white, signals Jin's willingness to give up his soul, but soul in the sense of his Chineseness, which is his truthful self. While embracing whiteness has no apparent costs for someone like Jane in Park's novel, in Yang's graphic novel, the liabilities are severe, a complete loss of identity. In that way, Yang's graphic novel provides a contemporary and visually unique narrative of a not uncommon theme of the perils of passing as white in Asian American literature that dates back to at least the late nineteenth century in North America. As the writer Sui Jin Far, also known as Edith Maud Eaton (b. 1865, d. 1914), recounts in her autobiographical essay, "Leaves from the Mental Portfolio of an Eurasian":

> My employer shakes his rugged head. "Somehow or other," says he, "I cannot reconcile myself to the thought that the Chinese are humans like ourselves. They may have immortal souls, but their faces seem to be so utterly devoid of expression that I cannot help but doubt."
>
> "Souls," echoes the town cleric. "Their bodies are enough for me. A Chinaman is, in my eyes, more repulsive than a n****r."
>
> "They always give me such a creepy feeling . . ."
>
> "I wouldn't have one in my house," declares my landlady.
>
> . . .
>
> A miserable, cowardly feeling keeps me silent . . . I have no longer an ambition to die at the stake for the sake of demonstrating the greatness and nobleness of the Chinese people.
>
> . . .
>
> With a great effort I raise my eyes from my plate. "Mr. K.," I say, addressing my employer, "the Chinese people may have no souls, no expression on their faces, be altogether beyond the pale of civilization, but whatever they are, I want you to understand that I am—I am a Chinese."[32]

Jin, in Yang's novel, confronts a similar ethno-racial reckoning and reconciliation. He can continue to be white Danny, but to do so would be perhaps cowardly, a betrayal of not only his true self but also his racial allegiances to his Chinese friends. For Jin, who he is is defined by his Chineseness, and Jin finally comes to that realization at the end of the novel when he

---

32. Cited from Chu, *Assimilating Asians*, 101.

eventually accepts how good it is to be himself, Chinese, not white. That realization is affirmed at the end of the novel when he reunites with an estranged Chinese American friend, Wei-chen, and agrees to meet over the best pearl milk tea in town.

Passing as Asian
(Celeste Ng, Lisa Ko, and Viet Thanh Nguyen)

Both Yang's and Park's novels display the cultural power and social promise of whiteness. For Jane in Park's novel, she finds liberation and affirmation of self in whiteness, more specifically, in embracing the whiteness that is possible in her mixed-race status as Korean and white. Jin in Yang's graphic novel seeks a similar form of affirmation in whiteness inasmuch as he desires to be white in order to relate with other white peers (to be noticed by them, to be Amelia's boyfriend, more precisely). In that way, Jin's desire to be white underscores the allure of whiteness as a form of belonging. Yet, Jin ultimately differs from Jane when at the end of the graphic novel he "sheds" his white body (when he reverts back to being Jin from Danny) for his essential Chinese self. That ultimate affirmation of himself as Chinese and not as white can be read as a kind of rebuke to the liberation and affirmation of self that Jane finds in whiteness.

Novels by Celeste Ng, Lisa Ko, and Viet Thanh Nguyen, however, complicate that rebuke. This complication is not so much about questioning the merits of Jin's rejection of whiteness as he moves toward reaffirming his Chineseness. Instead, the complication pertains to the question of whether Jin's reaffirmation of his Chineseness can be taken as a reaffirmation of some Chineseness (or Asianness) that is inherent to his identity or sense of self. In other words, when Jin reverts from being white Danny to Chinese Jin, can that reversion be understood as somehow a return to some truthful sense of himself? Is his return to and rediscovery of his Chinese American identity an identity that is in fact his own? Posited more broadly, is such an identity—an Asian American identity that is of one's own choosing—possible to begin with?

(1) Consider first Ng's 2014 novel *Everything I Never Told You*. Ng's book has resonated with diverse reading publics for a variety of reasons but not necessarily for the theme of racial passing. Yet, working with characters who are explicitly aware of their status as Asian Americans of mixed-race heritage in white middle America, her novel astutely, albeit implicitly,

imagines the centrality of passing for how Asian Americans think of themselves. In this novel, passing is less about passing as white and, perhaps surprisingly so, more about passing as Asian.

Ng's novel, set in 1970s Ohio, tells the story of an interracial, Asian-white family: James Lee, a Chinese immigrant, and Marilyn Lee, a white Southerner who meets James while both are studying at Harvard, and their children Lydia, Nathan (or "Nath"), and Hannah. While the mysterious death of Lydia, the eldest of the three Lee family children, structures and drives the narrative momentum of Ng's novel, Ng enlivens the main plot of the book with racial encounters centered on the social liabilities of the Lee family's "Chinese appearance." It is in the ways in which the Lee family deals with the social liabilities of their "Chineseness" that we are able to imagine how the very concept of passing underlines their daily interactions with others.

At least two narrative moments from the novel are particularly revealing. First, unlike their missing sister Lydia, Nath and Hannah take after her Chinese father more so than their white mother. Nath recalls when "a woman stopped the two of them in the grocery store and asked, 'Chinese?' and when they said yes, not wanting to get into halves and wholes, she'd nodded sagely. 'I knew it,' she said. 'By the eyes.' She'd tugged the corner of each eye outward with a fingertip."[33] Despite their interracial status, it is their morphology that defines who they are; they cannot hide it. And while Nath and his sister Lydia recoil from such imposed identity, they find it easier to yield to it, rather than expending the kind of intellectual and rhetorical effort that might be necessary to introduce complexity to racially simplistic either/or notions (assuming such effort would, in the end, make a difference in the way they are perceived). So they choose to pass as Chinese, given their inability to hide those features that signal their Asianness. Though biracial—Chinese and white—they remain too Chinese in appearance to be accepted as anything but Chinese, in some sense of that identity.

That same fate applies to Lydia even though she looks more like her white mother Marilyn: "But Lydia, defying genetics, somehow has her mother's blue eyes."[34] Those blue eyes, rather than disrupting racial perceptions, are found perplexing to Lydia's white school friend Jack (who Nath suspects is behind the disappearance of Lydia). In a passage that explores the early relationship between Lydia and Jack, we are given a glimpse of the

33. Ng, *Everything I Never Told You*, 23.
34. Ng, *Everything I Never Told You*, 23.

kind of alienation and distance Lydia experiences in her Ohio town. "I've never seen a Chinese person with blue eyes," Jack declares. Then, the reader is told, "Even with blue eyes, [Lydia] could not pretend she blended in."[35]

Ng, however, does not portray Jack as a person who is simply unwilling to be challenged by his racial perplexity. That perplexity, perhaps out of his closeness to Lydia, leads Jack to a moment of attempted empathy, to see the world from Lydia's point of view. He asks, "What's it like?"[36] Lydia begins to form a response:

> "What's it like?" . . . Sometimes you almost forgot: that you don't look like everyone else. In homeroom or at the drugstore or at the supermarket, you listened to morning announcements or dropped off a roll of film or picked out a carton of eggs and felt like just another someone in the crowd. Sometimes you didn't think about it at all. And then sometimes you noticed the girl across the aisle watching, the pharmacist watching, the checkout boy watching, and you saw yourself reflected in their stares: incongruous. Catching the eye like a hook. Every time you saw yourself from the outside, the way other people saw you, you remembered all over again. You saw it in the sign at the Peking Express—a cartoon man with a coodie hat, slant eyes, buckteeth, and chopsticks. You saw it in the little boys on the playground, stretching their eyes to slits with their fingers—*Chinese—Japanese—look at these*—and in the older boys who muttered *ching chong ching chong ching* as they passed you on the street, just loud enough for you to hear. You saw it when waitresses and policemen and bus drivers spoke slowly to you, in simple words, as if you might not understand. You saw it in photos, yours the only black head of hair in the scene, as if you'd been cut out and pasted in. You thought: *Wait, what's she doing there?* And then you remembered that *she* was *you*. You kept your head down and thought about school, or space, or the future, and tried to forget about it. And you did, until it happened again.[37]

This response, however, remains hidden in her own thoughts. Instead, Lydia responds to Jack's question of what it is like to be Chinese in a white town with "I dunno," hesitant to reveal her sense of alienation and distance from a community she calls home, resigning herself instead *to pass* as an uncontroversial, inconspicuous Chinese kid in Ohio.[38] In fact, that is the

35. Ng, *Everything I Never Told You*, 192.
36. Ng, *Everything I Never Told You*.
37. Ng, *Everything I Never Told You*, 192–93.
38. Ng, *Everything I Never Told You*, 193.

only recourse she has given her white neighbors' fixed regard for her as Chinese. Thus, while Lydia is like Henry's parents in Ardsley, New York, in Lee's *Native Speaker* insofar as she tries to be inconspicuous, she cannot help but be seen as and, thus, be Chinese in some sense. As she realizes, when looking at photos of her and her school friends, she *is* different, just as her white neighbors and friends keep reminding her. She can be inconspicuous, but it has to be inconspicuously Chinese.

Both Lydia and her brother Nath cannot be who they wish to be; they are denied the possibility of self-determination in their inability to be non-Chinese, or in being forced into a kind of reverse passing, passing as Asian. Both Lydia and Nath are tragically curtailed and circumscribed by racial ideals that enfold and discipline their interracial existence, notwithstanding their interraciality. That they are mixed-race persons hardly disrupts the racial imagination of their white neighbors and friends. Thus being Chinese, or at least being accepting of and resigned to the kind of Chineseness that acknowledges difference from whiteness but at the same time is not so different that it is imminently taken as threatening, is Lydia's and Nath's way of surviving the alienating effects of the prevailing whiteness of their town. Sometimes just passing as any kind of Asian (whether Japanese, Chinese, Vietnamese, or Korean, etc.) is the simplest or easiest way to survive, or as Grace, one of the Chinese American characters in Jade Chang's *The Wangs vs. the World* puts it after being pestered by a white man's poor attempt at trying to guess her ethnicity, "Sometimes in these situations the only way to get out was to play dumber than dumb."[39]

(2) The denial of self-determination as Asian American is brought into further relief in Ng's second novel *Little Fires Everywhere*, especially within the context of adoption.[40] What is so interesting about her depiction of adoption in this second novel is how she avoids the almost reflexive admiration for adoption as an act of parental self-gift that is typical in popular culture. Instead, her depiction of a white couple, the McCulloughs of Shaker Heights, Ohio, who have adopted a Chinese American girl, May

---

39. Chang, *The Wangs vs. the World*, 260.

40. A helpful review of the emergence of transracial adoptions as a critical site of inquiry in Asian American studies and literature can be found in Schlund-Vials and Wu, "Rethinking Embodiment," 201–6. The interest in transracial adoption as a theme in Asian American literature is not new, and the two novels referenced below, from Ng and Lisa Ko, continue that literary legacy reflected in novels such as Gen, *Love Wife*, Lee, *Happy Family*, and Truong, *Bitter in the Mouth*.

Ling, is unvarnished, revealing the messy terrain of interracial adoption and the questions of racial identity that it raises.

If Lydia and Nath in Ng's first novel feel alienated precisely because they are pressed to embody and remain within an Asian American identity that is not their own but of prevailing racial perceptions of Asian Americanness, then the adoption of May Ling serves as a more intimate portrait of that kind of alienation and forced passing as Asian American (or at least, a certain kind of Asian American—a stereotypical one). But unlike Lydia and Nath, May Ling is pressed into such an Asian American identity less as a matter of survival and more decisively as a matter of paternalism. The notion that racial paternalism is what presses her into a specific Asian American identity is magnified by the fact that May Ling is not only an adoptee but also an *infant* adoptee who has no real agency of her own. As such, she is, in no uncertain terms, subject to the paternal benevolence of her adopted parents who claim that they know what is best for her, even when it comes to her identity as an Asian American.

Such racial paternalism is on vivid display when the birth mother, Bebe Chow, discovers that the McCulloughs are the ones who have adopted May Ling, now named Mirabelle, and wishes May Ling to return to her custody. (We soon learn that Bebe Chow abandoned May Ling at the Shaker Heights fire station when she was only a couple months old out of dire economic hardship and has since then recovered financially and never intended to give up May Ling permanently.) The McCulloughs refuse to rescind the adoption and Bebe Chow, with the help of Mia Warren, the main character of the novel, forces the issue into public view, appealing to local news outlets and suing the McCulloughs in court. As the controversy swirls, supporters of the McCulloughs insist that they "were rescuing Mirabelle . . . They were giving an unwanted child a better life."[41] Supporters of Chow, however, insisted, "She's a *Chinese* baby. She's going to grow up not knowing anything about her heritage. How is she going to know who she is?"[42] In an interview with Channel 3, a local news station, the McCulloughs respond to such questions with the following: "'We're trying to be very sensitive to that,' she said. 'You'll notice that we're adding more and more Asian art to our walls.' She waved a hand at the scrolls with ink-brushed mountains that hung by the fireplace, the glazed pottery horse on the mantel. 'We're committed, as she gets older, to teaching her about her

41. Ng, *Little Fires Everywhere*, 152.
42. Ng, *Little Fires Everywhere*, 152.

birth culture. And of course she already loves the rice. Actually, it was her first solid food."[43] When the trial to determine permanent custody of May Ling finally takes place, the McCulloughs reiterate their cultural-ethnic custodial responsibilities, "Pearl of the Queen is one of our very favorite restaurants. We try to take her there once a month. I think it's good for her to hear some Chinese, to get it into her ears. To grow up feeling this is natural. And of course I'm sure she'll love the food once she's older . . . Perhaps we could take a Chinese cooking class at the rec center and learn together. When she's older."[44]

The McCulloughs's insistence that they in fact know what it means for May Ling to be Chinese—eating rice, enjoying the cuisine at Pearl of the Orient, speaking Chinese—echoes the kind of cultural-racial paternalism we find in Pete and Kay Wilkinson in Lisa Ko's *The Leavers* (2017). Pete and Kay are the adopted parents of Deming Guo, who as an adolescent was left behind after his mother, an illegal Asian immigrant, was deported to China. Deming often wonders of his birth mother's whereabouts, yearning to be reunited with her and living once again with his childhood Chinese friends in both the Bronx and, earlier, in Manhattan's Chinatown.

That desire is in one sense denied inasmuch as he is now in the legal custody and guardianship of the Wilkinsons; he is no longer Deming but renamed Daniel by them. But that desire is also denied insofar as Deming, or Daniel, is persistently confronted with Peter's and Kay's imposition of what *they think* constitutes Daniel's Chineseness. So while we find them throughout the novel fretting over whether they and Daniel are genuinely bonded as a family, Pete and Kay also worry about whether they are sufficiently attending to the preservation and cultivation of Daniel's Chinese identity and heritage, the legitimacy of which they do not question but assume they know what that means as if almost obvious. Note Kay's somewhat rhetorical question, "I mean, should we cook Chinese food? Or start Mandarin lessons again?" as if being Chinese goes hand-in-hand with eating Chinese food and speaking Mandarin.[45] Or, when in New York City, visiting friends Elaine and Jim, who are also parents of a Chinese adoptee named Angel, Elaine proclaims, "The lion dance and the fan dance, all the different dances. I can't keep track. It's so good for the kids to connect to their culture. That way they'll still know how to be Chinese." And

43. Ng, *Little Fires Everywhere*, 153.

44. Ng, *Little Fires Everywhere*, 260–61.

45. Ng, *Little Fires Everywhere*, 75.

then, while at a Chinese restaurant on Mott Street in Manhattan, Elaine's husband Jim turns to Deming and asks, "You must miss this, Daniel, having authentic Chinese food."[46]

In asking such questions, Pete and Kay, as well as their friends Elaine and Jim, are not too removed from the McCulloughs in Ng's *Little Fires Everywhere*. Not only do they assume that they know what it means to be Chinese or do Chinese things, but they see it as their responsibility to ensure that their adoptees experience and learn what they know of their supposed Chineseness. In the case of the McCulloughs, May Ling has no choice given her status as infant. In the case of the Wilkinsons, Deming, who was adopted as an older child, finds himself in a sustained struggle to exert his own sense of himself as Chinese American in the face of his adopted parents ethno-racial and cultural tutelage. For the most part, he is consigned to being Chinese American in his white adopted parents' image and not his own.

(3) Just as the motif of Asian American adoption sharpens the ways in which Asian Americans are unable to determine their own sense of themselves as Asian American, so too the motif of American imperialism in Viet Thanh Nguyen's *The Sympathizer* (2015). Like Deming and May Ling, the main character and narrator in Nguyen's novel, who remains nameless throughout, bears the pressure to embody and remain within, that is, pass into an Asian American identity that is not his own, or not one that he desires. And like Deming and May Ling, he is pressed to embody such an Asian American identity because that is the identity that is *considered for him* by non-Asians as truthful. In Nguyen's novel, it is white America that knows what is best for Asia and Asian Americans alike. That sense of American imperialism, and the sense of enlightened stewardship that goes with it, is weaved in the very setting of the novel, in the immediate aftermath of the Vietnam War.

Relocated to California, the narrator, a Vietnamese communist (who we learn is a double agent, working for the Viet Cong) struggles to transcend myopic representations of Vietnamese people that he encounters almost everywhere he goes in his adopted home of Los Angeles. In other words, he struggles to be seen in the way he desires to be seen. That desire to be seen on his own terms takes on multiple dimensions. Interestingly, Nguyen provides a narrator who is half French and half Vietnamese. The nameless narrator soon discovers that such interraciality benefits him little

---

46. Ng, *Little Fires Everywhere*, 87, 88.

even if it enables him to act more white, since he appears more Vietnamese, which overridingly governs the way he is perceived. Consider how he begrudges the way he thinks Violet, the assistant to a Hollywood movie director who we will discuss below, looks at him: "But now, even though I was a card-carrying American with a driver's license, Social Security card, and resident alien permit, Violet still considered me as foreign, and this recognition punctured the smooth skin of my self-confidence. Was I just being paranoid, that all-American characteristic? . . . The flawlessness of my English did not matter."[47]

While he is unable to be white, or accepted as fully white, the narrator also discovers that he is only permitted to be the kind of Asian that white Americans think he is, or perhaps want him to be. We gain a sense of that constriction in his continued resentment over Violet's attitude toward him when he thinks that her inability to see him as genuinely American is a function of "her retinas [having been] burned with the images of all the castrati dreamed up by Hollywood to steal the place of real Asian men." He continues, "Here I speak of those cartoons named Fu Manchu, Charlie Chan, Number One Son, Hop Sing—*Hop Sing!*—and the bucktoothed, bespectacled Jap not so much played as mocked by Mickey Rooney in *Breakfast at Tiffany's*. The performance was so insulting it even deflated my fetish for Audrey Hepburn, understanding as I did her implicit endorsement of such loathsomeness."[48]

But the persistence of those myopic, dehumanizing representations is none other than a particular iteration of a larger insistence Asian Americans are subjected to. Consider the narrator's exchange with Ms. Mori, the Japanese American woman who is the assistant to the chair of the Oriental Studies Department at a local university in Los Angeles. In response to the narrator's question about the length of Ms. Mori's employment with the chair of the department, Ms. Mori responds sharply:

> Call me Sofia, for Chrissakes . . . I can't help he's a little disappointed in me because I don't bow whenever I see him. When he interviewed me, he wanted to know whether I spoke any Japanese. I explained I was born in Gardena [California]. He said, Oh, you nisei, as if knowing that one word means he knows something about me. You've forgotten your culture, Ms. Mori, even though you're only second generation. Your nisei parents, they hung on to

47. Nguyen, *Sympathizer*, 127.
48. Nguyen, *Sympathizer*, 127, emphases original.

their culture. Don't you want to learn Japanese? Don't you want to visit Nippon? For a long time I felt bad. I wondered why I didn't want to learn Japanese, why I didn't already speak Japanese, why I would rather go to Paris or Istanbul or Barcelona rather than Tokyo. But then I thought, *Who cares?* Did anyone ask John F. Kennedy if he spoke Gaelic and visited Dublin or if he ate potatoes every night or if he collected paintings of leprechauns? So why are *we* supposed to not forget *our* culture?[49]

Not only are Asian Americans confined to being Asian Americans—we are expected to not forget our culture; to be a particular kind of cultural being—Ms. Mori's (or Sofia's) frustrations powerfully capture the kind of paternalism that characterizes the Asian American confinement to a particular kind of Asian Americanness. Whereas Sofia and Nath in Ng's first novel must remain Asian American in order to fit in a predominately white society, Ms. Mori indicates the need for Asian Americans to remain Asian American because that is what non-Asian Americans think is best for Asian Americans. "You've forgotten your culture . . . Don't you want to learn Japanese?" recalls Ms. Mori being asked by her employer the department chair as if he knows her better than she knows herself. But while she rejects such paternalism, she sadly resigns herself to it, feeling the force of its discipline. As she notes, in response, "I just smiled and said, You're so right, sir."[50]

The practical futility of resisting such paternalistic representations is imaginatively depicted in part of the novel where the narrator is asked to serve as a consultant to a movie about the Vietnam War. The movie, the narrator tells us, portrays Vietnamese soldiers and villagers who lack any speaking roles, other than the requisite scream when killed by American GIs. Appalled by the depiction of Vietnamese as essentially nameless, personality-less, and voiceless, the narrator attempts to convince the director of the movie, who the narrator refers to as the "Auteur," to have the Vietnamese, when dying, at least scream in a way that is more "Vietnamese," not "AIIIEEEEE!!!" as the script has it, "when villager #3 is impaled by a Viet Cong punji trap . . . Or when the LITTLE GIRL sacrifices her life to alert the Green Berets to the Viet Cong sneaking into the village." But instead, "AIEYAAHHH!!! . . . That's how we scream in my country."[51]

49. Nguyen, *Sympathizer*, 75, emphases original.
50. Nguyen, *Sympathizer*, 75.
51. Nguyen, *Sympathizer*, 131.

Whether there is a characteristically Vietnamese scream is not really the narrator's point. Rather, the point of the narrator's sarcastic correction of the sounds of Vietnamese death is to impress upon the Auteur that the movie's portrayal of its Vietnamese characters is debasing. Where is the particularity that animates these characters as Vietnamese persons? Yet, the Auteur is unmoved and, instead, indignant at the narrator's lack of his own self-understanding and, thus, unmerited correction of the Auteur's script. Aggressively, the Auteur responds by claiming learned superiority, "I researched your country, my friend. I read Joseph Buttinger and Frances FitzGerald. He's the foremost historian on your little part of the world. And she won the Pulitzer Prize. She dissected your psychology. I think I know something about you people."[52] Despite the narrator's continued protestations of the script's inaccuracies, the narrator, like Ms. Mori, resigns himself to the sad conclusion that "in this forthcoming Hollywood trompe l'oeil, all the Vietnamese of any side would come out poorly, herded into the roles of the poor, the innocent, the evil, or the corrupt. Our fate was not to be merely mute; we were to be struck dumb."[53] The only agency that he or his fellow Vietnamese had was to be represented by their American, self-described liberators. For the narrator, the control that Hollywood exerts over how Vietnamese are depicted parallels how American society controls the representation of Asian Americans more generally.[54]

BEING WHITE AND BEING ASIAN: MIRROR OPPOSITES

In Janice Y. K. Lee's *The Expatriates* (2016), we are introduced to two Asian American expats in Hong Kong. The first, Mercy, a Korean American woman and a recent graduate of Columbia University. The second, Margaret, the mother of three children who will eventually be cared for by Mercy as their nanny. In one of their first introductions, Mercy, almost as an epiphany, asks Margaret, "Are you half [Asian]?" "A quarter," Margaret responds. The reader is told that Margaret is "a little surprised" that she would be asked such a question, perhaps partly because she was taken aback that someone would see her as other than white. "Most people can't tell," as Margaret states. She then adds that her Asian heritage was never emphasized by her parents given that she was raised "in a very homogeneous [white]

52. Nguyen, *Sympathizer*, 130.

53. Nguyen, *Sympathizer*, 134.

54. Nguyen, *Sympathizer*, 179.

neighborhood." While her father was half Korean, he "didn't like growing up Asian in California at the time. There wasn't very many."[55]

Margaret simply assumes two racial possibilities for herself and her children who, like her, are of racially mixed heritage. For Margaret, they can be either Asian or white. That assumption reveals itself more explicitly in one tragic instance when we find her obsessing over the possible reasons for her youngest son G's disappearance during a family vacation to Seoul, South Korea. As she obsesses over what could have happened to G, she also begins to think about how if he had only looked more white rather than Asian then he would have been in the clear:

> But sometimes she'll read in the paper that in China and India, children are kidnapped and maimed so that they become more compelling and effective beggars. In other countries, kids are taken for their organs, but those are usually the older ones, older than G. There's the sex trade, of course. This is what she has to digest. G, her one-eighth Asian child, who actually could pass for Asian. They would never have taken light-haired Daisy, who looks white. Too much trouble, a foreigner's child, too much media attention, potential for international conflict. But Daisy and Philip look white. G looks Asian. Only G had that one recessive gene pushed to the fore, that stubborn Asian DNA strand that burst when he was made, so that while he's recognizable as her child— only one person has ever asked her if he's adopted—he looks quite recognizably Asian. So he has dissolved into the fifty million other Korean people on the peninsula.[56]

That Margaret assumes the possibility of only two racial modalities—Asian or white—is maintained by the narrowness of genetic heritage, or at least her unwillingness to imagine outside those genetic confines. Whatever the reasons, her assumption succinctly encapsulates the range of racial options that are presented to us in our discussion above of the novels by Park, Yang, Ng, Ko, and Nguyen. But against the backdrop of these novels, Margaret's assumption that there are only two racial possibilities for someone like her and her children takes on an added dimension. If Asian Americans can only be either white or Asian, then they can only be white or Asian in *predefined* senses of those identities, which means they are identities made available to them to be received, adopted, enacted, performed.

55. Lee, *Expatriates*, 40.
56. Lee, *Expatriates*, 122.

As predefined, the choice between white or Asian, however, cannot be taken as a choice between embracing a false, corrupted identity (whiteness) and a more truthful identity (Asianness). But that does not necessarily mean that being white is something to be celebrated either. Both racial identities are problematic and, in a way, tragic. That judgment may seem unfair in the case of Jane's embrace of whiteness in *Re Jane*, an embrace that enables her to find a level of freedom she did not experience prior to her living into the celebrity status of being a "California blond." Yet, we can be uneasy with her embrace of whiteness and the liberation she ultimately finds in that embrace, not only because, as we discussed in chapter 3, Asian Americans are subject to the manipulating allure of whiteness and, ultimately, its false promise of full social inclusion and acceptance. To be sure, she is half white and half Korean, so ignoring her "white half" would be equally questionable. But, as discussed earlier, Jane does not find liberation in some innovative hybrid reimagination of herself but in the envy that her friends show in the fact that she looks white. In claiming that the new California blond (meaning California white) is all the rage, that affirmation leads her to embrace herself as white and not someone in between whiteness and Korean or different from both (neither/nor), and certainly not just Korean. She ends up re-inscribing the prevailing privileges and sense of freedom that are commonly associated with whiteness in American society. For instance, to be white is to be free of the kind of familial expectations that white persons do not seem to be burdened by. Viewed from Yang's *American Born Chinese*, her turn to whiteness amounts to no more than a denial of the fullness of who she is. She is the antithesis of Jin's reversion back to his true self, to his Chineseness.

But being Asian is not necessarily what it appears to be, or at least that is what we can glean from Ng's, Ko's, and Nguyen's novels. What is so unsettling about the Asian American characters who are depicted in their novels is that they are in one way or another forced to be a certain kind of Asian. Put in a slightly different way, they cannot escape their Asianness or, more specifically, a caricatured sense of that identity. Nath and Lydia in Ng's first novel are emblematic of that inescapability, that is, the power of white racial conventions to overtly constrain and delimit Asian American identity and agency. Inasmuch as Ng's characters cannot escape their Chineseness—because they look foreign, different, not white—they are forced to live into a predefined sense of that identity. In the case of Deming in *The Leavers* and the nameless narrator in *The Sympathizer*, the inescapability of their Asianness (Chinese and Vietnamese, respectively) is regarded less as a malevolent imposition, but as a benevolent act of those who know the truth of a people better than they know themselves. That Ng and Ko help us to think about being Asian American in such a paternalistic way through the metaphor of Asian American adoption unsettles the very magnanimity of Asian adoption and the assumed givenness of what it means to be Asian American.

The inability of Asian Americans to be Asian American on their own terms is summarized well in the anger of the narrator in Weike Wang's *Chemistry* (2017). Consternations over whether her American identity has eroded her Chinese identity spills over into anger while watching a cooking competition television show featuring a Chinese American chef. The narrator tells us that the chef shares her upbringing with the judges, how her family dissuaded her from a chef's life. "But here she is. Ready to fight." "I am a chef and not a sheep," she roars. "There is then a round of applause from the judges. Bravo, they say, to have found your own voice and rebelled," the narrator recounts. "But something about the way she tells her story frustrates me," the narrator retorts.[57] She continues, "I am also angry at these judges. Why encourage this of us, to constantly rebel, without understanding why some of us do not?"[58] But if that question were to suggest that Asian Americans can choose to be someone other than what the judges—proxies for white America—tell Asian Americans to be, note the narrator's sarcastic resignation: what kind of Asian can one be other than what will be inevitably perceived by white Americans as a miserable existence. "And my mother is quiet like a lot of Asian mothers. And my father is strict like a lot of Asian fathers. And we are unhappy like a lot of Asian families."[59] If the judges think being that kind of Asian is dismal, then it must be dismal. Can Asian Americans who seek to be "traditionally" Asian somehow shake off that perception, or are they only permitted to be dismal people, lest they decide to be rebellious Asians? But is not rebelliousness also a definition of Asianness that is predefined by another?

57. Wang, *Chemistry*, 154.
58. Wang, *Chemistry*, 155.
59. Wang, *Chemistry*, 154.

PASSING AND THE DISEMBODIED ASIAN AMERICAN:
THE BLACKNESS OF ASIAN AMERICAN IDENTITY

The normative pressure that predefined racial identities exert on Asian Americans in the novels discussed above is characteristic of the general logic of passing. So while these novels are not literary studies in racial passing per se, to the extent that they present characters whose choices with respect to identity are limited and yet find the need to choose within that confine, their characters collectively raise the question of passing. That is, the question of whether the identities Asian Americans have are no more than the identities that they *must* have as dictated by the prevailing racial preferences and assumptions of society.

Recalling Bantum's observation, the practice of passing reveals the inescapability of predefined racial ideals that necessarily constrain and orient agency toward the performance of those predefined racial ideals. Performativity in this context differs slightly from the philosopher Judith Butler's use of it to connote "a way of understanding the materialization of gender and sex as seemingly natural categories." That applies to race as well.[60] For Bantum, however, the performance of predefined racial ideals reveals the very falsity of those ideals insofar as they must be enacted, they are not "natural" to any one person or group of persons; they are an act. That is in large measure the fate of the characters depicted in the novels by Park, Yang, Ng, Ko, and Nguyen, among others referenced above. In their whiteness or Asianness, their characters perform—or at least face the constant pressure to perform—identities that are made available to them by others, namely, white persons or, more broadly, a culture of whiteness. Accentuating or elevating the lightness of one's skin, the blondness of one's hair, or, simply, the whiteness of one's appearance are all performative in some sense, an act of following a predefined script of what it means to be a particular kind of person or identity so that one looks like, and can pass for, that identity. In that way, the "phenomenon of deliberate racial passing" is more than, as Nguyen puts it, simply a "close second" to "the successful assimilation of a minority onto whiteness."[61] They are one and the same. But if assimilating in its performativity is a kind of passing, then *not* assimilating, that is, not being white or, more specifically, in this case, being Asian, is also a form of passing. For Nath, Lydia, Deming, and the nameless narrator

60. Chuh and Shumukawa, "Adjudicating Asian America," 38.
61. Nguyen, *Race and Resistance*, 36.

(in *The Sympathizer*), being Asian American, *performing* a certain kind of Asianness, is the only real option that they are allowed.

There are attempts at resistance, to be sure. We see signs of resistance in Ko's *The Leavers* when Deming, in learning that his birth mother was deported to China, leaves his adopted parents Kay and Peter for China. However, barring the complete removal of oneself from the United States and its racial pressures, resistance to racial performance is an uphill battle. The nameless narrator's attempt at sarcastic praise of the Auteur's script about the Vietnam War, as we saw, fails spectacularly, resulting in the narrator, despite having gone through the Vietnam War, being lectured on what the Auteur has learned from the leading scholars of the war. Even recall, in Choi's *American Woman*, Jenny Yamada's sharp but ultimately fruitless retorts to Juan's unwavering characterization of her as third world. Given the futility of resistance, it is disquieting—or maybe understandable—that, for instance, Nath and Lydia resign in conformity to a particular racial performance, which for them means passing as a certain kind of Asian, one that is stereotypically relatable, palatable, or recognizable to white America.

What, then, are the realistic possibilities of being Asian on one's own terms rather than the disciplining terms of prevailing cultural, ethno-racial stereotypes? One critical value of construing the characters discussed thus far in this chapter as passing into either one racial modality or another is how such passing necessarily brings to the fore the question of agency. To be sure, there are social advantages to passing, most obviously when it comes to passing as white. Jane's sense of freedom in her embrace of whiteness given whiteness's cultural hegemony and, to an extent, Jin's transformation into Danny in his desire to be liked by his white peers, all testify to the advantages of assimilating or passing into whiteness. Even passing as Asian, in the ways Ng's, Ko's, and Nguyen's characters are apt to do, indicate the advantages of passing; in their cases, perhaps more so than in the cases of Park's and Yang's characters, passing as Asian ensures their survival, a survival that is made possible by accepting their minority status—their Asianness—in the social order. Thus, while the social advantages to passing make passing a not unreasonable mode of being in the world, the trade-off for passing is the curtailment of one's agency. That is not to suggest that the trade-off is a fair or, ultimately, just one. It is, more precisely, tragic. Whatever the social advantages that are gained from passing, whether as white or Asian, to pass is to be somebody always on someone else's terms. That reality comes into sharp relief when we come to grips with, especially, the struggles of passing as Asian. If Asian Americans cannot even be Asian on their own terms, then what it means for Asian Americans to be agents is problematic. Even more so if the only other viable option is to be white; this is Jane's option in Park's novel.

We can ask the question of agency in a more pointed manner by noting Nguyen's narrator's bleak assessment of white America's power over Asian America, mediated through Hollywood's representations of Asian Americans, as in the Auteur's Vietnam War movie. The narrator asserts, "They owned the means of production, and therefore the means of representation, and the best that we could ever hope for was to get a word in edgewise before our anonymous deaths."[62] But how realistic is that hope? To what extent are Asian Americans able—allowed—to "get a word in edgewise," a word that is their own rather than the voice of another? Given that the narrator was unable to get the Auteur to rewrite the way the Vietnamese soldiers in his movie yell in pain with a different intonation dims those prospects. Inasmuch as the narrator is resigned to their eventual "anonymous deaths," those dim prospects are sealed. If so, Asian Americans, metaphorically speaking, are dead already. If dead, then incapable of self-determination indeed.

The inability of Asian Americans to get a word in edgewise before their anonymous deaths recasts the question of Asian American agency in a markedly embodied, or more accurately, disembodied way. To some extent, an anonymous death is an oxymoron of sorts. To be anonymous is akin to being dead inasmuch as being nameless is to be nobody (or, literally, to have no body). But Asian Americans are not disembodied if by that we mean they have no identities; they are not completely anonymous. As Margaret in *The Expatriates* reminds us, the racial options availed to Asian Americans are to be either Asian or American (white). But given the provenance of those identities—identities that are made available to them to have—those identities raise the question of whether Asian Americans are only able to live in or "pass" into bodies sculpted by the ideals and perceptions of those other than themselves.

This question is centrally about the state of Asian American self-determination and the importance of the Asian American body as the site for that evaluation, and casts an ominous shadow over the proposition the "city" places before its residents, as we saw earlier with Henry Park in Lee's *Native Speaker*. Either one is to make oneself belong to the city or one must

62. Nguyen, *Sympathizer*, 179.

go. The terms of belonging, however, may very well be the city's terms (if the city is taken as a symbol of white assimilationist discourse) and not necessarily the terms of its individual residents. As the literary scholar Patricia P. Chu insightfully observes, Henry's assertion that the city requires its residents to belong prefigures the nature of that belonging for the non-white person. *Native Speaker* ends with Henry accompanying his white wife, Lelia, a substitute teacher of English to kids who are non-English as first language speakers. After spending three hours with these students in a Lower East Side school, Lelia offers a sticker to each student. "She uses the class list to write their names inside the sunburst-shaped badge. Everybody, she says has been a good citizen," narrates Henry Park. "She will say the name, quickly writes on the sticker, and then have me press it to each of their chests as they leave."[63] Lelia's act of recognizing these foreign students as good citizens, Chu notes, affirms that "these pupils of English will one day be assimilated subjects." This is only the beginning of their journey toward inhabiting white bodies, or having the cultural and social skills to pass as white. Yet, Chu draws attention to Henry's positionality in this last scene, for "only Lelia is empowered to recognize the children [as citizens and affirm their subjectivity], while Henry, her husband, is merely her assistant." But this is not simply a case of playing second fiddle, serving as sidekick; Henry's status as assistant goes more problematically deeper than that. For it is Lelia who "becomes the person who calls the names" of the students and in so doing affirms who they are, and Henry becomes like the students, "who can only be called."[64] His agency, therefore, is only subordinate to the life-granting, life-affirming agency of Lelia. Their names and, thus, their embodied existence, is rendered present, belonging to the city, in her recognition and affirmation of their names as *she* speaks and pronounces them. Without her affirmation, their names are perhaps inferior in their foreignness; she renders their names respectable.

Why it matters to reflect on the names or, more specifically, the bodies, that *are made available* for Asian Americans to adopt—assimilate or pass into—is starkly laid out by Ta-Nehisi Coates's *Between the World and Me*, a book penned as a father's letter to his son about being black in America. Coates writes that the goal of the so-called "American Dream," by which he euphemistically means whiteness, is to force and maintain disembodied black persons. In other words, in order to sustain, protect the white middle

63. Lee, *Native Speaker*, 349.
64. Chu, *Assimilating Asians*, 3.

class ideal, black bodies have to be disciplined into behaving in a manner that is appropriate to that ideal. Part of that discipline is to render the black body inferior. That includes "the larger culture's erasure of black beauty," which Coates concludes is "intimately connected to the destruction of black bodies."[65] What makes a black body—the life of a black person—respectable is if it acts, dresses, talks, and moves according to (that is, yields or passes into) the ideal of the white body. For Coates, such a disciplined, inferior black body is, in effect, to be *no-body* at all—to be disembodied—since it means having a body that is not one's own but defined and controlled by another. And such control is tantamount to violence, the use of violence to induce fear and, ultimately, submission to the normativity of whiteness:

> Disembodiment is a kind of terrorism, and the threat of it alters the orbit of all our lives and, like terrorism, this distortion is intentional. Disembodiment . . . The demon that pushed the middle-class black survivors into aggressive passivity, our conversation restrained in public quarters, our best manners on display, our hands never out of pockets, our whole manner ordered as if to say, "I make no sudden moves." Disembodiment.[66]

Coates underscores the pressures of whiteness on African Americans to pass as a certain kind of African American, one who is passive, restrained, or disciplined by the whiteness that seeks to maintain its social hegemony. To be a different kind of African American, a non-passive kind, is to be marginalized from the center of American social and political life as explicit threats to that center. Whichever path African Americans take, the point for Coates is that African Americans are in essence disembodied beings with no real capacity to determine for themselves the terms of their own existence and rightful place in American society. Such pessimism stands in tension with Coates's recollection of a mother who pleads, even though her son was murdered by a white man for simply being black, to be fearless in being one's own person: "You exist. You matter. You have value. You have every right to wear your hoodie, to play your music as loud as you want. You have every right to be you. And no one should deter you from being

---

65. Coates, *Between the World and Me*, 44. On the negative, violent impact of body image or aesthetics on black bodies, see also Copeland, "Body, Representation," 180–98. On the sexualized nature of this impact, see, for instance, Massingale, "Erotic Life of Anti-Blackness," 173–94, and Douglas, "More than Skin Deep," 3–18.

66. Coates, *Between the World and Me*, 114.

you. You have to be you. And you can never be afraid to be you."[67] Despite his remembrance of that extraordinarily courageous exhortation, Coates intimates that the prospects for African Americans to be some body in their own ways can seem grim at best and unrealistic at worst.

In surveying the range of characters that populate the novels by the Asian American authors discussed above—in paying attention to the motives behind the kind of lives they choose or adopt—does the condition of the black body (the disembodied black body), as Coates describes, also apply to Asian American bodies? It is debatable whether Asian American bodies are under the identical kind of daily assault that black bodies bear. Asian Americans, unlike African Americans, were not subject to the brutality of American chattel slavery. Yet, as discussed in chapter 3, Asian Americans have not been immunized from that legacy, as the history of exclusionary sentiments suggest. Also recall earlier in this chapter Sui Jin Far's recollection of a town clerk who asserts, "Souls . . . Their bodies are enough for me. A Chinaman is, in my eyes, more repulsive than a n****r." Such exclusionary sentiments continue in contemporary anti-immigration discourse. Hate crimes and discriminatory police actions are also not uncommon elements of Asian American experience, even if they go unnoticed in mainstream media outlets, as noted in chapter 1. Still, one-to-one comparisons between Asian Americans and African Americans misses the larger, more disquieting, picture of the nature of whiteness and its effects on the agency of nonwhite persons, black or Asian. It is this larger picture that makes Coates's account of violence against black bodies universally relevant, and specifically, that binds the experience of black bodies to Asian American bodies. Inasmuch as many of the characters in the Asian American novels surveyed in this chapter are pressed to pass, whether as white or Asian, these novels together portray a world in which Asian Americans are under a kind of bodily assault too, if by assault we mean to be the subject of a hostile external power. So, just as "the Dream," as Coates puts it, of the white American middle-class ideal demands disembodiment of African Americans so that they can ultimately pass into neutered, "sanitized" black bodies deemed appropriate to the safety and prosperity of "the Dream," that same racial dynamic appeals to and oftentimes outright expects and demands Asian Americans to embody or pass into identities that are not of their own determination but rather conform to prevailing racial ideals, perceptions, or stereotypes. Recall once more, for instance, Ng's characters,

67. Coates, *Between the World and Me*, 113.

Nath and Lydia in particular, who find it so hard to be someone other than Chinese, or in Park's novel, Jane who finds the "California blond" aesthetic the object of social, cultural desire and, ultimately, the path to personal wholeness and social acceptance. Are they not disembodied Asian Americans, situated in worlds that do not value their bodies *as they are* but only in relation to a standard set by a white racial imagination?

What is perhaps particularly insidious, however, is the ways in which the white racial imagination disembodies Asian Americans. If, as Coates notes, the threat and actual use of physical and legal force (i.e., discriminatory policing, mass incarceration, etc.) are often, for "the Dream," the tools of choice for black disembodiment (or the disciplining of the black body), then for Asian Americans, the primary tools of our disembodiment are more cunning and surreptitious. At least two examples can be drawn. First, disembodiment by way of Asian American self-hatred, which positions the Asian American psyche to be open to more suitable selves. A narrator in Zhang's *Sour Heart* surmises as much when recounting how she acquired her American name Mandee:

> She'll go by Mandee here [after the clothing store Mandee in the Queens Center Mall in New York City], my father said, and just like that, I was renamed. I would have two names, just like all the other Chinese people in America did, just like how my father went by Jerry and my mother went by Susan . . . My father said they needed "American" names on their resumes when applying for jobs; they had to have names that were pronounceable to white American English speakers because they already had faces that were considered vile to look at and who was going to hire someone with their faces *and* their names? I thought my mother and father had beautiful faces but my father corrected me, Not in America. We're ugly, and it's that simple. They look at us and think we're cretins. You think they like us going to their schools? You think they're okay with us working in their offices? Taking their jobs? You think they're happy to pick up laundry and takeout from businesses we've opened? You think they want to go to the corner store and see our eyes and our teeth and our skin looking back at them from behind the counter? No! They don't want us here. They don't want to have to try to pronounce Chinese names. X-U. Q-I-U. They don't want to see that![68]

68. Zhang, *Sour Heart*, 212–13.

Once her father's tirade comes to a conclusion, the narrator adds her own conclusion, "The more my father went on about how much they hated us, the more I started to suspect maybe he was the one who hates us."[69]

Second, there is disembodiment by way of self-forgetfulness, to lack sufficient self-awareness of the identity one in fact is embodying. Such is the modus operandi of assimilationist discourse, which Chang dramatizes in *The Wangs vs. the World*:

> Yes, Barbra [Saina's Taiwanese step-mother] was alone in [Saina's] house, with the keys to her rickety Saab and her [white boyfriend] Graham's phone number in case she needed anything. It had been strange leaving someone else in the house that she'd spent the last few months hiding in and obsessing over. When they were saying goodbye, a thought had struck her.
>
> She's asked Barbra, "Isn't it weird?"
>
> "*Zen yang?*"
>
> "That you're here. I mean, when you were growing up in Taiwan, would you ever have thought that you'd end up spending time alone in a farmhouse in upstate New York? When I bought the place, they told me it was built in 1902. I bet that first farmer would never have expected that some Asian lady would end up in his house."
>
> Barbra had looked at her for a moment, confused. "But you are also some Asian lady."
>
> *Oh god,* [Saina] remembered thinking. *How could I be so obtuse?* "You're right. I guess it felt . . . different? But you're right. That's dumb. It's the same thing."[70]

Being "so obtuse," as Saina puts it, is exactly the point, for being imperceptive of one's identity, that one's identity may not have always been one's identity, masks the ways in which one's own agency is not necessarily dictating the terms of one's own existence.

When we consider how passing plays an integral role in the ways Asian Americans approach their sense of self and exercise their agency, we are necessarily reoriented to thinking about Asian American identity in terms of our bodies. That is, what kind of bodies do Asian Americans have? Why do Asian Americans live in the bodies that they do? And, more normatively, are the bodies Asian Americans have the bodies Asian Americans should have? That latter question goes to the question of Asian American

69. Zhang, *Sour Heart*, 213.

70. Chang, *The Wangs vs. the World*, 312.

agency in a more direct manner, whether the bodies we have are simply consequences of adopting, that is, receiving and accepting, bodies that are "marketed" or in some cases forced upon us by the cultural and social pre-eminence of whiteness, or whether the identities Asian Americans embody are innovative constructs of our own creativity. In asking whether Asian Americans are able to determine who we are in our own self-determinative way, that question is not meant to suggest that Asian Americans, or any persons for that matter, can create themselves *ex nihilo*; I do not want to contravene the case against cultural authenticity mapped out in chapter 2 of this book. But in asking the question of self-determination, that question demands personal and collective soul searching among Asian Americans. It demands that we examine ourselves, who we think we are and, thus, the state of our bodily existence, within an explicit and incontrovertible racial frame; we cannot avoid the racial constraints that bind Asian Americans together as a community of persons and informs how individuals within this community understand themselves. Insofar as passing is a phenom-enon that is made uniquely possible by modern racial constructs—by the performativity of modern conceptions of what it means to be racial be-ings—reflecting on how the logic of passing plays into who Asian Ameri-cans are forces reflective confrontation with how Asian Americans are racially constituted.

In sum, thinking about who we are as Asian Americans in terms of how our bodies are constrained, manipulated, undermined, or disciplined by racial conventions, ideals, and hierarchies is centrally important since it disabuses any sense that Asian Americans are immune from the force of whiteness. Whiteness does not tack toward exclusion on the one hand or the demand to assimilate on the other hand, if by assimilate we mean simply to conform to whiteness or, more specifically, the expectations that whiteness places on nonwhite persons. The white racial demand to assimilate also includes the "option" for Asian Americans to remain Asian American, albeit as Asian Americans who are chastened, disciplined, or, as Coates might put it, rendered passive. Inasmuch as the force of white-ness exerts itself on Asian Americans to inhabit or embody identities that it constructs and insists upon, identities that are either white or, perhaps more disquietingly, Asian, not only is it questionable that Asian Americans have the kind of agency that is befitting full, equal participation in Ameri-can society, it is questionable whether Asian Americans, either individually or collectively, have or have ever had identities that are truly their own.

We have good reasons to wonder, then, whether Coates's refrain for the plight of African Americans is also the refrain that befits the plight of Asian Americans. Disembodiment.

5

Relationality

That's it, thought Barbra. *Now, finally, that was it.* She was going to leave all of them . . . She made a life on her own, and she could do it again! . . . She could marry someone else, or she could move back to Taiwan and make her own fortune! . . . Or better yet, she'd go back to Los Angeles and inform all of their acquaintances that she was actually a feng shui expert . . . And then just like that, with a smack of her own red lips, Charles reclaimed his place. Barbra cursed.

—*The Wangs vs. the World*[1]

To PROPOSE, AS I have, that Asian Americans are constrained in their capacities to determine their own selves is to call attention to the contested nature of Asian American bodies, that is, the ways in which Asian Americans have bodies that are acted upon rather than bodies of their own meaningful freedom. But as I acknowledged at the end of chapter 4, to say that Asian Americans are "acted upon" does not mean that a capacity to create oneself (self-determination) ought to be the goal for Asian Americans if that means freedom apart from relationality. Rather, it is to call distinct attention to how Asian Americans are overdetermined in their relationality; a relationality that is preponderantly misaligned toward the centripetal forces of white racism. Such overdetermination delimits Asian American

---

1. Chang, *The Wangs vs. the World*, 223–25.

agency and calls into question whether Asian Americans can speak of hav-ing a coherent sense of self at all. Furthermore, such overdetermination delimits Asian American agency in ways that are more complicated than, say, how antiblackness operates in the overt subjugation of black bodies. I say overt to indicate the crude bodily violence that disciplines black bodies, including discriminatory policing, incarceration, racial profiling, and aes-thetic disfigurement, though to say such forms of discipline are overt does not necessarily mean that such violence is clearly evident to all persons, black and nonblack alike, even if it is in plain sight. Not simply overt as in the case of antiblackness, the operative logic of whiteness acting on Asian American bodies is more covert and calculating, employing the tactics of allure, sycophantic gestures, beguiling camaraderie, or even a kind of mag-nanimous paternalism, as both chapters 3 and 4 describe. The logic of the model minority myth (almost whiteness) represents a prime form of the distillation of the first three tactics; the affirmation of racial difference and the distinctiveness of Asian American culture, the fourth tactic.

Considering the overdetermination of Asian American agency by the asymmetrical pull of whiteness, what does that reality reveal about the nature of relationality for agency? More specifically, how should Asian Americans think of themselves as relational beings? Is being Asian Ameri-can a radically constitutive mode of being, one that is intrinsically subject to, as Ephesians 6:12 might say, the powers and principalities that work on our bodies, our fleshly existence? Chapter 2 called attention to the impor-tance of relationality for thinking about our cultural selves—the concept of relationality not only undermines the idea of cultural authenticity but, in so doing, accounts for the governing logic of cultural pluralism. I do not wish to flout that claim now, but rather, in light of Asian American experi-ence, I want to ask about the moral traps set by relationality, that is, how relationality serves as threat to the self. This question, furthermore, is not about whether relationality should be questioned as a basic anthropological truth of human personhood, but instead whether the overdetermination of Asian American agency suggests a reconsideration or, at the very least, a broadening of what relationality as a basic anthropological truth entails, that is, about what it means to be relational or social beings.

Those are, of course, fundamental theological matters, but my interest in those questions goes beyond simply articulating how the vitiated free-dom of the Asian American self may weigh in on those questions of theo-logical anthropology, as important as they are. In addition to adjudicating those questions, my interest concerns whether Asian American agency is possible, an agency that is "capable of withstanding and rising above" the imposition of whiteness on the Asian American body.[2] In other words, what are the prospects for Asian American self-determination, or what would it mean for Asian Americans to be self-determining rather than being determined by (and under the constant threat of being determined by) the logic of whiteness? If, as chapter 4 proposes, the only sense of self that Asian Americans can live into is either the white self or Asian self that similarly emanate from whiteness's own imagination of who Asian Americans are, then what might an alternative path that is realistic look like for Asian Americans?

The path must be one of resistance and certainly not one of conformity, since conformity is the situation that threatens Asian American bodies. Again, conformity does not simply mean conforming to some vision of whiteness, but also yielding to a vision of Asianness that whiteness deems truthful. It is the weight of such a twofold conformity that Asian Americans bear. So, the priority must be placed on resistance, if the opposite, which is conformity, names the racial disciplining of Asian American bodies. But what exactly would resistance mean?

It merits noting that it would be a mistake to think that yielding to whiteness in either of the two ways just described simply amounts to submission or capitulation to whiteness. As we discussed in chapter 4, Asian American novels depict conformity in diverse ways, not simply as forms of false liberation or self-betrayal and deception. Yielding to whiteness can itself be a strategy for survival, a mode of enduring the racialized world in which Asian Americans are situated precisely by accepting the racial masks that we are pressed to wear, or pass into. In calling for resistance in this final chapter, however, I am looking beyond resistance in the form of survival to resistance as a means of social rupture and transformation. As such, I am asking whether a theological ethics of resistance that is more than survival is possible. At the same time, I am looking for alternatives to an ethics of resistance as racial sectarianism, or the hope of remaking ourselves on our

2. The formulation of this question is borrowed from Andrew Prevot's parallel articulation of the question of the integrity of the black self. See Prevot, "Sources of a Black Self?," 79. In so borrowing, I am trying to signal that the question of the black self in relation to antiblackness is not unique but reflects a universal struggle for all persons of color under the disciplining regime of whiteness. This is even more apparent on the question of Asian American representation as a possible form of resistance to whiteness that will be discussed below.

own terms while cloistered from popular culture and mainstream society. In such isolationism, whiteness is not so much challenged and dismantled as it is that which one hopes to escape. Such isolationism may also too easily support the impression that what Asian Americans need to do is reclaim, foster, and defend our original cultures and identities, but as I proposed in chapter 2, such hopes for authenticity are not unproblematic. Resistance in the hopes of a post-racial future is not what I have in mind either. Post-racialism can too easily slide into a kind of racial denial and ignorance, trivializing the entrenchment and tenacity of racism's grip on the world.

This final chapter considers the possibility of resistance as social transformation by reconsidering what it means to be relational beings. Reconsideration should not be taken as questioning the fundamental relatedness of human personhood but the need for a fuller description of how we are constituted by our relationships. Such a description is already intimated in our account of the delimited nature of Asian American agency. The task now is to make that description more explicit. Is relationality detrimental to moral agency? How, then, should we approach relationality? How does the delimited nature of Asian American agency inform the adjudication of these questions?

THE TROUBLE WITH RELATIONALITY

In developing an account of black selfhood, the theologian Andrew Prevot responds to those who claim the need to promote more complex and "positive associations with blackness" in contradistinction to those that whiteness advances.[3] It is interesting that such calls for more positive representations correspond to similar calls with respect to Asian American identity. As an example, the literary scholar Karen Fang describes one caustic reaction of a 2002 film by Asian American director Justin Lin called *Better Luck Tomorrow* when shown at the Sundance Film Festival. Unhappy with the film's lead Asian American characters who, despite their professional and educational achievements, turn to a life of crime, a "Sundance audience member . . . demanded of Lin, 'Don't you have a responsibility to paint a more positive and helpful portrait of your community?'"[4] Fang refers to this demand as "'the burden of representation,' or the predicament that minority filmmakers often face when audiences expect them to depict

3. Prevot, "Sources of a Black Self?," 80.
4. Fang, "Globalization, Masculinity," 79–80.

stories that explicitly promote their public identity."[5] Interestingly, this burden is not simply foisted on Asian American producers of culture by Asian Americans themselves, but also white persons who see themselves as allied to the cause of minority recognition; one of the criticisms directed at Lin's film is recounted by Fang as coming from a white attendee of the Sundance Film Festival.

Responding to the burden of representation within an African American context, Prevot outlines at least two reasons why efforts at promoting positive representations of blackness, while important, are problematic. It is worth noting that these problems confront Asian Americans in practically the same way he describes them. First, according to Prevot, "it may underwrite a 'politics of respectability' in which black people are asked constantly to prove their work according to white-centric or perhaps just overly demanding standards of cultural value." In his judgment, this "is a cruel soteriology of works righteousness."[6] From an Asian American frame, it is because Asian Americans have been justified or pardoned as model minorities that works righteousness is possible. Second, Prevot observes that "the goal of promoting positive associations with blackness" ends up focusing "on black persons' supposed conformity to such constructed meanings of blackness," which are often "narrow forms of musical, athletic, comedic, or otherwise stereotypical excellence."[7] As we considered in our study of contemporary Asian American fiction, being Asian American is often no more than conforming to similarly constricted meanings of Asianness, if not the alternative of being white, of a sort.

Both problems, at least in their Asian American iterations, underscore the extent to which the relationality that is constitutive of Asian American identity is one of distortion, pivoting on the asymmetrical pull of whiteness. Even the promotion of positive representations of Asian Americanness cannot escape whiteness as the standard of behavioral appropriateness; that standard is the background against which so-called positive representations are defined. That inescapability is perhaps underscored by the fact that, as noted above, white moviegoers took center stage in taking Lin to task for "making a movie so 'empty and amoral for Asian Americans.'"[8] One can only wonder what the white moviegoer considered as empty and

5. Fang, "Globalization, Masculinity, 79.
6. Prevot, "Sources of a Black Self?," 80.
7. Prevot, "Sources of a Black Self?," 80.
8. Fang, "Globalization, Masculinity," 79.

amoral representations of Asian Americans, what the reference point was for the white critic.

The specter of such relational overdetermination is insufficiently attended to in contemporary attempts at highlighting the centrality of relationality for moral agency. The philosopher Charles Taylor's account is a revealing example of such an inadequacy. Others have observed that Taylor's account of the relationally constituted self falls short of addressing the social and cultural forces (or relations) that undermine the agency of black persons and, more generally, non-Europeans and women.[9] Rehearsing and adding to such finely attuned critiques is not my interest here. While Taylor may not sufficiently attend to the ways in which white racism, along with, for instance, colonialism and patriarchy, have malformed the agency and identity of black persons, in turning to Taylor, my aim is to highlight an example of how the concept of the relational self does not provide an adequate account of how persons are to be self-determining agents within their relational matrixes. In other words, the concept of the relational self, while rightly questioning the conceptual incoherence of the unencumbered self (a self that can be apart from any attachments other than one's own will), does not satisfactorily attend to the ways in which our relationships can go awry. The reality is that our relationships do go awry—racism and sexism are only two indisputable examples of that reality—but how does such a reality come to pass? Paying attention to how Asian American agency is delimited reveals the significance of that question and signals directions toward a fuller reply to it.

For Taylor, relativism is only one instance of modernity's disregard for the relational context of the self. In *The Ethics of Authenticity*, Taylor argues that relativism corresponds to some form of the idea that persons need "no allegiance higher than their own development."[10] Such an idea, therefore, champions a form of reasoning that is fundamentally disentangled from "external" sources, the burdens of tradition, religion, family, and so on. The problem with such a relativistic stance, for Taylor, is that what it means to be someone—that is, the values one champions, what they mean, and why one should prefer them—have no reference point. While the typical retort to such a concern is that "I" should be able to freely determine who I am (identity) and what is important to me, Taylor finds such claims incoher-

9. Prevot, "Sources of a Black Self?," 83. He calls attention to critiques by, among others, Susan Wolf; see Wolf, "Comment," 75–86.

10. Taylor, *Ethics of Authenticity*, 31.

ent. That is not to deny the importance of being an individual person as opposed to simply being one who follows blindly what one is dictated to do, or the kind of person who is beholden to fads, trends, or corporatized visions of happiness. All those result in something other than authenticity. Authenticity is the term Taylor uses to describe the generally held belief that being unique or self-determinative is a personal and social good to be embraced and defended; authenticity, however, does not mean that one can be one's own self simply through one's own decisions as if choices can be made apart from relational reference points. (In this way, Taylor's use of the term authenticity does not diverge from my earlier critique of cultural authenticity in chapter 2.) The premise that decisions can emanate from one's own inner being (as if it is a matter of discovering what one's true passions are, as is often said, for instance) is where the incoherence of the unencumbered self comes in. One cannot, as Taylor argues, simply "determine what is significant, either by decision, or perhaps unwittingly and unwillingly by just feeling that."[11] For instance, "I couldn't just *decide* that the most significance action is wiggling my toes in warm mud. Without a special explanation, this is not an intelligible claim . . . So I wouldn't know what sense to attribute to someone allegedly *feeling* that this was so. What could someone *mean* who said this?"[12]

The determination of significance—that is, why one choice is meaningful rather than another choice and why it is a choice I ought to make—is made possible because of our intrinsic relationality. Far from being the kind of atomistic, individualistic beings that we think we are, it is because we are related to others, in dialogue with these others, that we develop a sense of what is important. As Taylor writes,

> We are expected to develop our own opinions, outlook, stances to things, to a considerable degree through solitary reflection. But this is not how things work with important issues, such as the definition of our identity. We define this always in *dialogue with, sometimes in struggle against*, the identities our significant others want to recognize in us. And even when we outgrow some of the latter—our parents, for instance—and they disappear from our lives, the *conversation* with them continues within us as long as we live.[13]

11. Taylor, *Ethics of Authenticity*, 36.
12. Taylor, *Ethics of Authenticity*, 36, emphasis original.
13. Taylor, *Ethics of Authenticity*, 33, emphases added, cf. 47–48.

Our relationships, he later describes, constitute "the background against which our tastes and desires and opinions and aspirations make sense."[14] Note that he refers to this "background of intelligibility" or "horizon" as "pre-existing."[15] As such, our sense of what "things are worthwhile and others less so, and others still not at all," are matters "anterior to choice"; our choices are made always against this horizon of intelligibility.[16]

Also noteworthy, especially in the foregoing larger citation, is the nature of how we are tied to this horizon; we are in dialogue with it, we are in conversation with it, or we struggle against it. That sense of the dialogic paints a picture of the formation of our identity as a function of active engagement with the values, aspirations, ideas, experiences, or traditions of those with whom we are in relationship; our identities are not passive inheritances. Chapter 2, in discussing the relational nature of cultural construction, I allude to this notion of the dialogic but more in the language of negotiation. Yet, Taylor's sense of the dialogic too easily misses the ways in which engagement with our preexisting horizon of intelligibility are supplanted. This is not to deny the truth of relationality but to call more specific attention to the fact that the idea of dialogue, conversation, struggle, or deliberation is in practice undermined. But undermined not only in the sense that Taylor recognizes when he admits, "The projecting of an inferior or demeaning image on another can actually distort and oppress, to the extent that it is interiorized. Not only contemporary feminism but also race relations and discussions of multiculturalism are undergirded by the premiss [sic] that denied recognition can be a form of oppression."[17] Taylor is indeed right that such racial distortions happen (and not just episodically), which can lead to the "misrecognition" of persons.[18] However, what Taylor does not attend to well enough is how such distortions and misrecognitions are made possible. In other words, his conception of relationality as fundamentally dialogic *too easily underestimates the power of whiteness* as one of the "external" sources that form our background of intelligibility.

14. Taylor, *Ethics of Authenticity*, 35.

15. Taylor, *Ethics of Authenticity*, 38.

16. Taylor, *Ethics of Authenticity*, 38

17. Taylor, *Ethics of Authenticity*, 50–51.

18. See Taylor, "Politics of Recognition," 65. Taylor refers to Frantz Fanon's *Wretched of the Earth*, and as Prevot points out, this is one of the rare instances where Taylor, at the very least, acknowledges the force of racism as more than simply individual instances of bias. See Prevot, "Sources of a Black Self?," 85.

The delimitation of Asian American agency is a sobering example of such an underestimation.

It is perhaps instructive to turn once again to the author and journalist Jay Caspian Kang, but this time to his reflections on his own Asian American myopias:

> While wandering around an empty street in Flushing [Queens, New York], I overheard two kids talking to one another in Korean. When I turned around, I saw that the kids were Black. They must have read the disbelief on my face for what it was—an ignorant outsider who was about to take a mental photo for his cultural tourism scrapbook—because they gave me a dirty look and crossed the street.
>
> How did I, who, prior to moving to New York, had lived in Boston, North Carolina, Maine, Los Angeles and Seattle, make it to the age of twenty-three without having ever met an Asian-American kid who had grown up much differently from me? It's true that I spent my childhood in nice, college towns that my exposure to other Asian-Americans was limited to bi-monthly potluck dinners where all the alumni of my father's high school would sit around and discuss God knows what, but I cannot help but wonder if this vacancy of identity might be the inevitable product of an entire generation of kids who were pushed directly into the structures of American success. Almost all of the Asian-American kids who grew up with me have lost the ability to speak the native language of our parents. When we watch *Old Boy* or *In the Mood for Love*, we alternate between an unfamiliar, displaced pride to a connection we cannot quite delineate and the shame of having to access it through subtitles. This distance, at least for me, came from a desire to duck out from the traditional immigrant shelter of family and culture, and *although it felt like a conscious choice at the time*, I sometimes look around at my Asian-American friends who suffer from the same blind spots, and *wonder if we have had any say at all.*
>
> The truth is, I really don't know.[19]

Kang's reckoning with his own prejudices as an Asian American that precluded the possibility of alternative versions of Asian Americaness is tinged with abjection. That despair is punctuated by the admittance that he really does not know how he arrived at his Asian American identity, one that is about "American success," by which he means, as he describes later in the

19. Kang, "Lives of Others," emphasis added.

essay, an identity and notion of success conditioned by the white imaginary. While he felt that he was choosing his identity as Asian American, he now wonders whether it was in fact a "conscious choice." More disconcerting is that whatever identities that may be considered alternatives or, as he puts it, "alien" to his present and rather ubiquitous Asian American identity, these other identities "belong to other races" that are also imagined and scripted by whiteness: for example, "the stand-up comedian, the police chief, the mass murderer, the potential first round pick in the NBA Draft."[20]

Kang's introspection on how he has come to be the kind of Asian American that he is casts a shadow over a central feature of Taylor's account of the self: that as relational, our identity forms in dialogic engagement with "others." Such engagement intimates a self that is not simply inundated by the force of others but exists in openness to her relationships or horizon of intelligibility. In other words, such openness indicates the reality of our existence as one of receiving *and* responding to the kind of questions that issue forth from our relationships. It is not insignificant that Taylor refers to the project of self-definition as "existing in a horizon of important *questions*" and not simply as "demands emanating beyond the self."[21] In another instance he will refer to being situated relationally as being open to the criticisms that our relationships offer of our own explanation of things; such criticism is part and parcel of the process of inquiry.[22] Yet, if we take Kang's consternations over his supposed consciously chosen identity (but perhaps in reality not so conscious and no so chosen) as a cautionary tale, oftentimes those questions emanating from our horizon of intelligibility are hardly recognized as questions but as answers.

How might we retrieve a regard for the horizon within which we gain and discern meaning as questions rather than as preexisting, perhaps even *a priori*, answers? How do we mitigate arriving somewhere before we even know that it is the destination we think it should be?

RECLAIMING AUTONOMY

That our horizons of intelligibility are commonly regarded as answers rather than as questions points to an important lacuna in Taylor's account of the relational self: the uncritical acceptance of our horizons as preexisting

20. Kang, "Lives of Others."
21. Taylor, *Ethics of Authenticity*, 40, emphasis added.
22. Taylor, *Ethics of Authenticity*, 36–37.

answers corresponds to a desire for them as answers. Taylor does at least intimate the importance of such approval when he notes that the subjectivist impulse in modernity is in part helped by what he calls "the affirmation of ordinary life."[23] What Taylor means to underscore here is the ways in which the scientific method, the reliance on technology, and the rise of state bureaucratism have animated a regard for the kind of individual self that underlies subjectivism by proving the instrumental worth of life in terms of "production and reproduction." That approach to life "is important for us" because it has "made a crucial contribution" to the obtainment of "abundance and the relief of suffering on an ever-wider scale."[24] But to characterize our affirmation of the ascendency of scientific, technological, and bureaucratic thinking as based on, referring to Francis Bacon, "instrumental efficacy"[25] is to overlook a more basic desire for the veracity (or at least perceived veracity) of that way of thinking. That more basic desire is crucial to unpacking how our horizons of intelligibility pull us into thinking about its questions as answers, especially when it comes to race.

Cornel West hints at this deeper sense of desire in his explanation of what is needed for an adequate genealogical inquiry into how African Americans are marginalized by Anglo-European logics and ideologies of racial hierarchy and homogeneity. Such a genealogical inquiry, West proposes, would be positively aided by turning to the "conception of societies as codified hero-systems or as symbolic-action systems that produce, distribute and circulate statuses and customs in order *to cope* with human fears of death or extreme otherness."[26] The idea that persons need to cope with or make sense of such dimensions of human finitude is key. He elaborates further:

> For example, with the lessening of religious influence in the modern West, human immortality quests were channeled into secular ideologies of science, art, nation, profession, race, sexuality and consumption. The deep human *desire for existential belonging and for self-esteem*—what I call the need for and consumption of existential capital—results in a profound, even gut-level, commitment to some of the illusions of the present epoch. *None of us escapes.*

23. Taylor, *Ethics of Authenticity*, 104.
24. Taylor, *Ethics of Authenticity*, 104.
25. Taylor, *Ethics of Authenticity*, 104.
26. West, "Race and Social Theory," 264, emphasis added.

And many Western peoples get much *existential capital from racist illusions*, from ideologies of race.[27]

In this passage, West's Augustinian inflected Niebuhrian leanings reveals its countenance.[28] West's observation on the deep human desire for existential belonging and self-esteem echo Reinhold Niebuhr's theological anthropology rooted in anxiety, by which he means a basic worry that persons have over their existence stemming from our inherent freedom or transcendence. In our freedom, that is, in our capacity to transcend our finitude, we recognize that we are, ultimately, finite. This paradoxical situation leads to the strategy of "undue self-assertion" or the desire to be "self-sufficing" as a way of resolving the problem of our basic finitude or temporality, when we are in fact not. No one escapes this existential dynamic that results in the sin of pride, as Niebuhr famously emphasized. "Not even the most idealistic preacher," asserts Niebuhr, "who admonishes his congregation to obey the law of Christ is free of the sin which arises from anxiety. He may or may not be anxious for his job, but he is certainly anxious about his prestige. Perhaps he is anxious for his reputation as a righteous man. He may be tempted to preach a perfect ethic the more vehemently in order to hide an unconscious apprehension of the fact that his own life does not conform to it. There is no life which does not violate the injunction 'Be not anxious.'"[29] West, following this anthropological logic, adds how racist illusions, the confused regard for the truthfulness of the social hierarchies such illusions demand, is yet another mode, if not one of the defining modes, of alleviating the anxiety of finitude or what West calls, as we saw above, the existential desire for belonging and self-esteem, that is, the need for meaning. For so many, racist illusions have met this desire for belonging, the need to be someone rather than simply a finite being.

The desire to belong and the desire to be someone is befitting the situation that Asian Americans find themselves in. To some extent, that desire is the Asian American story, if we can say there is in fact an Asian American story or metanarrative. Rather than inviting Asian Americans to occupy a space for the creative satiation of that desire, whiteness demands that Asian Americans occupy either the space of whiteness, to the extent that it is allowed, or the space of Asianness, as whiteness defines it. In that respect,

27. West, "Race and Social Theory," 264, emphasis added.

28. For West's Augustinian Niebuhrian leanings within the context of his positions on race, see, for instance, Stout, *Democracy and Tradition*, 53–58.

29. Niebuhr, "Why the Christian Church Is Not Pacifist," 108.

rather than encountering a horizon of intelligibility that presses Asian Americans to engage in their own self-understanding as an open-ended project, Asian Americans are thrust against a horizon of intelligibility that presses itself as the completion of that project. To belong, that is, to be someone, is to be that which is already given to or determined for us. That is why Kang's uncertainty of whether his identity as Asian American is of his own determination is so unsettling. Rather than thinking that he chose his identity as a means of distancing himself from "the traditional immigrant shelter of family and culture," the reality may have been that he chose to distance himself as such because that is an unchallenged prerequisite to "American success." Thus Asian American "choices" to be countercultural, that is, to stand at a distance from or, to use a phrase from Taylor, struggle against conceptions of Asianness expected of them by preceding parental generations, may not be acts of resistance after all. Instead, they merely amount to the following of a script that is not of their own making but one that succeeding generations of Asian Americans have simply assumed as countercultural when in fact it is an inconspicuous form of being "American," belonging to whiteness. To belong to America as an Asian American, in other words, is to be a certain kind of non-immigrant immigrant and Asian Americans have simply taken that for granted, as a matter of course. "The truth is," to reappropriate Kang's concluding line, that is the only answer Asian Americans are given (the ideal of white American success) and perhaps allowed to have, to what it means to belong, to be someone (and not no one, a no-body) in the United States.

If the question of belonging is presented as an answer of which only whiteness possesses and permits, then the problem that besets modernity is not only social fragmentation, as Taylor argues. "A fragmented society is one whose members find it harder and harder to identify with their political society as a community," writes Taylor, and the difficulty of forming and identifying with "effective common purpose" is abetted by a view of the self as unencumbered.[30] So a subjectivist understanding of the self and the kind of non-relationality it assumes is not only conceptually incoherent but has deep political-ethical implications that are not necessarily favorable to democratically driven collective identification and action. Yet, an Asian American perspective recasts the problem that subjectivism creates for society not so much as the problem of fragmentation but its opposite, the desire to readily, if not unwittingly, identify with a community that is

30. Taylor, *Ethics of Authenticity*, 117.

rooted in an untenable racial hierarchy as a central problem. Community rather than fragmentation is a problem that besets Asian Americans and non-Asian Americans alike.[31] If fragmentation, or at least racial fragmentation, exists, it does so in part because persons are excluded from concretely identifying with and participating in American social and political life as self-determinative agents. The consequences of such exclusion are manifold, such as the sowing of divisions between communities of color, and racial self-hatred and debasement, "the painful struggle of accepting and rejecting internalized negative and disenabling self-conceptions (for instance, pervasive lack of self-confidence in certain activities, deep insecurities regarding one's capacities) among people of color."[32]

If human persons as West suggests have a desire to belong and thus to be someone, then that desire is also a susceptibility to belong to communities, to be related to others that satisfy that desire, even if problematically. That susceptibility marks a significant downside of our relational constitution. The genius of whiteness is its ability to obscure itself as a problematic satiation of our desire to belong, to find a sense of self in relationship. Rather than encountering whiteness as a horizon of challenging, maybe even perplexing, questions, it convinces as a horizon of settled answers. Asian Americans' susceptibility to those persuasions is indicative of the depth of whiteness's grip on how the United States conceives of itself and thus its members. To underestimate that grip is to too easily fall back onto an insufficiently nuanced conception of the self as relationally constituted. That we engage our relations or our background of intelligibility dialogically, conversing with it, sometimes struggling against it, is the ideal, but practically speaking, we fall short of that ideal.[33] Is this shortcoming inevitable? Is it inescapable?

31. See, for instance, Ta-Nehisi Coates's critical essay on the hip-hop artist Kanye West and his turn to Trumpism. Coates, "I'm Not Black."

32. West, "Race and Social Theory," 264.

33. Note Taylor's description of the self in volume 1 of his *Philosophical Papers*. He sets out the claim that the self as self exists in deliberative relationship with sources that she is in relationship with, such as a particular culture, and those sources provide at least partial answers to questions of value: "To be a *full* human agent, to be a person or a self in the ordinary meaning, is to exist in a space defined by distinctions of worth. A self is a being for whom certain *questions* of categoric value have arisen, and received at least partial *answers*. Perhaps these have been given authoritatively by the culture more than they have been elaborated in the *deliberation of the person* concerned, but they are his in the sense that they are incorporated into his self-understanding, in some degree and fashion. My claim is that this is *not just a contingent fact* about human agents, but is *essential to*

This is the same type of question Taylor posits with respect to the primacy of instrumental reason (and, correlatively, individualism) in modern technological-bureaucratic society, a thesis that Max Weber famously advanced. Taylor is unwilling to accept the "iron cage" of instrumental reason as fate and notes that a first step toward averting that fate is to recognize and "understand the moral sources of our civilization" and how those sources have enabled instrumental reasoning.[34] But recognizing these sources is not enough given that it assumes that we are able to recognize them *as sources* rather than as normative givens. I am not questioning Taylor's claim that the sources that frame our sense of self and society are "not unidirectional." Society has to be receptive to a variety of sources for them to gain traction. In the case of bureaucratism in modernity, "it's not just that the institutions breed the philosophy; the outlook also had to begin to have some force in European society before the institutions could develop."[35] But given that the sources of bureaucratism have constrained us into instrumental reasoning, what are the prospects of seeing outside this constraint? Can we see that we are constrained, especially with respect to race, and can such insight in fact get us to stand in tension with it? Susannah Heschel adds a more distressing hurdle to those prospects when she observes, "Exposing the many ways in which racism functions in societal institutions does not always overcome its effects, leading to the question of why racism continues to maintain such a tenacious hold on the imagination."[36] It is worth recalling Kang's despairing surrender: "The Truth is, I really don't know," he confesses, and thrusts upon us the depths of whiteness's tenacity and entrenchment and

---

what we would understand and recognize as full, normal human agency" (Taylor, *Human Agency*, 3, emphasis added). However, does not Taylor's conception of the human agent predicate that she recognizes the distinction between questions and answers, or that she exists in actuality or in practice as an inquiring, deliberative agent? To regard a particular source as providing answers to questions of value suggests that one is in the position of deliberation or of wanting to make deliberative judgments about the reasonableness or truthfulness of those answers. But does this adequately capture the situation that the ordinary human agent, particularly, the Asian American agent, is in? The point I am attempting to raise from an Asian American perspective is that persons typically take what culture provides *as givens* rather than answers (taking them as answers implies that they recognize the questions culture raises and find its answers reasonable to accept). In making that distinction, between givens and answers, I am trying to paint a picture of persons who exist not necessarily dialogically but monologically as a matter of course. Dialogical would be the aspiration, while monological is the reality of the situation.

34. Taylor, *Ethics of Authenticity*, 99, 101.

35. Taylor, *Ethics of Authenticity*, 99.

36. Heschel, "Slippery Yet Tenacious," 3.

the formidable challenge of being able to dialogically relate to the sources of the Asian American self rather than simply as a passive audience of them.

Passivity can breed abjection, and Kang's introspective account of the formative power of whiteness, the extent to which Asian Americans are rendered passive in the face of whiteness, feels like a prime confirmation of that proposition. Taylor too can sound despairing when describing the hold that technological-bureaucratism has on modern society: "Instrumental reason has also grown along with a disengaged model of the human subject, which has a great hold on our imagination. It offers an ideal picture of a human thinking that has *disengaged from* its messy embedding in our bodily constitution, *our dialogical situation* . . . in order to be pure, self-verifying rationality."[37] The extent to which the displacement of our dialogical situation with a monological situation, one that offers self-verifying ideals of human life, has taken hold would suggest the deep challenges to being free, or self-possessive and determinative. "We don't want to exaggerate our degrees of freedom," Taylor cautions. "But they are not zero," he also insists, redirecting us to his anti-fatalism that we noted above.[38]

If we are fundamentally dialogic creatures, then cultivating, enlivening, and securing autonomy in our conception of selfhood takes on renewed urgency. In other words, if our freedom is not zero, then we are not simply subsumed by or an epiphenomenon of our relationality but related to others in a way that does not threaten the integrity of our independence from them. Maintaining autonomy and relationality may sound somewhat paradoxical, the need to hold together two anthropological features that are seemingly at odds with each other. However, one critical way of maintaining the capacity to engage with one's relations rather than being overdetermined by them is to advance autonomy, to recognize its intrinsic importance, in line with an early conviction of contemporary feminism. The theological ethicist Margaret Farley describes that conviction in the following manner:

> What is good for women is autonomy, in the sense of both self-legislation and self-determination. Women needed to take hold of their own lives, to refuse the subordinate position that rendered them passive in relation to an active male, to thrust their own insights and articulate their own self-understanding. Because autonomy belongs to women as personal beings with the capacity

37. Taylor, *Ethics of Authenticity*, 101–2, emphasis added.
38. Taylor, *Ethics of Authenticity*, 100–101.

to determine the ultimate meaning of their own lives, they could make claims for respect as persons, valuable in themselves and not merely as instruments in the service of community.[39]

While autonomy is depicted in contrasts, on the one side advocating for women to be respected as persons and on the other side resisting the ways in which community undermines that kind of respect, autonomy is not a denial of relationality but "ultimately for the sake of relationship . . . that relationships without respect for individuality and autonomy are destructive of persons."[40] Without acknowledging the "need for moral limits to community," relationality, as Farley points out, fails to be genuinely mutual. What is required is a sufficient sense of autonomy, which checks unjust relationality and restores right relationship. Genuine mutuality cannot be had unless those in relationship are in a position to engage one another—to give and to receive, to receive and to give—rather than simply to be disciplined unidirectionally. Without maintaining the integrity of the self as self even though we are desirous of relationality, such desire for the other devolves into self-negation by the other. Without such self-possession, self-transcendence for the other devolves into self-negation by the other.

An equally instructive way of conceptualizing and retrieving the importance of autonomy, especially for Asian American agency, is to draw the distinction between the claim that personhood is relational and personal existence is relational. The nuance of that distinction is outlined succinctly by the theologian Harriet A. Harris: "We cannot jump from recognizing the relationality involved in being a person to affirming that persons are relational entities. Persons are ontologically prior to relations. It is one thing to say that human beings develop characteristics which we regard as personal through having persons to relate to them . . . It is quite another to suggest that relations precede persons."[41] Harris then explains that the latter proposition, which is typically formulated with the shorthand *persons are relational*, "seems to imply that [a] human being can fail to become a person" if not in relationship. The Catholic philosopher Robert Spaeman underscores the gravity of such a conceptually sloppy implication: "Do we not want to say that all people have value and that we will be judged in

39. Farley, "Feminism and Universal Morality," 181–82.
40. Farley, "Feminism and Universal Morality," 182.
41. Harris, "Should We Say," 336.

our failure to recognize value in others? . . . Otherwise a person's value is dependent on the richness of her relations."[42]

Referring to the Anglican theologian John Macmurray's metaphor of the mother-child relation, Harris points out, "It is not that relations precede persons so much as that personal existence is created as relational."[43] A child is already a person, and given "the impulse to communicate is his sole adaption to the world in which he is born," it is through communicative relationship with the child's mother, parents, and other relations that the child develops a persona, an identity.[44] But that is only possible because the child is already a person. A more explicit Trinitarian formulation of this principle may be that persons are created by God and we are personally related to God, the former claim underscoring our personhood by divine event and the latter underscoring how our personal existence with God is relationally constituted, emerging and forming in dialogic relationship with God (with discipleship as the exemplary form of such dialogical relationality). We might say, then, that the principle of autonomy is an affirmation of this Trinitarian premise, that is, a way of recognizing that being in relationship with others dialogically rather than monologically is to respect and maintain the integrity of our personhood. Only persons can dialogue, and to deny or violate personhood is to undermine the very condition for dialogue. As Spaeman puts it, the very capacity or condition for dialogue is "selfdifference" or "the self-differentiation of a human subject from everything that may be different about him."[45]

---

42. Spaeman, "Persons," 339–40.

43. Harris, "Should We Say," 335.

44. Harris, "Should We Say," 335.

45. "Speech differs from the cries of living things in nature, in that it anticipates the standpoint of the one who is to hear what is spoken. When someone says 'I am in pain,' that statement is not merely a cry by other means. The immediate expression of pain must be suppressed, in order to form a communication about the pain as an event in the world and to make that communication intelligible to another. To this end, far from merely 'expressing ourselves,' we must submit to a prescribed system of rules that makes understanding possible. Correspondingly, the system of speech itself prompts the emergence of selfdifference [sic], the distance from ourselves that gives rise to our talk of 'persons.'" It is because of our self-difference that "makes reflection possible." See Spaemann, "Persons," 348.

CRITICAL SELF-LOVE AS DEFIANCE

One way of accounting for the susceptibility to whiteness is forgetfulness that we are persons apart from the ideals of life that whiteness advocates and demands. Retrieving a stronger sense of autonomy that incorporates the foregoing insights on personhood and relationality places greater scrutiny on the liabilities of such forgetfulness and elevates the alternative of critical self-love. The modifier critical should not be overlooked. I refer to critical self-love to underscore autonomy as a necessary posture in the face of deformed relationality; in other words, only by loving oneself as a self-possessive self is one in a more secure position to better maintain independence from the force of whiteness. But I refer to such self-love as critical self-love to underscore the risks of autonomy conceived as a form of self-love.

On those risks, consider, for instance, the journalist Wesley Yang's powerful refusal to follow the script of his Asian American identity. Not long after Amy Chua's publication of *Battle Hymn of the Tiger Mother* and its solidification of the Asian American, on the one hand, as the overbearing, hyper-disciplining parent and, on the other hand, as the stressed out, standardized-test-prepping, classical-music-practicing, overachieving student, Yang proffered this salty, provocative manifesto: "Let me summarize my feelings toward Asian values: F**k filial piety. F**k grade-grubbing. F**k Ivy League mania. F**k deference to authority. F**k humility and hard work. F**k harmonious relations. F**k sacrificing for the future. F**k earnest, striving middle-class servility."[46] This expletive-laden tirade is not gratuitous but serves to punctuate the point that Asian Americans are not necessarily the demure, disciplined achievers of tiger parent tutelage that popular culture makes them out to be. But even if Asian Americans (some if not many) have bought into this image and abetted the perpetuation of it, the crudeness of his language is meant to provoke the question of what Asian Americans have gained from the perpetuation of this image. Yang in part has in mind, among other discriminations, the phenomenon of the "bamboo ceiling," which is not unlike the glass ceiling many women experience restricting them to middle management throughout corporate America.[47] The bamboo ceiling is only one symptom of "the bitter undercurrent

46. Yang, "Paper Tigers."

47. In regards to the bamboo ceiling, Yang observes, "If between 15 and 20 percent of every Ivy League class is Asian, and if the Ivy Leagues are incubators for the country's

of Asian-American life that so many Asian graduates of elite universities find that meritocracy as they have understood it comes to an abrupt end after graduation."[48] This unfair ending coincides with the perception that Asian Americans are "easily pushed around by more assertive people, and thus basically invisible."[49]

What, then, is the alternative but to rage against the popular image that Asian Americans find themselves sedimented in—trapped in an iron (or bamboo) cage, perhaps? Yang maps out alternatives, one of which is to abide in the present reality of Asian American marginalization and attempt to succeed within the rules of white American success, if not gaming them to one's own advantage, even though both tactics will require revising what it means to be successful. For that reason, Yang finds the option of making the best of an unjust situation unattractive, for that would ultimately mean that the only status that Asian Americans can have in white America is a secondary one. "I see the appeal of getting with the program. But this is not my choice. Striving to meet others' expectations may be a necessary cost of assimilation, but I am not going to do it," declares Yang.[50] Another option is to opt into society in a slightly different way: to recognize that Asian Americans are in fact not equal to white Americans, which would behoove Asian Americans to "love the world twice as hard," that is, to prove beyond a reasonable doubt that they merit full equality.[51] But whatever intuitive logic that such a call to labor harder than anyone else might have, it is one that is all too familiar to Asian Americans, leading to no more than the status of model minority. Working twice as hard as anyone else simply proves that one is a hard worker but not necessarily a fully equal worker. Laboring to gain the approval of the other (the white American other) is a kind of other-regarding love that sacrifices oneself not for the other's genuine well-being but for their approval. Such an other-regarding love, therefore, sows the seeds for its perversion, resulting in self-sacrifice that is unworthy of love. Yang opts instead to opt out by way of a radical self-love: "In lieu of loving the world twice as hard, I care, in the end, about expressing my obdurate singularity at any cost. I love this hard and unyielding part of myself

---

leaders, it would stand to reason that Asians would make up some corresponding portion of the leadership class." But this is not the case, he argues. See Yang, "Paper Tigers."

48. Yang, "Paper Tigers."
49. Yang, "Paper Tigers."
50. Yang, "Paper Tigers."
51. Yang, "Paper Tigers."

more than any other reward the world has to offer a newly brightened and ingratiating demeanor, and I will bear any costs associated with it."[52]

But what exactly does it mean to love oneself to a point of expressing one's obdurate singularity at any cost? Does loving one's singularity imply a kind of social isolationism, the need to withdraw from society in order to protect the integrity of one's agency, self, and identity? It would be understandable to want to isolate oneself and retreat from the world, like Ralph Ellison's narrator in *Invisible Man*, who occupies an underground room. Seeking refuge from the pervasive demands and expectations of white America on the Asian American body by retreating to a fortified social space is not an unreasonable response. Yet such isolation can also feed a festering resentment and limit the kind of freedom one hopes to gain by withdrawing, since it does little to chip away at the fundamental problem that besets Asian Americans—the persistence and prevalence of white racism. Thus isolationism concedes defeat. Isolationism only confirms whiteness's power over Asian American bodies inasmuch as it succeeds in sequestering Asian Americans from participation in American life. Not only are Asian Americans rendered invisible by whiteness's definitions of who Asian Americans are and can be, it renders Asian Americans invisible in the literal sense of removing Asian Americans from public consciousness. Rather than extolling the virtues of hiding from the world and its threats, manipulations, and impositions, ultimately, Ellison's unnamed narrator's underground room is a metaphor of how white racism renders nonwhites invisible in those ways.

While Yang can sound like a separatist, Yang's sense of self-love ultimately moves in a different direction. His primary concern in turning to a radical self-love, an obdurate love for his singularity and efforts at nonconformity, is meant as a kind of social protest to destabilize and transform how Asian Americans are perceived and expected to be: demure, quiet, hardworking or, in other words, a good Asian or a good minority. While he begins his essay by observing how Chua's *Battle Hymn of the Tiger Mother* was criticized for burying Asian Americans even deeper into their popular stereotypes, at the end of the essay, Yang attempts to rehabilitate the negative reputation that Chua's book has garnered:

> She had set out, she explained, to write a memoir that was "defiantly self incriminating"—and the result was a messy jumble of conflicting impulses, part provocation, part self-critique. Western readers rode roughshod over this paradox and made of Chua a

52. Yang, "Paper Tigers."

kind of Asian minstrel figure. But more than anything else, *Battle Hymn* is a very American project—one no traditional Chinese person would think to undertake. "Even if you hate the book," Chua pointed out, "the one thing it is not is meek."[53]

Especially striking is the claim that her book is a very American project and not necessarily a Chinese one. In claiming as much, the book is meant to do exactly the opposite of what it has been perceived to be doing to Asian Americans. Yang characterizes the aim of the book as rebellion against how Asian Americans are typically perceived and how they are expected to behave—as meek. But the book is the exact opposite, not meek but the epitome of assertive. As Yang quips, "'The loudest duck gets shot' is a Chinese proverb. 'The nail that sticks out gets hammered down' is a Japanese one. Its Western correlative: 'The squeaky wheel gets the grease.'"[54]

I am not particularly interested in whether Yang's characterization of Chua's book (or even Chua's own characterization of it) is accurate. His characterization of it, however, is noteworthy for it reveals the inherent risks of the kind of radical, almost Nietzschean love of his own Asian American self Yang advocates. He concludes the essay with the following:

> There is something salutary in that proud defiance [motivating Chua's book]. And though the debate she sparked about Asian-American life has been of questionable value, we will need more people with the same kind of defiance, willing to push themselves into the spotlight and to make some noise, to beat people up, to seduce women, to make mistakes, to become entrepreneurs, to stop doggedly pursuing official paper emblems attesting to their worthiness, to stop thinking those scraps of paper will secure anyone's happiness, and to dare to be interesting.

A good deal is commendable in Yang's call for defiance, to be interesting rather than simply residing within the identities that Asian Americans have been given and come to accept, apprehensively or not. "Daring to be interesting" speaks to the best of the values implied in the principle of autonomy and reflects the priority of reclaiming the kind of self-love that rejects and resists the deformed other-regarding love all too familiar in the enabling of abusive relationships. (How else might we describe the hold that white racism has on Asian American agency as anything but abusive?) But how self-love as a kind of resistance to such abuse—resistance to "being pushed

53. Yang, "Paper Tigers."
54. Yang, "Paper Tigers."

around by more assertive people," to recall Yang's characterization of Asian Americans in white America—avoids falling into identities and patterns of behavior that are morally dubious remains unanswered. Simply doing those things that controvert or upend conventional perceptions of Asianness seems lacking. His examples in the foregoing citation leave much to be desired even if he means them to be only provocative. Are there not other ways of provoking the point without appealing to misogyny and pugilism? Even the more positive images that suggest Asian American defiance, such as not fearing mistakes or becoming entrepreneurs, require more definition. The Taiwanese American restaurateur and television personality Eddie Huang, who we encountered briefly in chapter 2, appears in Yang's essay as an example of someone who embraces the kind of entrepreneurial spirit that Yang thinks defies the typical expectations and perceptions placed on Asian Americans in popular culture. As Yang describes, "Rather than strive to make himself acceptable to the world, Huang has chosen to buy his way back in, on his own terms. 'What I've learned is that America is about money, and if you can make your culture commodifiable, then you're relevant,' he says. 'I don't believe anybody agrees with what I say or supports what I do because they truly want to love Asian people. They like my f**king pork buns, and I don't get it twisted.'"[55] If Yang is correct that Huang is making it in the world "on his own terms" rather than on someone else's terms (the implication being the terms of mainstream white America), is Huang's brand of self-determination the kind of autonomy that Asian Americans ought to emulate? Huang's entrepreneurialism is self-determination of a sort, but it is one that rests on seeing the world in dog-eat-dog terms, where survival, if not flourishing, depends on the drive to out hustle the other. Radical self-love indeed. But critical self-love it is not.

Such radical self-love takes autonomy to the extreme and perhaps represents the far opposite of the equally extreme position that there is no personhood apart from relationships. I do not want to suggest Yang is ultimately advocating that Asian Americans adopt a radical self-love that results in a wanton disregard for the non-Asian American other. But Yang's call that Asian Americans revel in a self-love that expresses their singularity, uniqueness, or unconventionality (that is, a love of one's own Asian Americanness rather than a desire to be Asian American as it has been defined) is not wholly capable of meeting its own call. Most problematically, Yang, in daring Asian Americans to be defiant or interesting, falls back on

55. Yang, "Paper Tigers."

individual desire rather than some larger account of what is or is not authoritative with respect to value. It is at this point that Taylor's critique of subjectivism is relevant here. Without a clearer sense of what it means to be defiant or interesting, his call to action is susceptible to emulating (or has no choice but to rely on and accept) prevailing notions of value or meaning. As his earlier examples of defiance or being interesting suggest, his brand of self-love opens him up to imitating forms of life that are patriarchal, misogynistic, and self-indulgent. And there is no reason to exclude racist from this list, even if he does not provide an example of defiance that would suggest as much. So long as self-love is advanced without a normative account of what love of one's "obdurate singularity" means and a standard by which such normativity is to be derived and defended, then there is little reason to think that such self-love can sufficiently avoid patterns of life that, while they may "appear" interesting, end up promoting, wittingly or not, the interest of white racism. (It is interesting in this regard, that Yang praises Chua's *Battle Hymn* book for being "American" and not typically Chinese in its assertiveness rather than meekness.) To some extent, what I am describing here is the threat of post-racialism, the notion that one is moving beyond the strictures of race, when in fact one is reinforcing them by ignoring the ways in which the very conditions for one's purported post-racialism is race-based.

So, if not radical self-love, or at least the kind of self-love that Yang calls for, then what might be an alternative? We now return to *critical* self-love. We might do well to recall Farley's observation that autonomy does not need to mean that persons do not need the other. While knowing and loving oneself, or self-possession, is not wholly constitutive of our relationality, persons are "capable of knowing and loving themselves not in spite of knowing and loving others, but through it and in it."[56] But what does "through it and in it" entail? How is that to be manifest in a way that does not lead to a subsuming of Asian American agency by dubious relationships? Let me propose, as a starting point the following: If not by self-love alone, then self-love in the service of the other. Ta-Nehisi Coates's reflections on his susceptibility to the trappings of fame signal what I mean to convey in that formulation of self-love. He writes of the allure of loving his own reputation and notoriety, for what those accolades provide him and only him, which would not be possible if he were no more than a typical

56. Farley, "Feminism and Universal Morality," 182.

African American male from Baltimore.[57] The love of his own fame "swept [him] away" from his "Baltimore ordinariness"; more distressingly, a part of him, he admits, "wanted to be swept away," to "love that small fame in the same terrible way that [he] wanted to live forever." It was only when he came to the realization that despite his love of his own fame his "pre-fame web of connections around [him]—child, spouse, brothers, sisters, friends—the majority of whom held fast and remained" that Coates began to come to terms with what he truly loves, not fame, but the love of his craft, writing.[58] The vulnerable tone of Coates's confessional powerfully conveys how self-love can go awry, toward self-indulgence, eventually, self-delusion. But notice that the problem of self-love is only apparent to him once he recognizes the steadfast commitments to him of his web of relations. As commendable as it is, his insight only leads him back to reaffirming his love of writing. It is the love that made him susceptible to the trappings of fame to begin with, since his love of writing, while expressive of his individuality ("I love how it belonged to me, a private act of creation"), is ultimately in the service of his own self. How does a non-delusional self-love (one that is not captivated by fame, in Coates's case) sufficiently resist the kind of freedom that he feared his susceptibility to fame would problematically lead to? How does a non-delusional self-love resist what he calls "white freedom, freedom without consequence, freedom without criticism, freedom to be proud and ignorant; freedom to profit off a people in one moment and abandon them in the next . . . a conqueror's freedom, freedom of the strong built on antipathy or indifference"?[59]

The *telos* of non-delusional, proper self-love is slightly reconfigured in Bryan Massingale's equally moving personal reflection on the vocation of black Catholic theology. He recollects:

> My grandmother was a major influence both in my life of faith and in nurturing my budding sense of scholarship. I was the first person in my extended family to attend and graduate from college, and my grandmother took special delight in that occasion. She dressed in her "Sunday best" for the commencement ceremony; she would not fail to witness this special event in our family's history. She glowed with pride after the ceremony as I showed her my degree. She took the folder in her hands, stared at it with a little

57. Coates, "I'm Not Black."
58. Coates, "I'm Not Black."
59. Coates, "I'm Not Black."

awe, and she said: "Look at that! This sure is something." Then turning to me, with love and pride and affection and wisdom, she asked: "Now, who are you going to help with it? Who are you going to use it for?"[60]

Massingale's grandmother's question, he finally concludes, is not only for black Catholic theologians, "but for all of us."[61] Note how that question diverges from Coates's conclusion that because of his abiding relationships he is reminded of what true self-love is, to love one's own projects rather than what others say they ought to be. But Massingale's grandmother's question challenges one's self-love to move outward rather than to simply reside in oneself. Otherwise, how else are we to know that what we (or I) love is in fact what ought to be loved? An expansive, *outwardly moving* self-love, or self-love in the service of the other, provides a measure of that question.[62]

The urgency and moral force of that question is absent in Yang's denunciation of the Asian American self that white America imposes on Asian Americans. Defiance simply as radical self-love too easily turns on itself, for the self, and nothing more. But self-love in the service of the other reconfigures Yang's call for Asian Americans to be defiant or interesting. Defiance is no longer simply about defending the self but also the interests of others. More specifically, defiance pivots on the reality that we are ineluctably tied to others who have been disciplined by social injustices, including whiteness. Defiance, therefore, is a discipline that aims at a kind of self-discovery that cannot be had apart from maintaining a remembrance of those who are similarly situated. Defiance construed in this way eschews moral ignorance and amnesia; it recognizes that not only I but others too are susceptible to malformed relationality, and to be defiant—to love oneself rather than to love oneself on the terms set out by the white racial imagination—is not simply a way of resisting that malformation for me but to do so in the hope that all will be free for right relationality.

60. Massingale, *Racial Justice*, 174–75.

61. Massingale, *Racial Justice*, 174.

62. Though Coates does at least hint at the spirit of the idea of loving oneself in the service of the other when he observes that self-love that deprives the lives of others is morally reprehensible: "It is often easier to choose the path of self-destruction when you don't consider who you are taking along for the ride, to die drunk in the street if you experience the deprivation as your own, and not the deprivation of family, friends, and community" (Coates, "I'm Not Black"). That the priority is not to deprive others in loving oneself is hardly as positive and forward moving as loving oneself in the service of others, however.

Linking defiance with the work of remembrance recalls the theologian M. Shawn Copeland's linkage of *anamnesis* with racial solidarity. Racial solidarity "begins in *anamnesis*—the intentional remembering of the dead, exploited, despised victims of history."[63] Copeland's primary focus, though not exclusively, is remembering society's systemic degradation of black female bodies. To that focus, we can add, from an Asian American perspective, that the centrality of such *anamnesis* makes the work of racial solidarity with women of color, black or nonblack, possible because such intentional remembrance is an act of defiance, a refusal to accept the societal legitimation of racial visions of life that afflict us and distort our sense of humanity not only personally but also collectively. Thus defiance, as rooted in the remembrance of others, to reformulate Copeland's characterization of the demands of racial solidarity, obliges us in the here-and-now to stand between the exploited and marginalized and the powers of oppression in society.[64] Thus, solidarity, at its core, is an act of defiance of the powers and principalities; alternatively, defiance, at its core, demands solidarity.

HOPE DEFERRED?

Yet, we must not gloss over Copeland's word of caution when it comes to the moral necessity of remembrance. Remembering the reality of the exploited, marginalized, and abused—this memory, Copeland warns, "cannot be a pietistic or romantic memorial, for always intentional recovery and engagement of the histories of suffering are fraught with ambiguity and paradox."[65] What Copeland has in mind here is the paradox of how solidarity is made necessary by the remembrance of those who are and have been exploited, marginalized, and abused; the moral weight of solidarity emerges from the moral cries of injustice. That paradox must not to be ignored. But Copeland's caution is also significant, at least within an Asian American context, for a different reason. Her warning against "romantic memorial" returns us back to the sober remembrance of the social reality that besets Asian Americans. As a sober remembrance of that reality, the moral force of defiance must be held in tension with the limits that white racism has placed on Asian American agency and identity. As argued in chapters 3 and 4, that hold implicates Asian Americans in the reinscription of white racist

63. Copeland, *Enfleshing Freedom*, 100, emphasis original.
64. Copeland, *Enfleshing Freedom*, 101.
65. Copeland, *Enfleshing Freedom*, 100.

discourse, while also indicating that such reinscription is a consequence of how white racism restricts the kinds of persons we can be. If not "white," then "Asian," but only on the terms set by whiteness. In that way, the range of racial identities that Asian Americans typically possess are of the same kind, emanating from whiteness's racial imagination. The extent to which the white racial imagination looms over the Asian American self should not be misjudged.

If we acknowledge soberly the deep constraints on Asian American agency by whiteness, one question that we need to wrestle with is whether self-love in the service of others is capable of generating more adequate, more alluring, more compelling visions of life (of the good). Such capability assumes, to recall Taylor's earlier assertion, that we can be free to engage and choose differently than the kind of freedom that whiteness champions. But the language of possibility is not the same as the language of actuality. What kind of freedom do Asian Americans have? What kind of freedom is concretely obtainable? Returning to Coates's struggle with his own fame, he remarks, "The incentives toward a grand ego were ever present."[66] By incentives, he means more specifically the incentives of white freedom. And as we noted earlier, he confesses to being enthralled by those incentives. The language of incentives is critical here in two ways, for it underscores a basic desire persons have for significance (the desire to be something other than, as Coates puts it, "unremarkable") and the way whiteness (white freedom) fills that desire. But are there alternative incentives, ones that are equally, if not more, enticing or captivating than the ones whiteness offers, and would we want to recognize them, desire them instead? As Thomas Aquinas puts it, "Every desire is for some good."[67] But not every good is equally commendable; desiring a sense of identity and a meaningful existence is a good, but the question is whether acting for the sake of some good, we knowingly act from a desire for what is bad (e.g., the incentives of white freedom), or are willing to recognize that we are doing so.[68] But why are those incentives so attractive to our desires that submission to them is not unexceptional even if they result in a restricted if not distorted freedom?

66. Coates, "I'm Not Black."

67. Aquinas, *Summa Theologica*, I-II, Question 8, Article 1, cited from MacIntyre, *Ethics in the Conflicts of Modernity*, 10.

68. This is a rewording of a sentence from MacIntyre, *Ethics in the Conflicts of Modernity*, 10.

Coates's willingness to imbibe in the self-delusion that white freedom offers the nonwhite person reaches a theological inflection (even though, interestingly, Coates is a self-avowed nonreligious person).[69] His willingness to yield to the incentives that white freedom markets to the ennui of ordinariness that so many if not all persons struggle with gives distinct voice to Niebuhr's reminder that the Christian gospel enjoins, "Be not anxious."[70] For Niebuhr, this command ought to inform the gospel's command to "love thy neighbor as thyself," or at least this love command needs to make sense of this additional injunction. In calling attention to the problem of anxiety, the implication is that human persons need to be formed in love as well as forgiveness.[71] For our anxiety over the question of meaning or significance leads to self-delusions about our *bodily existence*, that only a particular embodied existence can be the balm to such anxiety. For Niebuhr, the balm takes the form of pride, gaining advantage over another, satisfying one's own interest over and against others.

"Be not anxious" (RSV), "do not worry about your life . . . about your body" (NRSV), and yet, Asian Americans are in a persistent state of anxiety. How else to characterize the way Asian Americans are situated in the United States? Asian Americans are "other" while at the same time invited to be something other than "other," that is, the model minority. These are choices about the kind of bodies—forms of life—Asian Americans are to inhabit, and the very fact that a choice is demanded of us, either to remain as other or to be a "passable" other, underscores the deeply distressed conditions under which Asian American anxiety is to be managed or remedied. Under those circumstances, and if, as Niebuhr argues and Coates avows at least in his own life, all persons are afflicted with the need to soothe their anxiety for meaning, then are we, Asian Americans, able to resist whiteness's demands on Asian Americans? Are the demands of white racism on Asian Americans so overwhelming and of a kind that Asian Americans cannot refuse, not only because refusal is not a live option but because the incentives are

69. See, for instance, Coates, *Between the World and Me*, 12, 29, 88.

70. Niebuhr cites the Revised Standard Version (RSV) of Matthew 6:25; the whole verse goes as follows: "Do not be anxious about your life, what you shall eat or what you shall drink, nor about your body, what you shall put on. Is not life more than food, and the body more than clothing." The New Revised Standard Version (NRSV) translates it as, "Therefore I tell you, do not worry about your life, what you will eat or what you will drink, or about your body, what you will wear. Is not life more than food, and the body more than clothing?"

71. Mathewes, *Understanding Religious Ethics*, 191.

too attractive? What is it about whiteness's visions of embodied existence that elicit desire, trap the imagination, and create the perception that they are answers to rather than questions about our anxiety for meaning? While whiteness provides only a morally dubious freedom, that reality fails to convincingly disincentivize its appeal, or undermine its social sway. If we were to refuse whiteness's visions of embodied existence, then how would we go about refusing in a way that is true to the gospel's other command, "love thy neighbor as thyself"? In short, how do we worry less about what others deem as right for our bodies, assuming we can in fact worry less about them?

We could draw cues, as West does, from Martin Luther King Jr.'s discipline of nonviolence as a critical mitigating practice. Refusing the incentives of white racism, to see them as disincentives, requires disciplining one's own susceptibility to self-delusion and practicing the discipline of love of others, even the enemy.[72] As West explains, King saw that twofold discipline of nonviolence as the recognition "that evil is not simply external" but that he too was susceptible to the evil of racism. "He knew that there was white supremacy in him," West asserts. "That's what allowed him to love Bull Connor [the Commissioner of Public Safety for Birmingham, Alabama] even as he opposed Connor's white supremacy. That's the great Christian insight."[73] And yet, the gospel also recognizes that we remain anxious, and in our anxiety we are tempted toward self-delusion. As Niebuhr explains, "The ideal possibility is that perfect trust in God's providence ('for your heavenly father knoweth what things ye have need of') and perfect unconcern for the physical life ('fear not them which are able to lull the body') would create a state of serenity in which one life would not seek to take advantage of another life. But the fact is that anxiety is an inevitable concomitant of human freedom, and is the root of the inevitable sin which expresses itself in every human activity and creativity."[74]

Our susceptibility to self-delusion and the tenacious exploitation of that susceptibility by white racial discourse muddies the road to resistance, defiance. That Asian Americans struggle to be more than what they are perceived to be and yet are challenged to take up that struggle on terms that are truly theirs, witnesses to the depths and entrenchment that white

72. On nonviolence as a discipline, see, for instance, King, "Palm Sunday," 32–33.

73. West and Klor de Alva, "On Black-Brown Relations," 511.

74. Niebuhr, "Why the Christian Church Is Not Pacifist," 108. On the convergences between King and Niebuhr, see King, "Pilgrimage to Nonviolence," 46–47.

racial discourse has on the *American* imagination. Even while sounding a prophetic optimism in line with King, West's constant referrals to America's tendency to evade and avoid King by sanitizing him, "the clever gimmicks of mass distraction," or the American penchant for producing persons who simply sleep walk through history, is, paradoxically, reason enough, disquietingly so, to give pause to the possibility of resistance, the prospects for Asian Americans to be self-determining agents.[75] Beyond that pause is either abjection or pathways for hope yet unseen or imagined. Whether Asian American life can be imagined apart from, in defiance of, the watchful eye of whiteness is the hope we must hold out for.

75. West, "Radical King," x, xi, xii.

Bibliography

Aizenman, Nurith. "Baltimore Unrest Reveals Tensions between African-Americans and Asians." *NPR*, April 30, 2015. http://www.npr.org/2015/04/30/403231749/baltimore-unrest-reveals-tensions-between-african-americans-and-asian-owned-busi.

Alcoff, Linda. "Mestizo Identity." In *The Idea of Race*, edited by Robert Bernasconi and Tommy L. Lott, 139–60. Indianapolis: Hackett, 2000.

Ancheta, Angelo N. *Race, Rights, and the Asian American Experience.* New Brunswick, NJ: Rutgers University Press, 1998.

Anderson, Victor. *Beyond Ontological Blackness: An Essay on African American Religious and Cultural Criticism.* New York: Continuum, 1995.

Appiah, K. Anthony. "The Case for Contamination." *New York Times Magazine*, January 1, 2006. https://www.nytimes.com/2006/01/01/magazine/the-case-for-contamination.html.

———. *Cosmopolitanism: Ethics in a World of Strangers.* New York: Norton, 2007.

———. "Culture, Identity: Misunderstood Connections." In *Color Conscious: The Political Morality of Race*, edited by K. Anthony Appiah and Amy Gutmann, 30–105. Princeton: Princeton University Press, 1996.

———. "The Uncompleted Argument: Du Bois and the Illusion of Race." In *The Idea of Race*, edited by Robert Bernasconi and Tommy L. Lott, 118–35. Indianapolis: Hackett, 2000.

Arenson, Karen W. "Worried Colleges Step Up Efforts over Suicide." *New York Times*, December 3, 2004. https://www.nytimes.com/2004/12/03/education/worried-colleges-step-up-efforts-over-suicide.html.

Bantum, Brian. *Redeeming Mulatto: A Theology of Race and Christian Hybridity.* Waco, TX: Baylor University Press, 2010.

Bever, Lindsey, and Lynda Robinson. "'My Old Kentucky Home': The Kentucky Derby's Beloved, Fraught Singalong about Slavery." *Washington Post*, May 5, 2018. https://www.washingtonpost.com/news/retropolis/wp/2018/05/05/my-old-kentucky-home-the-kentucky-derbys-beloved-fraught-sing-along-about-slavery/?utm_term=.cc7f1f6b85d1.

Bilefsky, Dan. "Calling Poutine 'Canadian' Gives Some in Quebec Indigestion." *New York Times*, December 19, 2017. https://www.nytimes.com/2017/12/19/world/canada/quebec-poutine.html.

Booker, Karene. "Asian-Americans Often Feel Racial 'Microaggressions.'" *Cornell Chronicle*, April 24, 2013. https://news.cornell.edu/stories/2013/04/asian-americans-often-feel-racial-microaggressions.

Bouchard, James. "Chinaman or White Man, Which?" *San Francisco Catholic Guardian*, March 1, 1873.

Brody, Leslie. "Who Got into Stuyvesant and New York's Other Elite Public High Schools." *Wall Street Journal*, March 7, 2018. https://www.wsj.com/articles/who-got-into-stuyvesant-and-new-yorks-other-elite-public-high-schools-1520465259.

Bush, Melanie E. L. *Everyday Forms of Whiteness: Understanding Race in a "Post-Racial" World*. Lanham, MD: Rowman & Littlefield, 2011.

Cannon, Katie Geneva. *Black Womanist Ethics*. Oxford: Oxford University Press, 1988.

Chang, Andrea. "Why So Many Asian-American Women Are Bleaching Their Hair Blond." *New York Times*, April 9, 2018. https://www.nytimes.com/2018/04/09/fashion/why-are-so-many-asian-american-women-bleaching-their-hair-blond.html.

Chang, Jade. *The Wangs vs. the World*. Boston: Houghton Mifflin Harcourt, 2016.

Chang, Robert S. "Toward an Asian American Legal Scholarship: Critical Race Theory, Structuralism, and Narrative Space." *California Law Review* 81 (1993) 1241–323.

Chen, Cindy I-Fen, ed. *The Routledge Handbook of Asian American Studies*. New York: Routledge, 2017.

Chen, David W. "'A Huge Blind Spot': Why New York Asians Feel Overlooked." *New York Times*, July 4, 2018. http://www.nytimes.com/2018/07/04/nyregion/asians-overlooked-specialized-schools.html.

Cheng, Kevin. "What Role Do Asian Americans Have in the Campus Protests." *Atlantic*, December 8, 2015. https://www.theatlantic.com/education/archive/2015/12/asian-americans-campus-protests/419301/.

Choe, Sang-Hun. "South Koreans Struggle with Race." *New York Times*, November 2, 2009. http://www.nytimes.com/2009/11/02/world/asia/02race.html?scp=1&sq=South%20Koreans%20Struggle%20with%20Race&st=cse.

Choi, Hoon. "Gender and Sexuality." In *Asian American Christian Ethics: Voices, Methods, Issues*, edited by Grace Y. Kao and Ilsup Ahn, 19–40. Waco, TX: Baylor University Press, 2015.

Choi, Ki Joo (KC). "Racial Identity and Solidarity." In *Asian American Christian Ethics: Voices, Methods, Issues*, edited by Grace Y. Kao and Ilsup Ahn, 131–52. Waco, TX: Baylor University Press, 2015.

Choi, Susan. *American Woman*. New York: HarperCollins, 2003.

Chou, Rosalind S., and Joe R. Feagin. *The Myth of the Model Minority: Asian Americans Facing Racism*. Boulder, CO: Paradigm, 2008.

Chu, Patricia P. *Assimilating Asians: Gendered Strategies of Authorship in Asian America*. Durham, NC: Duke University Press, 2000.

Chua, Amy. *Battle Hymn of the Tiger Mother*. New York: Penguin, 2011.

Chuh, Kandice. "Asians Are the New . . . What?" In *Flashpoints for Asian American Studies*, edited by Cathy J. Schlund-Vials, 220–40. New York: Fordham University Press, 2018.

Chuh, Kandice, and Karen Shimikawa, "Adjudicating Asian America." In *The Cambridge Companion to Asian American Literature*, edited by Crystal Parikh and Daniel Y. Kim, 29–41. Cambridge: Cambridge University Press, 2015.

Coates, Ta-Nehisi. *Between the World and Me*. New York: Spiegal & Grau, 2015.

———. "The Case for Reparations." *Atlantic*, June 2014. https://www.theatlantic.com/magazine/archive/2014/06/the-case-for-reparations/361631/.

————. "I'm Not Black, I'm Kanye: Kanye West Wants Freedom—White Freedom." *Atlantic*, May 7, 2018. https://www.theatlantic.com/entertainment/archive/2018/05/im-not-black-im-kanye/559763/.

Cohen, Cathy J., et al. "The 'Woke' Generation? Millennial Attitudes on Race in the U.S." *GenForward Survey*. October 2017. http://genforwardsurvey.com/reports/.

Cone, James H. *A Black Theology of Liberation*. 20th anniversary ed. Maryknoll: Orbis, 1990.

Copeland, M. Shawn. "Body, Representation, and Black Religious Discourse." In *Postcolonialism, Feminism, and Religious Discourse*, edited by Laura E. Donaldson and Kwok Pui-lan, 180–98. New York: Routledge, 2002.

————. *Enfleshing Freedom: Body, Race, and Being*. Minneapolis: Fortress, 2010.

Denyer, Simon. "Thousands of Vietnamese, Including Offspring of U.S. Troops, Could Be Deported under Trump Policy." *Washington Post*, September 1, 2018. https://www.washingtonpost.com/world/asia_pacific/thousands-of-vietnamese-including-offspring-of-us-troops-could-be-deported-under-tough-trump-policy/2018/08/30/8de80848-a6d0–11e8-b76b-d513a40042f6_story.html?noredirect=on&utm_term=.a466653313ef1.

Douglas, Kelly Brown. "More than Skin Deep: The Violence of Anti-Blackness." In *Anti-Blackness and Christian Ethics*, edited by Vincent W. Lloyd and Andrew Prevot, 3–18. Maryknoll: Orbis, 2017.

Erlanger, Steven. "Goodbye, Steinbeck; All Hail, Shelley." *New York Times*, May 30, 2014. https://www.nytimes.com/2014/05/31/books/goodbye-steinbeck-all-hail-shelley.html.

Espenshade, Thomas J., and Alexandra Radford. *No Longer Separate, Not Yet Equal*. Princeton: Princeton University Press, 2009.

Fang, Karen. "Globalization, Masculinity, and the Changing Stakes of Hollywood Cinema for Asian American Studies." In *Asian American Literary Studies*, edited by Guiyou Huang, 79–108. Edinburgh: Edinburgh University Press, 2005.

Farley, Margaret A. "Feminism and Universal Morality." In *Prospects for a Common Morality*, edited by Gene Outka and John P. Reeder Jr., 170–90. Princeton: Princeton University Press, 1993.

Fessenden, Ford, and Sam Roberts. "Then as Now—New York's Shifting Ethnic Mosaic." *New York Times*, January 22, 2011. http://www.nytimes.com/interactive/2011/01/23/nyregion/20110123-nyc-ethnic-neighborhoods-map.html?_r=1&.

Fletcher, Jeannine Hill. *The Sin of White Supremacy: Christianity, Racism, and Religious Diversity in America*. Maryknoll: Orbis, 2017.

Freedman, Samuel G. "Building on U.S. Tradition, Camp for Hindu Children Strengthens Their Identity." *New York Times*, August 22, 2014. http://www.nytimes.com/2014/08/23/us/building-on-us-tradition-camp-for-hindu-children-strengthens-their-identity.html?src=xps.

Gen, Gish. *The Love Wife*. New York: Vintage, 2005.

Gibson, Rev. O. *Chinaman or White Man, Which? A Reply to Father Buchard, Delivered in Platt's Hall, San Francisco, Friday Evening, Mar. 14, 1873*. San Francisco: Alta California, 1873.

Goizueta, Roberto S. *Caminemos con Jesús: Toward a Hispanic/Latino Theology of Accompaniment*. Maryknoll: Orbis, 1995.

Grimes, Katie Walker. "Black Exceptionalism: Anti-Blackness Supremacy in the Afterlife of Slavery." In *Anti-Blackness and Christian Ethics*, edited by Vincent W. Lloyd and Andrew Prevot, 41–60. Maryknoll: Orbis, 2017.

———. *Christ Divided: Antiblackness as Corporate Vice*. Minneapolis: Fortress, 2017.

Greenberger, Scott S. "'Cheap Slaves': Trump, Immigration and the Ugly History of the Chinese Exclusion Act." *Washington Post*, August 3, 2017. https://www.washingtonpost.com/news/retropolis/wp/2017/08/03/cheap-slaves-trump-immigration-and-the-ugly-history-of-the-chinese-exclusion-act/?noredirect=on&utm_term=.e2d48c845267.

Guo, Michael. "An Open Letter to the Woman Who Told My Family to Go Back to China." *New York Times*, October 9, 2016. https://www.nytimes.com/2016/10/10/nyregion/to-the-woman-who-told-my-family-to-go-back-to-china.html.

Harris, Elizabeth A., and Winnie Hu. "Asian Groups See Bias in Plan to Diversify New York's Elite Schools." *New York Times* (June 5, 2018). https://www.nytimes.com/2018/06/05/nyregion/carranza-specialized-schools-admission-asians.html.

Harris, Harriet A. "Should We Say That Personhood Is Relational?" In *T. & T. Clark Reader in Theological Anthropology*, edited by Marc Cortez and Michael P. Jensen, 330–41. London: Bloomsbury T. & T. Clark, 2018.

Hartocollis, Anemona. "Asian Americans Suing Harvard Say Admissions Files Show Discrimination." *New York Times*, April 4, 2018. https://www.nytimes.com/2018/04/04/us/harvard-asian-admission.html.

———. "Harvard Rates Asian-American Applicants Lower on Personality Traits, Suit Says." *New York Times*, June 15, 2018. https://nytimes.com/2018/06/15/us/harvard-asian-enrollment-applicants.html.

Heschel, Susannah. "The Slippery Yet Tenacious Nature of Racism: New Developments in Critical Race Theory and Their Implications for the Study of Religion and Ethics." *Journal of the Society of Christian Ethics* 35 (2015) 3–27.

Hiltner, Stephen. "Vietnamese Forged a Community in New Orleans. Now It May Be Fading." *New York Times*, May 5, 2018. https://www.nytimes.com/2018/05/05/us/vietnamese-forged-a-community-in-new-orleans-now-it-may-be-fading.html.

Ho, Emily. "Banh mi: The Sandwich That Marries the Flavors of French and Vietnamese Cuisine." *Chicago Tribune*, September 5, 2012. http://articles.chicagotribune.com/2012-09-05/features/sns-201209051500--tms--foodstylts--v-b20120905-20120905_1_banh-mi-pickled-carrots-and-daikon-place-tofu.

Ho, Jennifer Ann. *Racial Ambiguity in Asian American Culture*. New Brunswick, NJ: Rutgers University Press, 2015.

Ho, Soleil. "Do You Eat Dog?" *Taste*, July 12, 2018. https://www.tastecooking.com/the-dog-question/?ref=PRH0C8AF7CCBA3C&linkid=PRH0C8AF7CCBA3C&cdi=6E11C33E460DDE41E0534FD66B0A324B&template_id=9823&aid=randohouseinc7308-20&utm_campaign=taste&utm_source=Crown&utm_medium=Email&cid=75515&mid=981807070.

Huang, Eddie. "Hey, Steve Harvey, Who Says I Might Not Steal Your Girl?" *New York Times*, January 14, 2017. https://www.nytimes.com/2017/01/14/opinion/sunday/hey-steve-harvey-who-says-i-might-not-steal-your-girl.html.

Jacobson, Matthew Frye. *Whiteness of a Different Color: European Immigrants and the Alchemy of Race*. Cambridge: Harvard University Press, 1999.

Jennings, Willie James. *The Christian Imagination: Theology and the Origins of Race*. New Haven: Yale University Press, 2010.

Jeung, Russell. "Creating an Asian American Christian Subculture: Grace Community Covenant Church." In *Asian American Religions: The Making and Remaking of*

Borders and Boundaries, edited by Tony Carnes and Fenggang Yang, 287–312. New York: New York University Press, 2004.

Joshi, Hrishikesh. "Stop Anti-Asian Bias." *Inside Higher Ed,* May 13, 2016. https://www. insidehighered.com/views/2016/05/13/elite-colleges-should-not-penalize-asian-applicants-essay.

Kang, Jay Caspian. "How Should Asian Americans Feel about the Peter Liang Protests." *New York Times,* February 23, 2016. http://www.nytimes.com/2016/02/23magazine /how-should-asian-americans-feel-about-the-peter-liang-protests.html.

———. "The Lives of Others." *Freedarko.com,* January 14, 2010. http://freedarko.blogspot. com/2010/01/lives-of-others.html.

———. "What a Fraternity Hazing Death Revealed about the Painful Search for an Asian-American Identity." *New York Times Magazine,* August 9, 2017. https://www. nytimes.com/2017/08/09/magazine/what-a-fraternity-hazing-death-revealed-about-the-painful-search-for-an-asian-american-identity.html.

Kao, Grace Y., and Ilsup Ahn, eds. *Asian American Christian Ethics: Voices, Methods, Issues.* Waco, TX: Baylor University Press, 2015.

Kearney, Dennis, and H. L. Knight. "Appeal from California. The Chinese Invasion. Workingmen's Address." *Indianapolis Times,* February 28, 1878. http://historymatters. gmu.edu/d/5046.

Keh, Andrew. "An Olympic Challenge: Eat All the Food Visitors Won't." *New York Times,* February 21, 2018. https://www.nytimes.com/2018/02/21/sports/olympics/korean-food-visitors.html.

Kim, Claire Jean, and Taeku Lee. "Interracial Politics: Asian Americans and Other Communities of Color." In *Contemporary Asian America: A Multidisciplinary Reader,* edited by Min Zhou and J. V. Gatewood, 542–55. 2nd ed. New York: New York University Press, 2007.

Kim, Elaine. "Korean Americans in U.S. Race Relations: Some Considerations." *Amerasia Journal* 23 (1997) 69–78.

Kim, Grace Ji-Sun. "Chris Rock Should Know That Racism Isn't Black and White." *Time,* February 29, 2016. http://time.com/4241460/chris-rock-racism/.

Kim, Janine Young. "Are Asians Black? The Asian American Civil Rights Agenda and the Contemporary Significance of the Black/White Paradigm." In *Contemporary Asian America: A Multidisciplinary Reader,* edited by Min Zhou and J. V. Gatewood, 331–53. 2nd ed. New York: New York University Press, 2007.

Kim, Sharon. *A Faith of Our Own Book: Second-Generation Spirituality in Korean American Churches.* New Brunswick, NJ: Rutgers University Press, 2010.

King, Martin Luther, Jr. "Palm Sunday Sermon on Mohandas K. Gandhi." In *The Radical King,* edited by Cornel West, 23–38. Boston: Beacon, 2015.

———. "Pilgrimage to Nonviolence." In *The Radical King,* edited by Cornel West, 39–54. Boston: Beacon, 2015.

Kochhar, Rakesh, and Anthony Cilluffo. "Income Inequality in the U.S. Is Rising Most Rapidly among Asians." *Social and Demographic Trends,* Pew Research Center, July 12, 2018. http://www.pewsocialtrends.org/2018/07/12/income-inequality-in-the-u-s-is-rising-most-rapidly-among-asians/?utm_source=Pew+Research+Center&utm_campaign=ae470ffaad-EMAIL_CAMPAIGN_2018_07_12_01_09&utm_medium=email&utm_term=0_3e953b9b70-ae470ffaad-399903993.

Ku, Rober Ji-Song. *Dubious Gastronomy: The Cultural Politics of Eating Asian in the USA.* Honolulu: University of Hawai'i Press, 2014.

Kwok, Jean. *Girl in Translation*. New York: Riverhead, 2011.

————. *Mambo in Chinatown*. New York: Riverhead, 2014.

Kwok, Pui-Lan. "The Conversation That Is Chinese Christianity." *Boston College Magazine*, Fall 2011.

Lee, Chang-rae. *Native Speaker*. New York: Riverhead, 1995.

Lee, Erika. "Immigrants and Immigration Law: A State of the Field Assessment." *Journal of American Ethnic History* 18 (1999) 85–114.

Lee, Janice Y. K. *The Expatriates*. New York: Penguin, 2016.

Lee, Jennifer. *Civility in the City: Blacks, Jews, and Koreans in Urban America*. Cambridge: Harvard University Press, 2006.

Lee, Robert G. "The Cold War Construction of the Model Minority Myth." In *Contemporary Asian America: A Multidisciplinary Reader*, edited by Min Zhou and J. V. Gatewood, 469–84. 2nd ed. New York: New York University Press, 2007.

Lee, Sang Hyun. *From a Liminal Place: An Asian American Theology*. Minneapolis: Fortress, 2010.

Lee, Wendy. *Happy Family*. New York: Grove/Atlantic, 2008.

Lim, Audrea. "The Alt-Right's Asian Fetish." *New York Times*, June 1, 2018. https://www.nytimes.com/2018/01/06/opinion/sunday/alt-right-asian-fetish.html.

Linshi, Jack. "Why Ferguson Should Matter to Asian Americans." *Time*, November 27, 2014. http://time.com/3606900/ferguson-asian-americans/.

Liu, Lowen. "Why Chris Rock's Asian Joke Was Such a Disappointment." *Slate*, February 29, 2016. http://www.slate.com/blogs/browbeat/2016/02/29/why_chris_rock_and_ali_g_s_racist_asian_jokes_at_the_oscars_were_such_a.html.

Lloyd, Vincent W., and Andrew Prevot, eds. *Anti-Blackness and Christian Ethics*. Maryknoll: Orbis, 2017.

————. Introduction to *Anti-Blackness and Christian Ethics*, edited by Vincent W. Lloyd and Andrew Prevot, xv–xxx. Maryknoll: Orbis, 2017.

López, Gustavo, et al. "Key Facts about Asian Americans, a Diverse and Growing Population." *Fact Tank*, Pew Research Center, September 8, 2017. http://www.pewresearch.org/fact-tank/2017/09/08/key-facts-about-asian-americans/.

Lowe, Lisa. "Heterogeneity, Hybridity, Multiplicity: Marking Asian American Differences." In *Contemporary Asian America: A Multidisciplinary Reader*, edited by Min Zhou and J. V. Gatewood, 505–25. 2nd ed. New York: New York University Press, 2007.

————. *Immigrant Acts*. Durham, NC: Duke University Press, 1996.

Mabalon, Dawn Bohulano. "As American as Jackrabbit Adobo: Cooking, Eating, and Becoming Filipina/o American before World War II." In *Eating Asian America: A Food Studies Reader*, edited by Robert Ji-Song Ku et al., 147–76. New York: New York University Press, 2013.

MacIntyre, Alisdair. *Ethics in the Conflicts of Modernity: An Essay on Desire, Practical Reasoning, and Narrative*. Cambridge: Cambridge University Press, 2016.

Mak, Aaron. "'You're Asian, Right? Why Are You Even Here?'" *Politico*, August 23, 2016. http://politico.com/magazine/story/2016/08/milwaukee-protests-asian-american-black-lives-matter-214184.

Mak, Tim. "Ferguson's Other Race Problem: Riots Damaged Asian-Owned Stores." *Daily Beast*, August, 20, 2014. http://www.thedailybeast.com/articles/2014/08/20/ferguson-s-other-race-problem-riots-damaged-asian-owned-stores.html.

Massingale, Bryan N. "The Erotic Life of Anti-Blackness: Police Sexual Violation of Black Bodies." In *Anti-Blackness and Christian Ethics*, edited by Vincent W. Lloyd and Andrew Prevot, 173–94. Maryknoll: Orbis, 2017.

———. *Racial Justice and the Catholic Church*. Maryknoll: Orbis, 2010.

Mathewes, Charles. *Understanding Religious Ethics*. Malden, MA: Wiley-Blackwell, 2010.

Matsuda, Mari. "We Will Not Be Used." *UCLA Asian American Pacific Islands Law Journal* 1 (1993) 79–84.

McClain, Charles J. "Tortuous Path, Elusive Goal: The Asian Quest for American Citizenship." *Asian American Law Journal* 2 (1995) 33–60.

Medina, Jennifer. "Awe, Gratitude, Fear: Conflicting Emotions for Korean-Americans in the Era of Trump." *New York Times*, May 10, 2018. https://www.nytimes.com/2018/05/10/us/korean-americans-trump-immigration.html.

Min, Pyong Gap, and Rose Kim. *Struggle for Ethnic Identity: Narratives by Asian American Professionals*. Walnut Creek, CA: ALtaMira, 1999.

Mishan, Ligay. "Asian-American Cuisine's Rise and Triumph." *New York Times Style Magazine*, November 10, 2017. https://www.nytimes.com/2017/11/10/t-magazine/asian-american-cuisine.html.

New York Times Editorial Board. "It's Time to Integrate New York's Best Schools." *New York Times*, June 24, 2018. https://www.nytimes.com/interactive/2018/06/24/opinion/editorials/new-york-specialized-school.html.

Niebuhr, Reinhold. "Why the Christian Church Is Not Pacifist." In *The Essential Reinhold Niebuhr: Selected Essays and Addresses*, edited by Robert McAfee Brown, 102–22. New Haven: Yale University Press, 1986.

Ng, Celeste. *Everything I Never Told You*. New York: Penguin, 2014.

———. *Little Fires Everywhere*. New York: Penguin, 2017.

Nguyen, Viet Thanh. *The Sympathizer*. New York: Grove, 2015.

———. *Race and Resistance: Literature and Politics in Asian America*. New York: Oxford University Press, 2002.

O'Connor, Brendan. "Here Is What Appears to Be Dylann Roof's Racist Manifesto." *Gawker.com*, June 20, 2015. http://gawker.com/here-is-what-appears-to-be-dylann-roofs-racist-manifest-1712767241.

Okihiro, Gary. *Margins and Mainstreams: Asians in American History and Culture*. Seattle: University of Washington Press, 1994.

Omi, Mitchel, and Howard Winant. *Racial Formation in the United States from the 1960s to the 1990s*. New York: Routledge, 1994.

Ong, Anthony D., et al. "Racial Microaggressions and Daily Well-Being among Asian Americans." *Journal of Counseling Psychology* 60 (2013) 188–89.

Ono, Kent A., ed. *Companion to Asian American Studies*. Malden, MA: Blackwell, 2005.

Park, Andrew Sung. *Racial Conflict and Healing: As Asian-American Theological Perspective*. Maryknoll: Orbis, 1996.

Park, John S., and W. Park. "Race Discourse and Proposition 187." *Michigan Journal of Race and Law* 2 (1996) 175–204.

Park, Patricia. *Re Jane*. New York: Pamela Dorman / Viking, 2015.

Pew Research Center. "The Rise of Asian Americans." *Social and Demographic Trends*, Pew Research Center, April 4, 2013. http://www.pewsocialtrends.org/2012/06/19/the-rise-of-asian-americans/.

———. "Multiracial in America: Proud, Diverse and Growing in Numbers." *Social and Demographic Trends*, Pew Research Center, June 11, 2015. http://www.pewsocialtrends. org/2015/06/11/multiracial-in-america/.

Pham, Minh-Ha T. "De Blasio's Plan for NYC Schools Isn't Anti-Asian. It's Anti-Racist." *New York Times*, June 13, 2018. https://www.nytimes.com/2018/06/13/opinion/ stuyvesant-new-york-schools-de-blasio.html.

Phan, Peter C. *Christianity with an Asian Face: Asian American Theology in the Making*. Maryknoll: Orbis, 2003.

———. "'Reception' or 'Subversion' of Vatican II by the Asian Churches? A New Way of Being Church in Asia." In *Vatican II Forty Years Later*, edited by William Madges, 26–54. College Theology Society Annual 51 Maryknoll: Orbis, 2005.

Prevot, Andrew. "Sources of a Black Self? Ethics of Authenticity in an Era of Anti-Blackness." In *Anti-Blackness and Christian Ethics*, edited by Vincent W. Lloyd and Andrew Prevot, 77–95. Maryknoll: Orbis, 2017.

Punongbayan, Christopher. "What Asian Americans Owe African Americans." *Huffington Post*, October 2, 2015. https://www.huffingtonpost.com/christopher-punongbayan/ what-asian-americans-owe-_b_8234910.html.

Rodríguez, Rubén Rosario. *Racism and God-Talk: A Latino/a Perspective*. New York: New York University Press, 2008.

Roediger, David R. *Working toward Whiteness: How America's Immigrants Became White*. New York: Basic, 2005.

Rojas, Rick. "In New York, Thousands Protest Officer Liang's Conviction." *New York Times*, February 20, 2016. http://www.nytimes.com/2016/02/21/nyregion/in-new-york-thousands-protest-officer-liangs-conviction.html.

Rothstein, Richard. *The Color of Money: A Forgotten History of How Our Government Segregated America*. New York: Norton, 2017.

Ruskin, Bayard. "Do Not Forget Us!" *Worldview Magazine* (Carnegie Council, 1978). https://www.carnegiecouncil.org/publications/100_for_100/010.

Sardar, Ziauddin. "Who Are the British Asians?" *NewStatesman*, September 25, 2008. http://www.newstatesman.com/uk-politics/2008/09/british-asians-britain-india.

Schlund-Vials, Cathy J., ed. "Crisis, Conundrum, and Critique." Introduction to *Flashpoints for Asian American Studies*, edited by Cathy J. Schlund-Vials, 1–20. New York: Fordham University Press, 2018.

———. *Flashpoints for Asian American Studies*. New York: Fordham University Press, 2018.

Schlund-Vials, Cathy J., and Cynthia Wu. "Rethinking Embodiment and Hybridity: Mixed Race, Adoptee, and Disabled Subjectivities." In *The Cambridge Companion to Asian American Literature*, edited by Crystal Parikh and Daniel Y. Kim, 197–211. Cambridge: Cambridge University Press, 2015.

Semple, Kirk. "In Chinatown, the Sound of the Future Is Mandarin." *New York Times*, October 21, 2009. http://www.nytimes.com/2009/10/22/nyregion/22chinese.html ?scp=2&sq=mandarin%20in%20nyc&st=cse.

———. "Surge in Suicides Alarms Region's Koreans." *New York Times*, December 31, 2009. http://www.nytimes.com/2009/12/31/nyregion/31suicides.html?scp=1&sq=Surge%20 in%20Suicides%20Alarms%20Region's%20Koreans&st=cse.

Sharma, Nitasha. "The Racial Studies Project: Asian American Studies and the Black Lives Matter Campus." In *Flashpoints for Asian American Studies*, edited by Cathy J. Schlund-Vials, 48–65. New York: Fordham University Press, 2018.

Sherman, Ted. "In 'Life and Death' Stakes, Judge Stops N.J. Deportation of Indonesians." *NJ.com*. February 2, 2018. https://www.nj.com/news/index.ssf/2018/02/last_minute_court_appeal_halts_deportation_of_indo.html.

Song, Min Hyoung. "Asian American Literature Within and Beyond the Immigrant Narrative." In *The Cambridge Companion to Asian American Literature*, edited by Crystal Parikh and Daniel Y. Kim, 3–15. Cambridge: Cambridge University Press, 2015.

Spaeman, Robert. "Persons: The Difference between 'Someone' and 'Something.'" In *T. & T. Clark Reader in Theological Anthropology*, edited by Marc Cortez and Michael P. Jensen, 342–49. London: Bloomsbury T. & T. Clark, 2018.

Spickard, Paul R. "What Must I Be? Asian Americans and the Question of Multiethnic Identity." In *Contemporary Asian America: A Multidisciplinary Reader*, edited by Min Zhou and J. V. Gatewood, 393–407. 2nd ed. New York: New York University Press, 2007.

Sternbergh, Adam. "The Extinction of the Middle Child." *New York Magazine*, July 2018. https://www.thecut.com/2018/07/the-middle-child-is-going-extinct.html.

Stout, Jeffrey. *Democracy and Tradition*. Princeton: Princeton University Press, 2004.

Sue, Derald Wing, et al. "Racial Microaggressions and the Asian American Experience." *Cultural Diversity and Ethnic Minority Psychology* 13 (2007) 72–81.

Swanson, David. "Thousands in Philadelphia Protest the Conviction of NYPD Officer Peter Liang." *Philadelphia Inquirer*, February 20, 2016. http://www.philly.com/philly/blogs/real-time/Thousands-in-Philadelphia-protest-conviction-of-NYPD-officer-Peter-Liang.html.

Tan, Jonathan Y. *Introducing Asian American Theologies*. Maryknoll: Orbis, 2008.

Tanner, Kathryn. *Theories of Culture: A New Agenda for Theology*. Minneapolis: Fortress, 1997.

Taylor, Charles. *The Ethics of Authenticity*. Cambridge: Harvard University Press, 1991.

———. *Human Agency and Language*. Philosophical Papers 1. Cambridge: Cambridge University Press, 1985.

———. "The Politics of Recognition." In *Multiculturalism: Examining the Politics of Recognition*, edited by Amy Gutmann, 25–74. Princeton: Princeton University Press, 1994.

Truffaut-Wong, Olivia. "Why the Asian Character in 'Get Out' Matters So Much." *Bustle*, March 6, 2017. https://www.bustle.com/p/why-the-asian-character-in-get-out-matters-so-much-42569.

Truong, Monique. *Bitter in the Mouth*. New York: Random House, 2010.

Tsui, Bonnie. *American Chinatown: A People's History of Five Neighborhoods*. New York: Free Press, 2009.

———. "Choose Your Own Identity." *New York Times*, December 14, 2015. https://www.nytimes.com/2015/12/14/magazine/choose-your-own-identity.html.

Tuan, Mia. *Forever Foreigners or Honorary Whites: The Asian Ethnic Experience Today*. New Brunswick, NJ: Rutgers University Press, 1999.

Tucci, Sherry. "When K-Pop Culturally Appropriates." *Daily Dot*, April 2, 2016. https://www.dailydot.com/upstream/kpop-hip-hop-culture-appropriation/.

Vega, Tanzina. "Colorblind Notion Aside, Colleges Grapple with Racial Tension." *New York Times*, February 25, 2014. https://www.nytimes.com/2014/02/25/us/colorblind-notion-aside-colleges-grapple-with-racial-tension.html.

Wang, Weike. *Chemistry*. New York: Knopf, 2017.

Weaver, Hilary. "Rachel Dolezal Is Back, Refusing to Apologize for Lying about Being Black." *Vanity Fair*, February 28, 2017. https://www.vanityfair.com/style/2017/02/rachel-dolezal-refuses-to-apologize.

Wei, Clarissa. "The Struggles of Writing about Chinese Food as a Chinese Person." *Munchies*, April 18, 2017. https://munchies.vice.com/en_us/article/yp7bx5/the-struggles-of-writing-about-chinese-food-as-a-chinese-person.

West, Cornel. "Race and Social Theory." In *The Cornel West Reader*, edited by Cornel West, 251–68. New York: Basic Civitas, 1999.

———. "The Radical King We Don't Know." Introduction to *The Radical King*, edited by Cornel West, ix–xvi. Boston: Beacon, 2015.

West, Cornel, and Jorge Klor de Alva. "On Black-Brown Relations." In *The Cornel West Reader*, edited by Cornel West, 499–513. New York: Basic Civitas, 1999.

Wolf, Susan. "Comment." In *Multiculturalism: Examining the Politics of Recognition*, edited by Amy Gutmann, 75–86. Princeton: Princeton University Press, 1994.

Wong, Alia. "Asian Americans and the Future of Affirmative Action." *Atlantic*, June 28, 2016. http://www.theatlantic.com/education/archive/2016/06/asian-americans-and-the-future-of-affirmative-action/489023.

Wu, Jean Yu-wen Shen, and Min Song, eds. *Asian American Studies: A Reader.* New Brunswick, NJ: Rutgers University Press, 2000.

Wu, Jean Yu-wen Shen, and Thomas C. Chen, eds. *Asian American Studies Now: A Critical Reader.* New Brunswick, NJ: Rutgers University Press, 2010.

Xu, Wenying. *Eating Identities: Reading Food in Asian American Literature.* Honolulu: University of Hawai'i Press, 2008.

Yam, Kimberly. "9 Times Non-Asians Completely Screwed Up Asian Food and We Lost Our Appetites." *Huffington Post*, May 8, 2017. https://www.huffingtonpost.com/entry/non-asians-screw-up-asian-food_us_59011e43e4b0af6d718b4058.

Yamashita, Samuel Hideo. "The Significance of Hawai'i Regional Cuisine in Postcolonial Hawai'i." In *Eating Asian America: A Food Studies Reader*, edited by Robert Ji-Song Ku et al., 98–124. New York: New York University Press, 2013.

Yang, Gene Luen. *American Born Chinese.* New York: Square Fish / Macmillan, 2006.

Yang, Jeff. "Black-Asian Tensions: Not the Cause of Baltimore." *CNN*, May 8, 2015. http://www.cnn.com/2015/05/01/opinions/yang-asians-black-baltimore/index.html.

Yang, Wesley. "Paper Tigers." *New York Magazine*, May 8, 2011. http://nymag.com/news/features/asian-americans-2011-5/.

Young, Iris Marion. "Difference as a Resource for Democratic Communication." In *Deliberative Democracy: Essays on Reason and Politics*, edited by James Bohman and William Relig, 383–406. Cambridge: MIT Press, 1997.

Zeng, May. "Yes, We Play Jazz Too: 8 Asian American Jazz Artists You Should Know About." *Pacific Ties*, May 1, 2016. https://pacificties.org/?p=8234.

Zhang, Jenny. *Sour Heart.* New York: Lenny, 2017.

Zhou, Min. "Are Asian Americans Becoming White?" In *Contemporary Asian America: A Multidisciplinary Reader*, edited by Min Zhou and J. V. Gatewood, 354–59. 2nd ed. New York: New York University Press, 2007.

Zhou, Min, and J. V. Gatewood. "Transforming Asian America: Globalization and Contemporary Immigration to the United States." In *Contemporary Asian America: A Multidisciplinary Reader*, edited by Min Zhou and J. V. Gatewood, 115–38. 2nd ed. New York: New York University Press, 2007.

Index of Subjects and Names

ACLU, 19n53
Adoption, 127–128, 130, 136
Aesthetics, 4, 92, 141n65
Affirmative action, 4, 10–15, 85
Ahn, Ilsup, xi, xiin2
Alcoff, Linda, 80, 96n76, 100, 101n85
   on Malinche, 93
   on Pocahontas, 93
Alito, Samuel, 11n26
Alt-Right, 6–7
Ambivalence, toward Asian American
      identity, xiii, 1, 3, 5, 21, 30, 34
American dream, "the Dream," xiv, 95,
      140, 142–143
American Enterprise Institute, 13
Anderson, Victor, 89
Anti-Asianness, 29–30, 107
Antiblackness, xvii, 15–17, 21, 26, 28–29,
      33, 39, 107–108, 148, 149n2
Anxiety, existential, about meaning, 158,
      175–176
Appiah, K. Anthony, 46–47, 52–55,
      64n65, 113
Appropriation, and re-appropriation, 9,
      42–43, 46, 58, 62, 78–79
Aquinas, Thomas, 174
Asian Americans as
      exotic, 69, 82, 92
      invisible, 5, 27, 29n84, 116, 166–167

other, pertaining to immigrant
      otherness, xv, 25n73, 69, 70, 73,
      77, 83, 86n49, 99, 100, 102
perpetual foreigner or immigrant,
      pertaining to "foreigner axis," xv,
      82, 99, 25n73, 51, 69, 99n81, 134
scapegoats, 8–9, 24
Asian Americans Advancing Justice,
      13n37
Asian American affluence, ascendency,
      17, xiv, xv, 98, 103
Asian American church, 85, 86n49, 88
      pan-Asian American, 85
      panethnic, panethnicity in or of, 85,
      87
      multiracial, 86, 88
      second-generation, 90
      primordialist and instrumentalist
      views of, 87
Asian American Coalition for Education,
      11n27
Asian American fashion bloggers and
      models, 92
Asian American foodways, 57, 59, 77,
      83–84
      bahn mi, 49n34
      California roll, 84
      kung pao chicken, 84
      mandoo, 62
      SPAM, 84
      tuyo, 57–62

Asian American food studies, xvi, 84
Asian American identity, origin of, role of
    Yuji Ichioka, 4, 55
Asian American identity as (nationality)
    Bangladeshi, 4, 17, 98n79
    British Asian, 5n6
    Burmese, 98n79
    Chinese, Chineseness, 8–9, 21–23,
        44–45, 51–52, 56n48–49, 80–81,
        86n49, 91, 99, 101, 123–125,
        127–130, 135, 143, 168, 170
    Filipino/a, 49–50, 52n38, 57–59, 61
    Hmong, 17, 98n79
    Indian Asian, 4, 23, 44, 50n36, 56n49
    Indonesian, 19n54
    Korean, South Korean, 1–3, 18,
        19n54, 44, 48–50, 54, 56, 60,
        64n67, 88, 90, 94, 115, 119,
        133–134, 155
    Nepalese, 98n79
    Malaysian, 17
    Scotch-Korean, 64
    Taiwanese, 144, 169, 41, 63n63
    Vietnamese, 7, 19n54, 43, 45, 49n34,
        89n55, 130–133, 136, 139
Asian American identity as (racially)
    "Mongolian," "Asiatic," "yellow," 21
Asian American identity as (regionally)
    Central Asian, 98
    East Asian, xiv, 4, 33, 56, 98
    Pacific Islander, 13n37
    South Asian, xiv, 4, 23, 27, 33
    Southeast Asian, 4, 17, 29n84, 65n67,
        71, 98
Asian American Legal Defense and
    Education Fund, 13n37
Asian American literature, novels, or
    fiction, xvi, xvin11, xvii, xix, 110–
    111, 114, 118, 121–123, 127n40,
    142, 149, 151
Asian American studies, xvi, 127n40
Asian American theology, 74
Asian Americans Advancing Justice-Los
    Angeles, 13n37
Asian Catholic Bishops, or Synod of
    Asian Bishops, 72–73
Asian Christianity, Protestant and
    Catholic, 72

Assimilation, acculturation, 18, 94–98,
    100–102, 104–105, 107–109, 137,
    140, 144, 166
    "straight line" assimilation theory of
        immigration, 94
Atlantic Monthly, 10
Augustine, Augustianian, 111, 158
Autonomy
    a feminist account and connection to
        relationality, 162–163
    as self-possession, 163, 170
    as critical self-love, 165

Bacon, Francis, 157
Baltimore, 6, 171
Bamboo ceiling, and glass ceiling,
    165–166
Bantum, Brian, xvin11, 111–114, 119,
    137
Bhabba, Homi, 76
    on fixity, 100n85
Black Catholic theology, theologian,
    171–172
Black Justice League, 10
Black Lives Matters, 9, 25
Black theology, xvi, 28
Black-white dichotomy, paradigm, xvii,
    21, 23, 25n73, 28, 30–33, 113
Bleaching, hair, or ombré trend, 92–93
Blum, Edward, 13
Bouchard, Father James, 81
Bourdain, Anthony, 41–42, 45–46, 53
Bratton, William Joseph, former New
    York City police commissioner, 8
Breakfast at Tiffany's, 131
Brigham Young University, 39n9
Bronx Science, 14
Brooklyn, 3–9, 41, 120
Brooklyn Technical, 14
Brown, Michael, 6, 8
Butler, Judith, on performativity, 137

"California blond," 120, 135, 143
Camp Friendship, Stirling, NJ, 56n48
Cannon, Katie Geneva, xvin11
Carranza, Richard, New York City
    school's chancellor, 14
Chang, David, 49, 94

Chang, Jade, *The Wangs vs. the World*, 127, 144, 147

Charleston, 6–7

Chestnutt, Charles, *The House Behind the Cedars*, xvi, xviin11

Chew, Pat, 81n38

Chin, Vincent, 85

Chinese Exclusion Act of 1882, 22n64, 80–81, 89

Choi, Susan, *American Woman*, 114, 116, 138

Chu, Patricia P., 140, 117n18

Chua, Amy, *Battle Hymn of the Tiger Mother*, 5, 51–52, 165, 167–168, 170

Chuh, Kandice, 12–13, 21, 30, 103

Cleveland, 8

Coates, Ta-Nehesi, xiv, 20, 140–143, 145–146, 160n31, 170–172, 174–175

Colicchio, Tom, *Top Chef*, 43

Columbia University, 52n38, 133

Comparative race studies, 20

Complicity, xviii-xix, 97–110

Communist, communism, 29n84, 99, 105, 130

Cone, James, 28–29, 31

Confucian values, Confucianism, 39, 72, 85

Connor, Bull, 176

Copeland, M. Shawn, on *anamnesis*, 173

Cornell University, 54n44

Cultural authenticity, xviii, 5, 40–41, 45–46, 48, 53, 59, 101, 145, 148, 153

Curb Your Enthusiasm, Larry David, 83

DACA, 19n54

Dai, Serena, 99

DeBlasio, Bill, 14

Desire, racial, 120

Discrimination, xv, 9, 11–13, 17, 20n55, 24, 25n73, 32, 68–69, 70, 75–80, 82, 84–85, 88–90, 94, 97, 102–105, 165

Disembodiment, 141–146

Dolezal, Rachel, 79n31, 112

Drummond, Dee, 99n81

Du Bois, W. E. B., 64n65

Ebert, Robert, 109

Ellison, Ralph, *Invisible Man*, 167

Emanuel African Methodist Episcopal Church, 7

Engabachamiento, or whitening, 94

Ephesians 6:12, 148

Espenshade, Thomas J., 12

Essentialism, essentialist, 24, 47, 73

Fang, Karen, 150–151

Fanon, Frantz, *Wretched of the Earth*, 154n18

Far, Sui Jin, or Edith Maud Eaton, "Leaves from the Mental Portfolio of an Eurasian," 123, 142

Farley, Margaret, 162–163, 170

Ferguson, xv, xvii, 6, 8

Fisher v. The University of Texas at Austin, 11n26

Flag Foundation of India, Tiranga, 50n36

Fletcher, Jeannine Hill, 81

Food Network, 99

Fraternities, 85, 88, 102

Garner, Eric, 8

Gates Jr., Henry Louis, on cultural geneticism, 63

Gatewood, J. V., 45, 70–71, 73n15

Gaudium et spes, 72

Gen, Gish, *Love Wife*, 127n40

GenForward Survey, millennial attitudes on race, 90

Gibson, Reverend Otis, 81

Goizueta, Roberto, 61

Grace Community Covenant Church, Silicon Valley, CA, 86n49

Grey, Freddie, 6

Grimes, Katie Walker, 15–19, 21, 23, 98n80

Grutter v. Bollinger, 4n4

Guo, Michael, 82–83, 99

Gurley, Akai, 7–9

Harvard University, 11–15, 85, 100, 125

Harris, Harriet A., 163–164

Hawaiian cuisine, 58

Heschel, Susannah, 80, 161

Hindu Heritage Summer Camp,
    Macedon, NY, 56n49
Ho, Jennifer, 83
Honhyol, 119–121
Hope
    versus abjection, 173–174
    versus cheap optimism and
        unreasonable pessimism, xxi
Hoq, Laboi, 13n37
Huang, Eddie, 18n50, 41–45, 53, 169
Hybridity as
    interculturalism or intercultural
        exchange or innovation, xviii,
        69–70, 73, 77–79, 85–88, 93
    cultural cohabitation, 72
    consequence of borderlessness, 70,
        73, 79, 82
    consequence of in-betweenness, 72,
        74–76, 86n49
    hopefulness, 77, 86, 91, 97

Immigration, 23, 44, 82, 103–104
Immigration and Nationality Act of 1965,
    23, 82, 103–104
Immigration, Customs, and Enforcement,
    19n54
Imperialism
    American, 130
    colonial (colonialism), 24, 26, 33,
        99n34, 79, 152
    cultural, 58
Income inequality, 18, 98n80
In re Ah Yup, 22, 23n64
Interracial, 18, 86–87, 90, 93, 113, 120,
    125, 127–128, 130
Interracial dating, 86–87, 90
Ivy League, 12, 85, 165

Jeung, Russell, 78, 85, 86n49
Jim Crow, 104
Johnson, James Weldon, *Autobiography of
    an Ex-Coloured Man*, xviin11
Johnson-Reed Act of 1924, 82

Kang, Jay Caspian, 68–69, 84–85, 88,
    92n62, 155–156, 159, 161–162
Kao, Grace Y., xi, xiin2
Kearney, Denis, 80–82

Kentucky Derby, 79n32
Kim, Claire Jean, 11n26, 18, 91, 102
Kim, Grace Ji-Sun, 31
Kim, Janine Young, 30n87, 32n93, 25n73
Kim, Ron, New York State assemblyman,
    9
Kim, Sharon, 85
King, Rodney, 6, 89
King Jr, Martin Luther, 29n84, 176
Klor de Alva, Jorge, 32, 37
Ko, Lisa, *The Leavers*, 124, 127n40, 129,
    135, 138
Koo, Peter, New York City councilman,
    14
Koreatown, Los Angeles, 6, 89
Korematsu v. United States, 80
Ku, Robert Ji-Song, 84
Kwok, Jean, *Girl in Translation* and
    Mambo in Chinatown, 36, 67
Kwok, Pui-Lan, 72–73

Latinos/as
    as brown, 37–40
    and affirmative action and
        standardized testing, 11n26, 12,
        13n37, 14
    and whiteness, discrimination, 17,
        102
Larsen, Nella, *Passing*, xviin11
Lee, Chang-rae, *Native Speaker*, 115,
    116n16, 117, 127, 139–140
Lee, Janice Y. K., *The Expatriates*, 133,
    139
Lee, Sang Hyun, 74–77, 96
Lee, Taeku, 11, 18, 91, 102
Lee, Wendy, *Happy Family*, 127n40
Liang, Peter, 7–9, 24
Liberation, emancipatory, xxi, 28, 69, 87,
    118, 124, 135, 149, 154
Liminality, 75–79, 86–87
Lin, Justin, *Better Luck Next Time*, 109,
    150
Liu, John C., former New York City
    comptroller, 14
Lloyd, Andrew, 16, 26
Love as
    radical self-love, xx, 166–167, 169,
        170, 172

other-regarding self-love, xx, 166, 168
critical self-love, 165, 169
self-love in the service of the other,
170, 172
Lowe, Lisa, 78

Mabalon, Dawn Bohulano, 57–58
MacIntyre, Alistair, 174n67
Macmurray, John, 164
Mak, Aaron, 9
Massingale, Bryan, 26–27, 141n65,
171–172
Matthew 6:12, 175n70
McClain, Charles J., 22n62–64
McLaren, Peter, 94, 97n78
Mestizo/mestizaje, 46, 74
Michigan
Law School, 4n4
Univesity of, 102
Microaggressions, 82
Middle minorities, middle-agent
minorities, 23–25, 31
Migration, xiv, 57, 74
Miller, Laura, 93
Milwaukee, 9
Milwaukee Journal Sentinel, 9
Mishan, Ligaya, 68–70, 73, 77, 82
Mixed-race, 52n38, 71n10, 93, 113, 116,
119, 124, 127
Model minority, xv, xviii, xix, 18, 92, 98,
100–107, 110, 148, 166, 175
and Marshall Plan, 103n93
linked to ethnic assimilation theory,
104
Monolithic, Asian American identity,
experience and culture, 5, 45, 65
Morrison, Toni, The Bluest Eyes, 96n76
Multiculturalism, 46, 154
Myrdal, Gunnar, An American Dilemma:
The Negro Problem and Modern
Democracy, 104

National Asian American Survey, 13n37
National Policy Institute, 7
Nativism, xv, 20
New Orleans, 45, 89n55
New York City, 1, 7–8, 13–15, 20n55,
44–45, 83, 119, 129, 143

New York Times Editorial Board, 14
Niebuhr, Reinhold, 158, 175–176
Ng, Celeste, Everything I Never Told You
and Little Fires Everywhere, 124–
130 passim, 135, 137, 142
Nguyen, Viet Thanh, The Sympathizer,
1, 109, 110n3, 118n19, 124, 130–
133 passim, 134–135, 137–139
passim
No Reservations, 41
Nonviolence, 176

Okihiro, Gary, 31
Ong, Anthony, 82

Pan-Asian unity, 85
Pantaleo, Daniel, 8
Passing
concept of, 111–114
as white, 118–123 passim
as Asian, 124–133 passim
Paternalism, ethnic or racial, 128–129,
132, 148
Park, Andrew Sung, 23
Park, Patricia, Re Jane, 117–121 passim,
123–124, 134–135, 137–139, 143
Peele, Jordan, Get Out, 106
People v. George C. Hall, 21–22
Performance
cultural, 54, 68
racial, 112–113, 137–138
social, 34
Pew Research Center, xivn5, 5n7, 18,
71n10, 92, 98
P. F. Chang's, 43n14
Pham, Minh-Ha T., 20n55
Phan SJ, Peter, 72n13, 72–75
Philadelphia, 8n16
Plessy v. Ferguson, 27
Policing, 6, 143, 148
Politics of recognition, concept of, 47
Postracialism, 150, 170
Poutine, 51n36
Prevot, Andrew, 16, 26, 149n2, 150–151,
154n18
Princeton University, 10, 25
Proposition 209, xvii, 10–11, 11n26

Racial profiling, 19, 148
Radford, Alexandra, 12
Ramakrishnan, Karthick, 13n37
Representation, 31, 83, 93n67, 105, 111,
    130–133, 139, 144n65, 149–152
Resistance, xx, 24, 66, 73n15, 76, 78, 84,
    88, 90, 105, 110n3, 118n19, 138,
    149, 150, 159, 168, 176, 177
Rice, Tamir, 8
Ricker, Andy, Thai restaurant Pok Pok
    NY, 41–43, 45–46, 53
Rock, Chris, 18
Roman Catholic Church, 89n55
Roof, Dylann, 6–7
Rustin, Bayard, *Worldview Magazine*,
    Carnegie Council, 29n84

Schlund-Vials, Cathy J., 7–8
Settler colonialism, 24
Sharma, Nitasha, 9, 20, 25–26
Sin of pride, 158
Smith, Sylville, 9
Solidarity, 8, 53, 173
    Asian American, 86n49, 88–89
    racial, xvi, 19, 173
Spaeman, Robert, 163–164
Specialized High Schools Admissions
    Test or SHSAT, 14
Spencer, Richard, 7
Spickard, Paul R., 52n38
Starburst candy advertisement, 64
Students for Fair Admissions or SFA, 12
Stuyvesant, 14
Subjectivism, as consequence of
    modernity, 157, 159, 170
Suicide, 54, 55n44

Takao Ozawa v. United States, 22
Tan, Jonathan Y., 23
Tanner, Kathyrn, 46–48
Taylor, Charles, 46–48, 152–157, 159,
    160n33, 161–162, 170, 174
Tequila, Tila, 7
Thomas, Clarence, 4
Till, Emmett, 105

Trinitarian formulation of identity versus
    personhood, 164
Truong, Monique, *Bitter in the Mouth*,
    127n40
Tsui, Bonnie, 56n49, 65, 91, 94
Turner, Victor, 76

United States v. Bhagat Singh Thind,
    22–23, 27, 81n38
University of Texas at Austin, 11n26,
    13n37

Wang, Weike, *Chemistry*, 37, 136
Weber, Max, on the "iron cage," 161, 166
Wei, Clarissa, 42
West, Cornel, 37–38, 40–41, 80–81,
    157–158, 160, 176, 177
    on his Augustinianism,
    Niebuhrianism, 158
West, Kanye, 160n31
White freedom, 21, 171, 174–175
White supremacy, 16, 32–33, 38, 41, 176
Whiteness
    general definition, xiii-xiv
    Asian American whiteness, 102
    Asian American adjacency to, xiv,
    92n62, 17, 91, 107
    and European immigrants, 99n81
Wilson, Darren, 8
Wong, Alia, 13n37
Womanist theology, xvi
Workingmen's Party of California, 80

Xu, Wenying, 59, 83

Yang, Gene Luen, *American Born
    Chinese*, 118, 121–124 passim,
    134–135, 137–138
Yang, Wesley, 5–6, 165–170, 172
Young, Iris Marion, on social perspective,
    Pierre Bourdieu, 59–60

Zhang, Jenny, *Sour Heart*, 37, 67, 121,
    143–144
Zhou, Min, 70–71, 73n15, 95, 101

Made in the USA
Monee, IL
09 August 2021